Modern Methods of Teaching Psychology

Modern Methods of Teaching Psychology

K.C. Shukla
Tara Chand

Commonwealth

Modern Methods of Teaching Psychology

Edition : 2017

ISBN 81-7169-909-X

Published by :
COMMONWEALTH PUBLISHERS
4831/24, Prahlad Street,
Ansari Road, Darya Ganj,
New Delhi - 110002
Ph. : 23275511, 23257835
e-mail : commonwealthbooks@gmail.com

Typesetting by :
Rishu Computers
Delhi

Printed at :
Divine Digital Press
Delhi

PREFACE

This book is primarily meant for teacher educators in teachers colleges and departments of education. Methods of teaching generally and specifically apply equally to psychology. This book tries to help teachers in colleges of education as to how to train would be teachers who are to work in schools and colleges?

Psychophysics is that branch of psychology which is concerned with subjective measurement. Obviously a subjective unit of measurement is required. Psychophysical theory is concerned with the logic of subjective measurement [8], and psychophysical methods are concerned with experimental procedures.

In order to illustrate the difference between *the psychological continuum and the physical stimulus continuum,* let us consider an experiment in the differentiation of lifted weights, which has been investigated by hundreds of experimenters. The experimental subject is presented with a large assortment of small cylinders, all of them equal in size and appearance but different in weight. He is shown two of these cylinders which differ markedly in weight, and they are designated as *standards* for this experiment. Then the subject is asked to select one of the other weights that seems to be midway between the two standards. When the subject has satisfied himself that he has found a cylinder whose weight marks the midpoint between the standards, the three cylinders may be compared as to their "actual" weights. When the intervals are expressed in grams or other physical units, it is found that the lower interval is smaller than the upper one. In other words, the subjective on psychological continuum is not the same as the physical continuum. Measurement on the subjective continuum will be denoted *S*, and measurement on the physical continuum will be denoted *R*. The experimental method just described is called the *method of mean gradation*.

Psychophysical problems can be divided into several classes. Perhaps the most fundamental of these is that in which each one of a set of stimuli is allocated to a point in the subjective continuum without reference to physically measurable attributes. In a closely related class is the problem of predicating what people will do in terms of the subjective values of a set of stimuli. If their subjective values for a set of neckties are known, how many of the subjects will select a particular necktie as their first choice in any given assortment of neckties? Another large class of problems is concerned with the relation between the subjective and the physical continua. We shall see that relation is known as Fechner's law. One of the oldest types of psychophysical problem is that of determining the physical stimulus increment which the subject can just barely perceive. This increment is called the *just noticeable difference*. Since this is the simplest of the psychophysical problems, we shall start with the concepts and the experimental methods that have been used for determining such stimulus increments.

The author is grateful to the Ministry of Human Resource Development Govt. of India and the National Council of Educational Research and Training for their valuable contributions in the preparation of this volume. The author has heavily depended upon the literature produced by them.

K.C. Shukla
Tara Chand

Contents

1

Psychological Methodology

As the student surveys the literature of modern psychology, he is impressed with its wide scope and the extremely varied methods that are employed in its heterogeneous domain. The data that fall within the boundaries of psychology include such diverse subjects as loudness discrimination in dogs, factors of delinquency in urban areas, spinal reflexes, and psychotherapy. Yet all these are psychology. Not only do the data and sources of data show great diversity, but it naturally follows that the methods of the field must also exhibit some similar degree of diversity.

Within the gigantic framework of psychological science there is some system and order among the facts and among the methods. The purpose of this introductory chapter is to search into the bases of methodology and attempt to bring together some of the common features and differentiating features of the sundry methods that are being employed in the advancement of psychological knowledge. The remaining chapters of the book are devoted to the more specific methods and the technical details of their application in the different fields of interest.

The science of psychology faces several rather fundamental difficulties. One of these major difficulties can be appreciated by a comparison with the so-called natural sciences, in which the beginning points—the raw material—

are not under great controversy. Man does not ordinarily question the basic subject, matter of physics or of chemistry : such raw stuff constitutes the main stimulus objects of his physical environment. On the other hand, historically, psychology has had some difficulty in trying to decide the boundaries of its subject matter, which has ranged from consciousness to the more modern and operationally definable *discriminatory* response [3]. There are many ways of going about the analysis of the behaviour which we call the subject matter. As professor E.G. Boring has indicated, psychology has settled down to the attempt to account man's functional capacities and describe them [4].

During its historical difficulties concerning subject matter psychology has fostered the growth of several rather divergent points of view, out of which there have arisen several interesting controversies [11,12]. Certain psychologists have also felt compelled to expend considerable energy in trying to combat the easily made claim that their field should not be classified as a science. Perhaps the older subjects of analysis, such as consciousness, did not appear very scientific, but such a controversy is nevertheless a barren one. In this regard it is best to follow the rule, as stated by Karl Pearson [19], that any field is a science so long as it consistently employs scientific methods.

BACKGROUNDS OF SCIENTIFIC METHOD

Rationalism and Empiricism

If method is to be the major criterion of science, we can easily see the necessity for becoming conversant with the backgrounds and characteristics of scientific method.

The philosophical techniques used to evaluate and investigate behaviour and all other things are *rational* in nature. Rationalism is the more speculative philosophy which attempts to arrive at "truths" by reasoning from a few rather broad assumptions in accordance with some principles of correct procedure, rather than by turning directly to experience. It is evident that rationalism presupposes a very strong faith in man's power to reason.

There have been some quite satisfactory procedures and criteria for deduction form propositions [6], but a major criticism of the familiar syllogistic from is that it has never proved of value in obtaining really new information. Demonstrating by syllogistic reasoning such things as "Socrates is mortal" has not been sufficient to satisfy the more spirited and *empirical* truth seekers [16]. Also, the major premise (the large if) in such syllogisms is usually an untestable hypothesis. Waiting until the last man : has died in order to demonstrate that all men are mortal would not be a fruitful procedure.

Some investigators of a less speculative frame of mind were seeking new information, and so they scrapped most of the techniques of the rationalists and turned directly to nature and experience for the answers to their questions. These questions took on new forms; they were stated with greater precision and were more closely directed to the world of experience. Rather than remaining satisfied with a statement merely because the rules of logical deduction had been followed in deriving it, these investigators tested the statement by determining whether it concurred with other types of observation.

These newer techniques were carried out in an entirely different spirit. Instead of the syllogistic form, the reverse was applied—that of starting from particulars and going toward generalities. This principle of *induction*, however, did not allow the application of convenient criteria of "truth" that had been developed for a syllogistic deduction. Although a little more troublesome, this lack of complete criteria served a purpose, because it helped science to throw off the cloak of absolutism and become progressive by never feeling too certain about its results [15].

There were many verbal battles and some actual bloodshed before the more inductive and empirical techniques were fully launched on their way toward the development of the body scientific. In the division of the two camps, the more rugged and individualistic empiricists tended toward overcompensation by throwing completely overboard any connections with the despised speculative systems. During more recent years, however, there has been an interesting and profitable reversion to the extent that scientists are becoming more and more concerned about the philosophical bases of their methods and modes of discourse. Philosophy therefore, is still with us in all our scientific endeavors [5, 17, 20].

For purposes of the description and prediction of natural phenomena, the empirical and inductive methods of science have survived as the fittest. Nevertheless, whenever the scientist poses an hypothesis for investigation, designs an experiment, arranges precision instruments for purposes of recording, statistically analyzes the quantitative results of the investigation, and makes inferences about behaviour on the basis of the experimental results, he is making a large number of critical assumptions that are based on some one or another philosophical presupposition. In the following analysis of psychological methodology we shall see how the more abstract tools of science are inextricably mixed with philosophy.

The General Plan of Scientific Method

The scientist selects a tentative explanation as the beginning step in his inquiry, and this tentative suggestion is taken as an *hypothesis,* which directs the search for corroborative or negating facts. The hypothesis is merely a question and is usually quite narrow in scope. These hypotheses are piecemeal but not haphazardly so; each is a question recognized as belonging to a larger family of questions.

An investigation is designed in such a way that it involves a direct analysis of all the major conditions of the hypothesis. Preferably the investigation takes the form of an *experiment,* which is carried out under rigidly controlled conditions during the systematic variation of one of these conditions in particular. These characteristics allow the *reproducibility* of the conditions under which a given experiment is performed. When experimentation is impossible, however, the investigator may employ other methods. Psychological science is founded upon but not limited by the experimental method.

If the results of the investigation are not controversial, the hypothesis may be confirmed (although not proved), and the next step involves tying together the results of a large number of scientifically tested propositions, which have some system of relationship. The results of this last step may involve the formulation of a *scientific law*, which is only a type of mental shorthand by which a number of facts or relations are subsumed under one simplified statement. A natural law, then, is merely a resume of a longer and more detailed description.

Another stage, although not an absolutely necessary one, is the organization of *a theory* to account for the laws. The laws, as well as the theories, represent, generalizations from which formal deductions can be made. These deductions are then set up as hypotheses for further scientific investigation. A particular law or theory is thus tested objectively according to whether or not the things which it predicts (which may be deduced from it) are supported or discredited empirically. As more and more correct predictions are added for a particularly theory or law, we say that *truth is approached* (not *attained*) by the theory or law.

The process of induction from empirical evidence always involves a treacherous step because the evidence is never complete. In testing a certain hypothesis about human behaviour, we can never study *all* humans but must obtain what is believed to be a "representative" sample from the hypothetical population of all humans. Generalizations are thus of necessity made on the basis of partial evidence, and so they are made only as *probable inferences*. The degree of probability—or confidence—that can be attached to scientific inferences differs from one to another, and to this extent the business of science is directed toward diminishing error in the general process of scientific problem solving.

The scientific method becomes more than a mere circular game played by scientists when prediction directs investigation to seek something that has not been previously suspected. Furthermore, some of the most spectacular achievements of science have been produced by the rather straightforward system of inducing a generalization and then deducing from the generalization. Good experimentation, then, is not a hit-or-miss affair or purely random trial and error, and this fact led Darwin to the pregnant statement, "How odd it is that anyone should not see that all observation must be for or against some view, if it is to be of any service."

Theory and experiment are the helpmates of scientific pursuit, theory suggesting the pattern of the maze, and experiment determining the blind alleys and the short cuts. Whenever such a maze is found to be composed only of blind alleys, it is modified or discarded, or at least it should be. To this extent the term *science* should be reserved to describe a body of *verified knowledge*, and the most satisfactory criterion of science is in terms of the method of verification. Knowledge of facts without knowledge of the procedures to discover the facts does not constitute science, and this is especially true in psychology. Knowing about the behaviour of people does not qualify one as a psychologist.

Classification of Psychological Methods

When we try to catalog the many methods of investigation in psychology, we find that there are several types of general methods and several types of more specific techniques. The various fields of psychological study have their own specific techniques of research. The more general methods, however, are not peculiar to the separate fields but are used as common property by all psychologists. These general methods of investigation may be broadly classified in several different ways; one classification scheme is as follows :

1. Methods of selecting the individuals to be studied.
2. Methods of controlling extraneous stimulation during the investigation.
3. Methods of instructing or directing the attention of the individuals under investigation.
4. Methods of presenting the stimuli.
5. Methods of registering intermediate bodily changes.

6. Methods of observing and recording overt responses to stimulation
7. Methods of analyzing and synthesizing the data resulting from an investigation.

Although there is some overlapping among these classes of methods, each class pertains to humans or lower animals, to learning sensory motivational, motor, social, abnormal, child, personality, educational, or industrial investigations. This classification of methods is easily seen as depending to a considerable extent on the *stages of the investigation.*

Another and somewhat old-fashioned type of classification is based on a differentiation between *subjective* and *objective methods*. Because of the nature of many psychological phenomena there has always been some concern about this differentiation. In so far as the direct experience of an individual is to some extent a private and subjective phenomenon, many of the methods used to study direct experience and mental processes are called subjective. The general technique for investigating these phenomena—thought, images, feelings, sensations, perceptions—has been to ask the subject to report on these experiences, to introspect. This general type of observation has been distinguished from objective observation, which is not so dependent on the biases or judgments of the individual observer and better permits independent verification. Such a methodological distinction has become of less importance with the growing realization that all the subjective methods can be handled with a considerable degree of objectivity and that all the objective methods have some of the characteristics of subjectivity.

Still another and somewhat more fruitful classification of psychological methods are in terms of the conditions of control and the purposes of the observations. The general methods may be characterized as *experimental, differential, or clinical.* These classes overlap only slightly, and a choice between them is usually made on the basis of the specific problem to be solved and the nature of the assumptions that are possible or advisable for a particular investigation.

EXPERIMENTAL METHODS

Experimentation holds the central position in psychological science, as it does in all other sciences, for the reason that it best exemplifies the principles of scientific method [20, 22]. The experiment consists of objective observations of actions performed under rigidly controlled condition. The hypothesis for investigation is chosen and is stated in such a manner that it can be tested rather completely. One factor, the "causal" one, is usually varied through a predetermined range of values. In the more classical scheme, changes are produced in one variable at a time, and the effects of these changes are observed and measured or recorded while all other important variables of influence are held constant in their effects [2, 7].

The Independent and the Dependent Variable

One manner of illustrating a typical design for a psychological experiment is shown in Fig.1.1. This diagram indicates that a certain type of specified action, the *dependent variable*, is observed while it is influenced by arbitrarily produced changes in some specified stimulating condition, the *independent variable*. Other stimulating conditions that might influence the dependent variable are not allowed to vary during the course of the experiment; *i.e.*, their influences are held constant. On the other hand, actions other than those of one particular

Fig. 1.1. A diagram to represent the scheme of a psychological experiment.

dependent variable are quite naturally being carried on by the organism, and these are indicated by the lines R_1 and R_3. In some experiments measures of these other responses are recorded during the whole process, and under such conditions more than one dependent variable exists in the experiment. Such is the case in an experiment which is designed to determine the effects on both mood and efficiency (two dependent variables) of changes in oxygen content of the air breathed by the subjects in the experiment.

Thus there is only one independent variable in an experiment of the classical design, and so we often hear of the *law of the independent variable*. This law states what we are to keep all causal factors constant except one, which is to be systematically varied while observations of concomitant or successive changes in the dependent variables are made. Such a procedure rules out all other possibilities of producing in the results effects not attributable to the one independent variable. Certain systematic experimental designs are now available that enable the experimenter to employ more than one independent variable in a single experiment. A discussion of this important point will arise later.

The foregoing description is not to be taken as indicating that all the factors involved in any experiment are under the investigator's control. If the observations could be completely controlled, the experimenter would need to make only as many observations as there are degrees of change in the independent variable. This may be the situation in certain physical sciences, but certainly not in the behavioural sciences, where the behaviour of the organism is quite variable and is influenced by a multitude of factors, both internal and external. Because of the relatively great variability of behaviour, it is necessary for the experimenter to obtain several observations under each condition of the experiment. An average tendency among the observations for each level of the independent variable is then computed, and that average tendency is accepted as a more dependable and representative value for the dependent variable.

Importance of Controls

Many of the factors that would influence and modify the behaviour specified by a particular dependent variable must have their influence removed from the experimental situation. Insuring adequate controls is one of the most important problems for the experimentalist to face. The influences of uncontrolled factors may obscure the results of experiments that would otherwise be critical, and yet psychology cannot exert control over all the possible sources of influence that are extraneous to the independent variable. The result of this seeming impasse is that all experiments must be repeated (replicated) and must produce consistency of results under a variety of conditions before they become accepted as demonstrating "facts." The scientist must always be prepared to scrap his results whenever they are demonstrated to be untenable in the light of replication under more precise control.

A typical Psychological Experiment

Before going further into the logic of experimental design, the reader is referred to Buxton's description of experiment by Courts. Courts tested the hypothesis that there is a functional relationship between the degree of tension on the part of the learner and the efficiency of learning, and the description given of Court's study forms a good lesson in experimental design. The reader should study this description carefully before proceeding in this introduction.

Functional and Factorial Experiments

As a result of having carried out an experiment, the psychological investigator usually wishes to express a relationship between the independent and a dependent variable. Seeking for such *concomitant variations* is one of the most important endeavors in scientific work [6,23]. As a result of this type of information science is able to understand causal factors and make predictions.

Through experimentation we wish ultimately to establish statements of scientific law, or at least generalizations which approach the status of laws. The laws, our goal, express relations and thus become the model for an important type of experiment. When the researcher wishes to determine the functional relationship between two experimental variables, he first establishes the range of the independent variable within which he will experiment. As a next step he chooses several values within that range and stimulates his subjects with each of these values (or under the conditions of each of these values) while he observes and records the resulting changes in behaviour of a specified sort (the dependent variable). This general procedure identifies the experiment as being of the *functional type, i.e.,* one in which a functional relationship is sought. Such was Court's experiment.

Quite often, however, the researcher must cast about in a more exploratory fashion to determine factors that will offer some chance of showing important and useful relationships. Instead of using several values along the independent variable, the experimenter may use only two, as in the typical experiment wherein a difference is sought between the presence and the absence of a certain feature. The results of such experiments as this do not indicate the functional relations between variables but do show whether the factor which has been changed produces any measurable change in the dependent variable. We may classify experiments of this second type as *factorial.* Experiments of the factorial type are most useful as preliminary stages in an experimental programme; they are used mainly to answer the question *what,* whereas experiments of the functional type are designed to answer the question *how.*

The Control-Test Method

In order further to see how experiments are designed to answer psychological hypotheses, we may make another type of classification of experimental methods. One of these classes may be called the control-test method, which consists in the observation of performance under what may be called normal conditions and then again with one condition changed. The control-test method is an example of the factorial type of experiment at its simplest level. For example, visual acuity might be measured under ordinary conditions of illumination and then under the condition of glare. Actually the measure would be taken several times under each condition, but it would not be necessary to have two different groups of subjects for the experiment. The control-test method is sometimes called the *method* of *difference*.

The control-test method is used when there is little or no practice effect or transfer from one condition of measurement to the other. Visual acuity is not changed by its measurement, although the process of measurement is usually novel or complex to the degree that it may take the subjects a few practice trials to learn to follow the instructions and to give reliable reports. Such practice trials, of course, are not recorded.

The Control-Group Method

This technique consists in observing two equated groups of subjects who are performing under the same conditions except for the influence of one element. The scale of presence-absence of this one particular element represents the independent variable of the experiment and identifies it as factorial in type. The difference in performance between the two groups is the dependent variable and is a function of the independent variable if all other sources of influence are eliminated.

In this experimental design it is very important that the two groups involved have equal potentialities to begin with. In order to approximate this condition the groups are equated; *i.e.*, they are so chosen as to be at the same level of measured capacity on the variables that may conceivably affect the results, and ideally they should due equated for *all* characteristics which might bear on the investigation at hand. Because perfectly equated groups are a frank impossibility, the investigator is usually content to equate for those characteristics which seem most likely to influence the dependent variable.

An example of the control-group technique may be

described in the following manner. The general hypothesis may be that practice in memorizing increases memory ability. Such an hypothesis defies direct experimental test, and so a more particular aspect of the general statement is chosen : practice in memorizing certain prose increases ability to memorize certain poetry. In designing an experiment for an adequate test of this hypothesis, the first step is to select a group of subjects who are reasonably homogeneous in memorizing ability and do not differ from one another very much in intelligence. All the subjects are then given a test (the *fore-test*) to determine their ability to memorize poetry. On the basis of the scores from this fore-test, the subjects are divided into two groups such that the average poetry memorizing abilities (as measured by the test) are the same. It is also desirable that the variabilities of the two groups be equal. One of the two groups is now chosen as the *experimental group*, and a period of practice in memorizing prose is spent by this group. The other group becomes the *control group* and does not receive any of the practice on prose. Both groups are then given a final test on memorizing poetry.

The following hypothetical data may be used to indicate the expression and treatment of experimental results that might accrue from this investigation :

	Fore-Test (poetry)	*Training Period (prose)*	*Final Test (poetry)*
Experimental group	62	—	79
Control group	62	....	66
			Difference = 13

The two groups were equated at 62 (same measure of proficiency) on the fore-test, and the experimental group was 13 points better than the control group on the final test. This difference is now attributable to the effects of the training period on the experimental group, because the two groups were the same in most other important respects. It is to be noted that the control group in this hypothetical experiment became slightly better (by 4 points) at poetry on the final test, presumably due to the practice administered in the very taking of the fore-test. Therefore, we may assume that the experimental group likewise gained 4 of their 17 points as a result of the practice afforded by the fore-test.

The control-group method is used whenever it is possible that the function to be measured (memory in the experiment described) may change every time it is measured. That is, there may be and usually is some practice effect within the fore-test itself, and the only way to determine the amount of this unwanted practice effect is by the use of the control group.

The Matched-Pair Technique

The theory of the control-group method is applied to situations other than those involving growth or learning. When choosing two groups for the purpose of evaluating the effects of an independent variable, the investigator often selects the subjects in *pairs,* and this procedure is known as the *matched-pair technique.* In such cases the independent variable may from the basis of the selection. For example, an investigator may wish to determine whether bright children are more or less suggestible than dull children. This hypothesis is an interesting one and has been tested in a rather precise manner by Simmons [21]. Knowing that suggestibility may be influenced to a considerable extent by age and sex, Simmons chose children in pairs in such a way that the two members of each pair were exactly equal in age and were of the same sex. One member of each pair was dull, with an intelligence quotient below 90, and the other member was bright, with an intelligence quotient above 125. For our purposes we need not be concerned with the way in which suggestibility was measured. It will suffice to say that the groups were treated in exactly the same manner in the investigation and a numerical suggestibility score was obtained on each subject. Interestingly enough, the bright children averaged 30.7, and the dull children averaged 46.3, the later being definitely the more suggestible. In this factorial type of study by Simmons the independent variable was intelligence, which she "varied" in the manner in which she selected her groups.

It is worth pausing for a moment to note that Simmons's

investigation does not qualify as a read experiment, which necessarily involves the more purposive manipulation of the independent variable. It is, however, sometimes desirable to turn to nature and find conditions that conform rather closely to what is wanted and so to utilize these conditions without further manipulation. In such cases selection may replace control. After all, intelligence is not a variable which we can easily manipulate and vary and therefore we must run to individual differences for a scale, rather than to a physical scale which can be employed in the laboratory.

The Practice Method

This method consists in training the subject or subjects in the function to be used until no more improvement is made as a result of training or practice. After such a level of practice is reached, variations in performance may safely be ascribed to variations in the conditions under which they are made. When a subject is used as his own control in this manner, it is obviously necessary to reach a high practice level before beginning the experiment proper. The practice method is not frequently used in experimentation because a great deal of time is required for each subject, thus making it difficult to obtain a very large number of subjects; also the method is obviously not suitable for studies that pertain to the early stages of the learning process. These factors that weigh against the general use of the practice method clearly indicate a central problem in experimenting on organisms; *i.e.*, the organism is subject to change by the very measurement process itself—a feature especially peculiar to psychological experimentation.

The Rotation Method

The rotation method consists in presenting two or more stimulation situations to the experimental subjects in as many sequences as necessary to control the serial effects of fatigue or practice. For example, if we wished to determine the relative influence of two specified conditions, A and B, on a group of subjects, we would *not* measure all the subjects under condition A and then under condition B. Condition A might so fatigue or train the subjects that the measures under condition B would not be independent of the fatigue or training effects—another case in which the measuring process changes the behaviour. We would thus be faced with two alternatives. We might obtain half the measures for condition A, all the measures for condition B, and then the other half of the measures for condition A. This technique is sometimes called the ABBA order or *counterbalancing*. Another alternative is to separate the subjects into two equated groups, one of which receives treatment A and then B, whereas the other group receives treatment B and then A. Both sets of A results and both set of B results may then be combined, and the difference between them calculated.

The purpose of the rotation method in experimental design is fairly obvious. The advantage or disadvantage of placing one condition first in the sequence is balanced for the two conditions. An assumption is made in this logic, however, to the effect that the transfer effect form condition A to condition B is the same as from B to A. This assumption may or may not be sound, and it is probably made more often than is justified. At any rate, the rotation method should be applied only with some caution, and it is usually a compromise method. Ideally, large groups of carefully equated subjects should be used in an experiment, one for one condition and the other for the other condition. The rotation method, however, is usually resorted to when only a limited number of subjects are available, and with this method all the subjects are measured under all the conditions; the two groups are equated because they are the same persons. This assumption, however, may be a delusion because a subject is not the same after he has had a certain test—he may learn important elements or attitudes for the next test.

Let us briefly go through a typical situation in which the rotation method is employed as a group demonstration for classes in experimental psychology. Using the hypothesis that the three typical methods of measuring retention of verbal material give different results, we choose three lists of nonsense syllables in such a way that the three lists are of equal difficulty. (This equality can be obtained from lists published for the purpose.) Calling these lists A, B, and C, we have a large group of subjects memorize the lists in the order ABC and under standardized conditions. For each subject we obtain a score on each of the three lists, and three scores are then averages for each persons. We send the subjects away with the admonition that they should not rehearse the material in any way and that they should return to the laboratory at a designated time in the future.

From the set of scores we equate three groups of subjects, I, II, and III, such that they are equal in their demonstrated ability to memorize the material. When the subjects return for further observations, we instruct them in such a way that the different groups take the retention measures in the following manner :

Group I	*Group II*	*Group III*
Recall test on list A	Recognition test on list A	Relearning on list A
Relearning on list B	Recall test on list B	Recognition test on list B
Recognition test on list C	Relearning on list C	Recall test on list

Note that all three measures of retention occur in all three orders. Thus no method of measurement gets more practice or fatigue effect than any other when we combine the data for analysis. We pool the data simply by taking all the scores on *recall* together, those on *recognition* together, and those on *relearning* together. Remember that the lists were equated before the investigation began.

As a general result, in analyzing the data from such an experiment, we would probably find that methods of measuring retention differed and that recognition produced highest scores, relearning next highest, and recall lowest. In such an experiment the lists might be made up of different types of materials : one list of related words, another of unrelated words, and the third of nonsense syllables. Our retention tests would probably then indicate that the list of related words is retained best and the nonsense syllables least. An additional question of interest would then be whether there was considerable interaction between one of the lists and one of the measures of retention. For example, we might find that recalling the related words was relatively a very easy task, although recall in general did not produce high scores. This problem of interaction can be approached with proper experimental designs and is becoming an important aspect of experimentation in psychology [9].

If the lists of nonsense syllables were not equated in this experiment or if the lists were made up of different materials, a more complicated experimental design would be needed, and we would probably have our groups of subjects do different things. A characteristic to note in such a case as this is the possibility of interaction between a certain type of material and a certain method of measuring retention.

Notice that in the foregoing experiment two independent variables were involved and were active in conjunction with one another. This appears to contradict the statement made earlier to the effect that we employ only one independent variable at a time in an experiment. There are, however, some new types of experimental designs based on concepts that differ rather radically from the classical ones as to the number of inquiries that should be included in a single experiment. In the newer experimental designs all the factors to be tested are varied concurrently in all possible combinations. Such complicated experimental designs are really extensions of the rotation method and are based on a statistical method called analysis of variance [9, 13]. These techniques allow much greater efficiency than the classical technique of the single independent variable.

Artificial Characteristic of Experiments

A meaningless critcism has frequently been directed against experimental methods as used in psychology. This criticism is to the effect that real human behaviour, the kind of everday behaviour that we wish to understand, occurs outside of laboratories, and when it is studied in the laboratory under the usual conditions of rigid control and precise measurement, it is not the same behaviour. This statement is of course quite true, but the experimentalist does not take it as a serious criticism because he actively seeks for stringent and artificial conditions, rather than attempting to avoid them and study "daily life" behaviour as it occurs.

Because of the extreme variety and complexity of behaviour and of the forces which influence it, no one would be able to establish a science of behaviour by trying to study it under "normal" conditions. Whenever we begin a behavioural investigation, normal conditions do not exist because the measurement situation (even the interview situation) is not "normal." As stated near the beginning of this chapter, scientific hypotheses are necessarily quite limited in scope. It is only by the piecemeal selection of a few very limited aspects of behaviour at a time and by carefully planned and intensive analysis of those limited aspects that successive investigations may allow us to construct a picture of behaviour such that we may understand it, describe it, predict it, and control it. In all this work there is an obvious *error of fractionation,* but the error is important only when laboratory conditions are incorrectly thought of as counterparts of daily life activities.

Woodworth [24] has stated an analogous situation in the history of physics (the experimental techniques of which science are more easily "acceptable" to the layman). In order to test the law of falling bodies with adequate precision and control, objects of different mass are dropped simultaneously in a vacuum. The counterpart of this situation would be very unusual if it occurred in nature : what is more "unnatural" than a vacuum?

There are, of course, psychological methods of investigation which are not so rigorous nor quite so artificial as experimentation. The psychological investigator therefore must be acquainted with the psychological investigator therefore must be acquainted with the other techniques that may be applied to problems that temporarily defy laboratory experimentation. The second major class of psychological methods of investigation is called *differential,* and these methods will be seen to meet more nearly some of the objections leveled at the experimental methods.

DIFFERENTIAL METHODS

Non-experimental Variables

The class of methods called differential includes those systems of techniques which employ *individual differences* as variables of investigation. In such studies there usually is no purposive *manipulation* of the independent variable ; the investigator merely chooses his subjects according to certain criteria, and the measurements on the subjects themselves form the variable or variables for the investigation. The criterion of selection of the subjects may become the independent variable for an investigation (intelligence, in Simmons' study), but it is to be noted that this variable is not under the full control of the investigator, to be varied up and down a given scale at will and with full freedom.

At first view the above differentiation between experiments and differential methods may appear quite artificial, and it is true that all psychologists will not agree to such an apparently artificial classification scheme. Nevertheless, it should always be made clear that the independent variables resulting from individual differences are never under the investigator's control to the same degree that experimental variables are. Also the scales are different in kind.

Although the experimental methods are more precise and the inferences made from the results of these methods have greater likelihood of validity and can be more easily verified, it cannot be said that they are always more desirable than the differential methods. Experimental methods establishe the model of objectivity for the other methods of psychological investigatgations, but experiments obviously cannot be devised for all the problems that are raised in the heterogeneous subject matter of psychology, as will be seen in a perusal of the various techniques described later in this book.

Correlational Methods

It is easily seen that most correlation studies in psychology fall into the class of differential methods. The major studies of intelligence and aptitudes and personality and a large number of those on social behaviour are therefore classed as differential investigations. In these studies the psychologist takes people as they are and studies what they do, usually without changing the conditions under which they respond to the "tests" or perform the desired tasks. (If the conditions are changed, the situation becomes more like an experiment.) The subjects will naturally differ from one another in their behaviour, and the investigator is usually seeking *concomitant variations* in other ways in which they behave.

The importance of this general technique for purposes of prediction can easily be seen from a few simple examples. It is quite important to be able to predict what kind of work each person can do best in order to produce the most efficient matching of workers with jobs. Attempts at solution of this problem are handled mainly by correlational techniques, in which workers are rated in terms of success on the job, and these ratings are correlated with a number of test scores on the same workers. Those tests that produce the highest correlations with the ratings of merit are then employed in the screening of others for the job in question. Other persons may now be given the same tests, and those who score highest on them will be judged as having a higher likelihood of performing efficiently on the specified job.

The foregoing is an example of the use of correlation procedures in analyzing related scores, and the literature of psychology contains thousands of published studies on these problems. Another general type of application of the correlation method is directed toward the nature-nurture problem in psychology and involves studying pairs of persons who are genetically related. The score of one member of a pair is plotted against the score of the other member, and this is repeated for successive pairs. Most studies of this general sort indicate that in terms of intelligence test scores identical twins correlate quite highly (.90), fraternal twins less (.70), and siblings still less (.50), while relations as remote as grandparent-grandchild correlate hardly at all (,15). Such correlation studies as these on related pairs are really quite inadequate because of the presence of another correlating variable : similarity of environmental conditions during early development. The studies do, however, constitute examples of how correlational analyses are applied for the purpose of testing relations other than between one mental test and another.

The Longitudinal and the Cross-sectional Approaches

The problem of mental growth is a good one to illustrate differential methods in studying concomitant variations. In investigations on this problem mental progress, as measured by some type of test, is observed, and charted. There is no attempt on the part of the investigator to alter the normal course of development because it is the normal trend that is to be discovered. This general technique obviously raises an important issue, in which the investigator must choose whether to retest a group of individuals at successive ages, the *longitudinal approach,* or to test different age groups at the same time, the *cross-sectional* approach. Each of these approaches offers its own peculiar difficulties [1,10]. It is enough for our purposes here merely to indicate the general nature of the differential technique in contrast to the experimental approach. The experimental approach has no way of giving information on the general problem of mental growth, although certain more limited hypotheses concerning such growth may be studied experimentally. The issue in this case is that both age and mental ability go along without our being able to do much direct manipulation of either of them. The investigator merely takes things as they are and determines the relationship between two specified natural phenomena. In order to study the differences between males and females in terms of certain psychological or physical traits, differential methods must also be applied. We most certainly cannot experimentally vary the sex of the human subject.

The cross-sectional approach has become an extremely important technique in an active democratic society. By its use determinations may be made of such phenomena as the morale effects of certain government policies, of electioneering effects, of food habits during critical shortages.

General Statistical Methods

The differential methods have often been called statistical for the reason that statistical techniques become the major devices for studying individual differences. This fact can be seen from a brief listing of the more important characteristics of statistical methods : (*a*) efficiently describing masses of data in terms of relatively few numerical expressions, (*b*) expressing the relationships between variables, (*c*) allowing the extensions of scientific inferences to be tested under conditions of mathematical exactness.

The commonly noted relation between differential methods and statistical techniques does not mean that statistics are not considered important tools to be applied in experimental methods. The data that result from experiments are expressed in mathematical form, and statistical analyses are applied to these data in order to exhaust all the useful information from them. It is also through statistical methods that the most efficient experimental designs have been derived [8].

CLINICAL METHODS

The clinical methods have a different frame of reference from the experimental and differential methods in psychology. The word clinic originally referred to "something pertaining to a bed", and it has been extended to mean "directed toward the individual." Whereas the experimental and differential methods have been established to ascertain facts which transcend the individual case, the clinical methods are directed less toward investigations of general behavioral facts and more toward individual appraisal and adjustment.

No attempt will be made to elaborate upon clinical methods at this point because these techniques and their applications are thoroughly described in Chapter 19. The reference to clinical methods in this introductory chapter serves mainly to indicate a third and important general class of psychological methods.

ORGANIZATION OF THE CHAPTERS THAT FOLLOW

The plan of organization of the chapters in this book is fairly obvious and seems to represent a logical form. The chapters on acquiring behaviour changes—learning and thinking—cover the major types of investigation in these fields and indicate how the central problems have been attacked by properly devised methods and techniques.

The next section of the book is devoted to the topics of reception. Because of the psychological nature of measurement in sensory and perceptual research, this section is introduced by a chapter on psychophysics. The chapter on methods of studying perceptual phenomena was placed next because of the excellent discussion of the methodological relations between perception and sensation. Furthermore, this chapter serves as a bridge between the psychophysics and the psychophysiology of sensation.

The chapter on animal behaviour represents a transition of subject matter. It takes its present position because it serves as an indicator of how the learning and reception techniques are applied to lower animals, and it introduces the topic of motivation at a lower level. The next section, containing chapters on motivation and emotion recording action, neuropsychological and other bodily functions, and motor functions and efficiency, discusses the methods of psychology which have been applied to solving the significant problems of response mechanisms and tendencies.

The last section of the book is devoted to descriptions of the important methods of studying individual differences in the more specialized domains of psychological investigation. Here the non-experimental methods of psychology are seen in their important relations to investigating and appraising various capacities and traits of people classified in different manners.

SUMMARY

In this introduction we indicated some of the causes in the development of the scientific method and also some of the characteristic features of scientific method in the steps intervening between investigation and theory. A rather crude classification of psychological methods was made, and the more important features of each of the three types were described. In experimental methods the character features of the independent and dependent variables were discussed, and the difference between "factorial" and "functional" experimentation was evaluated. Some of the basic forms of psychological experiments were analyzed as (1) the control-test method, (2) the control-group method, (3) the matched-pair method, (4) the practice method, and (5) the rotation method.

Differential methods were characterized by their dependence on individual differences for the variables under investigation, and clinical methods by their individual-centered interests. Some of the interrelationships between the different classics of methods were shown, and it is hoped that the student will become more and more aware of this characteristic of interdependence among the psychological methods as he studies the topical chapters of this book.

REFERENCES

1. Anastasi, A., *Differential Psychology*. New York : Macmillan, 1939.
2. Bentley, M., The nature and uses of experiment in psychology. *Amer. J. Psychol.*, 1937, *50*, 452-469.
3. Boring, E. G., A psychological function is the relations of successive differentiations of events in the organism. *Psychol. Rev.*, 1937, *44*, 445-461.
4. Boring, E. G., Mind and mechanism. *Amer. J. Psychol.*, 1946,

59, 173-192

5. Churchman, C. W., *Theory of Experimental Inference.* University of pennsylvania, privately distributed.
6. Cohen, M. R., and E. Nagel, *An Introduction to Logic and scientific Method.* New York : Harcourt, Brace, 1934.
7. Dingler, H., *Das Experiment.* Munich : Ernst Reinhardt, 1928.
8. Fisher, R.A., *The Design of Experiments.* London : Oliver and Boyd, 1935.
9. Garrett, H. E., and J. Zubin, The analysis of variance in psychological research. *Psychol. Bull.*, 1943, *40*, 233-267.
10. Greene, E.B., *Measurements of Human Behaviour.* New York : Odyssey Press, 1941.
11. Griffith, C.R., *Principles of Systematic Psychology.* Urbana, Illinois : University of Illinois Press, 1943.
12. Heidbreder, E., *Seven Psychologies.* New York : Appleton-Century, 1933.
13. Jackson, R.W.B., Application of the analysis of variance and covariance method to educational problems. *Univ. Toronto, Dept. Educ. Research, Bull. No. 11*, 1940.
14. Jackson, T.A., *Principles of Experimentation.* (On file in Psychology Reading Room, Columbia University.)
15. Jaffe, H., The development of the experimental method. In *Philosophical Essays in Honour of Edgar Arthur Singer, Jr.* F.P. Clarke and M.C. Nahm, Eds. Philadelphia. University of Pennsylvania Press, 1942.
16. Jeffreys, H., *Scientific Inference.* New York : Macmillan, 1937.
17. Johnson, H.M., Pre-experimental assumptions as determiners of experimental results. *Psychol. Rev.*, 1940, *47*, 338-346.
18. Murray, H.A., *Explorations in Personality, a Clinical and Experimental Study of Fifty Men of College Age.* New York : Oxford University Press, 1938.
19. Pearson, K., *The Grammar of Science.* London : Adam and Charles Black, 1911.
20. Ritchie, A.D., *Scientific Method.* New York : Harcourt, Brace, 1923.

21. Simmons, R.M., A study of a group of children of exceptionally high intelligence quotients in situations partaking of the nature of suggestion. *Teach. Coll. Contrib. Educ.*, 1940, No. 788.

22. Westaway, F. W., *Scientific Method.* London : Blackie and Sons, 1937.

23. Wolf, A., *Essentials of Scientific Method.* New York : Macmillan, 1925.

24. Woodworth, R.S., Success and failures of experimental psychology. *Science,* 1941, 94, 265-270.

2

Psychophysical Methods

The Problem of Subjective Measurement

Psychophysics is that branch of psychology which is concerned with subjective measurement. Obviously a subjective unit of measurement is required. Psychophysical theory is concerned with the logic of subjective measurement [8], and psychophysical methods are concerned with experimental procedures.

In order to illustrate the difference between *the psychological continuum and the physical stimulus continuum,* let us consider an experiment in the differentiation of lifted weights, which has been investigated by hundreds of experimenters. The experimental subject is presented with a large assortment of small cylinders, all of them equal in size and appearance but different in weight. He is shown two of these cylinders which differ markedly in weight, and they are designated as *standards* for this experiment. Then the subject is asked to select one of the other weights that seems to be midway between the two standards. When the subject has satisfied himself that he has found a cylinder whose weight marks the midpoint between the standards, the three cylinders may be compared as to their "actual" weights. When the intervals are expressed in grams or other physical units, it is found that the lower interval is smaller than the upper one. In other words, the subjective on psychological continuum is not the same as the physical continuum. Measurement on the subjective continuum will be denoted *S*, and measurement on the physical continuum will be denoted *R*. The experimental method just described is called the *method of mean gradation.*

Psychophysical problems can be divided into several classes. Perhaps the most fundamental of these is that in which each one of a set of stimuli is allocated to a point in the subjective continuum without reference to physically measurable attributes. In a closely related class is the problem of predicating what people will do in terms of the subjective values of a set of stimuli. If their subjective values for a set of neckties are known, how many of the subjects will select a particular necktie as their first choice in any given assortment of neckties? Another large class of problems is concerned with the relation between the subjective and the physical continua. We shall see that relation is known as Fechner's law. One of the oldest types of psychophysical problem is that of determining the physical stimulus increment which the subject can just barely perceive. This increment is called the *just noticeable difference*. Since this is the simplest of the psychophysical problems, we shall start with the concepts and the experimental methods that have been used for determining such stimulus increments.

The Limen

The physical stimulus continuum is represented by the vertical line in Fig. 2.1. If the subject is being examined as to his ability to differentiate fine differences in the lengths of lines, then the stimulus unit might be the centimeter. If he is examined as to his ability to differentiate fine differences in pitch, then the stimulus unit would be cycles per second. The highest stimulus magnitude that the subject can perceive is called his *terminal stimulus or terminal threshold.*

In one type of experiment, the object is to determine the smallest stimulus difference that the subject can perceive. With a given standard R_s, the experimenter determines that stimulus threshold R_t which the subject can just barely differentiate from the standard. The magnitude of R_t is called the *differential threshold* for the given standard. The stimulus increment required for discrimination is called the *difference limen t.*

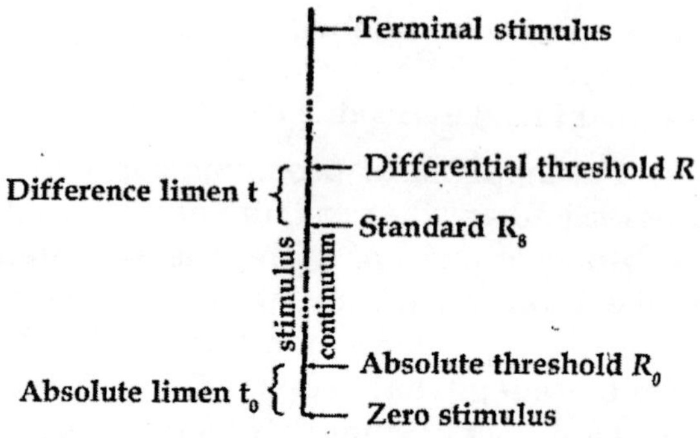

Fig. 2.1. The physicla stimulus continuum.

Sometimes the object is to determine the smallest stimulus magnitude that the subject can perceive. Various small intensities are then tried to find the *absolute threshold* R_0, which is the smallest stimulus intensity that the subject can identify. The increment between zero stimulus magnitude and the absolute threshold R_0 is called the *absolute limen* t_0. The absolute threshold R_0 and the absolute limen t_0 are numerically identical.

Another well-known problem in *psychophysics* is to determine the *two-point threshold.* This is the smallest distance between the two points of a special compass, called an *esthesiometer,* which the subject can just barely differentiate as two distinct points. For smaller separations between the compass points, the subject reports that he feels only one point. For further descriptions of the two-point threshold.

We have described the limen here as if it might be a sharply defined stimulus increment, but such is not the case. The subject varies from moment to moment in his sensitivity and attention, so that it usually becomes necessary to define the limen as a statistical measure. We say then that the limen is that stimulus magnitude, or that stimulus difference, which the subject can discriminate in a specified proportion of his attempts. In some experiments this proportion is set at 50 per cent, whereas in others it is set at 75 per cent, or higher. It is customary to define the absolute threshold as that stimulus magnitude which the subject can identify in half of his attempts.

The difference limen, however, is usually set at a higher proportion, such as 75 per cent, because otherwise the subject would be right in half of his attempts merely by guessing which of the two stimuli is the higher.

THE MAJOR PSYCHOPHYSICAL METHODS

Method of Reproduction

One of the simplest psychophysical methods is called the *method of reproduction* or the *method of average error*. The essential feature of this method is that the subject tries to reproduce the magnitude of a presented stimulus. For example, he is shown a straight line on a large card, which is placed at a specified distance in front of him, and is given a large sheet of paper with instruction to draw a line of exactly the same length. If he makes, say, one hundred such attempts, then his performance can be analyzed to determine how accurate it is.

In answering the question of how accurately the subject can reproduce the presented stimulus, we encounter in the subject's performance two kinds of error, which are investigated separately in many psychophysical experiments. One of these is the *constant error*, which is also called the *systematic error*. Another type is the *variable error*, which measures the *sensitivity* of the subject.

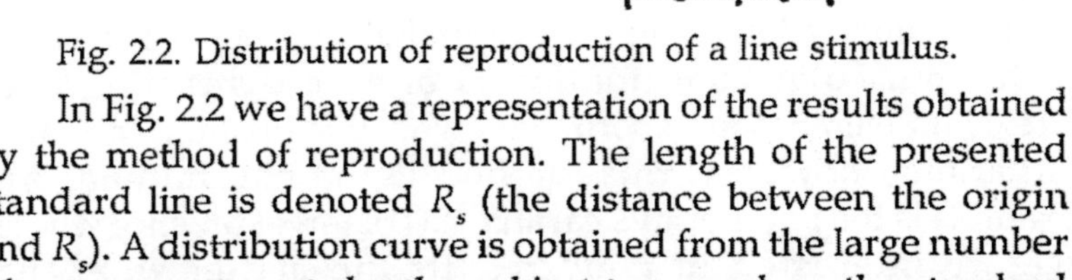

Fig. 2.2. Distribution of reproduction of a line stimulus.

In Fig. 2.2 we have a representation of the results obtained by the method of reproduction. The length of the presented standard line is denoted R_s (the distance between the origin and R_s). A distribution curve is obtained from the large number of separate attempts by the subject to reproduce the standard line. The mean of this distribution is denoted R_m. If the length of the standard line R_s and the average length R_m of the lines by the subject are unequal, then the discrepancy is a measure of the amount of *overestimation* or *underestimation*. This discrepancy is also called the *crude constant error* c. In the example of Fig. 2.2 we infer that the subject overestimated the standard line because his average line is longer than the standard R_s. The crude constant error can be defined by the relation $c = R_m - R_s$.

The consistency of the subject, sometimes also called the sensitivity, is measured by the dispersion of the distribution of his attempts. The standard deviation σ may be used to denote the amount of dispersion. In analyzing psychophysical data it is common to make a formal assumption that the subject's reproduction R is determined by two components : his average amount of overestimation or underestimation c and his variable error v at the moment of drawing a particular line. The formal result is then that his reproduced line $R = R_s + c + v$. Of course, we do not really believe that the degree of overestimation, positive or negative, is truly constant, but the result is treated as if it were the sum of one component that is constant, the constant error c and another component v that is variable from moment to moment.

There is an important limitation in the method of reproduction, namely, that the stimulus magnitude reproduced by the subject is determined in part by his ability to *perceive* the stimulus and in part by his *muscular coordination* in reproducing the standard stimulus, either by drawing a line, as in the present case, or by manipulating some apparatus that controls the stimulus magnitude of his reproductions. In psychophysical studies we are usually interested in the subject's ability to perceive the stimulus, and hence the effect of his muscular coordination is often a distracting and irrelevant element in experiments with this method. In many situations, however, this method is the natural one. An example is the psychophysical analysis of target practice where we are interested in good results, no matter what the perceptual and muscular components may be. Here it is useful to know the constant error, both in direction and in amount, and also the variability of the results over the target.

Weber's Law and Fechner's Law

The two best-known laws of psychophysics are Weber's law and Fechner's law. These two laws are frequently confused, and they are then described in a general way as the Weber-Fechner law, as if they were essentially the same law. The explicit formulation and experimental verification of these two laws will be described here. Their theoretical and experimental separation will be described in a later section in connection with the concept of the discriminal dispersion.

The older law is that of Weber, who stated "in comparing magnitudes, it is not the arithmetical difference, but the ratio of the magnitudes, which we perceive" [27, p. 430]. This law states what is well known in practical observation. In judging two suitcases as to which is the heavier, it is the ratio of the two weights that determines the ease with which we can perceive their difference. If their difference is only a few ounces, then it is unnoticed. If two letters differ by the same number of ounces, however, we easily perceive the difference. In the case of the letters a few ounces alter their weight ratio very markedly, whereas a few ounces have no significant effect on the ration of the weights of the suitcases. If a room is lighted by a single candle, then we notice readily the addition of a second candle because the light is then doubled. The addition of a single candle to a well-lighted room is unnoticed, however, because the two brightnesses are practically the same. This principle seems to be general.

Let us attempt to make an explicit scientific statement of Weber's law so that it can serve as a guide to what we actually do in the laboratory in trying to verify this law. We seek, then, an operational statement of Weber's law. Merely to say that it is the ratios of the stimuli that we notice rather than their actual differences does not say just what to look for in the laboratory. The statement will be improved if we say that *the differences limen is a constant fraction of the stimulus.* But the subject compares two stimuli. Which stimulus magnitude shall we take as the denominator? We can resolve this ambiguity by taking the average of the two stimuli as a standard. Then our statement would read : *the difference between two stimuli which can be just barely perceived is a constant fraction of their average magnitude.* When we come to the experiments, we find that this stimulus difference is not stable. Any fixed small difference is perceived by the subject in some trials and unnoticed in other trials. The greater the difference, the more often will the subject notice it. In fact, we are dealing with an experimentally continuous function which has no "jumping-off place" that can be called a limen. The proportion of correct judgments rises continuously with increase in the stimulus difference. Hence we must state Weber's law in terms of the relative frequency of correct judgments that we require in a definition of the limen. This difficulty can be resolved if we state Weber's law in the form, $P_{R<kR} = C$. Here C is any specified proportion of correct judgments except zero and unity. Let us take some arbitrary value, such as $C = 0.75$. If the stimulus value R is 100 grams, we may find that kR is 103 grams, as experimentally determined. The constant k is then 1.03. If we find that the value of k is the same for all values of R, then we have verified Weber's law for the constant $C = 0.75$. If we find that the relation also holds for all permissible values of C, then this formulation of Weber's law is experimentally verified [12].

The constant $(k-1)$ is called Weber's ratio. This ratio is about 1/100 for brightness, and about 1/30 for lifted weights. The smaller values of Weber's ratio indicate the greater sensitivity. The ratio is much higher for loudness, for which human perception is rather coarse. Weber's law has been found to hold fairly well over the major part of the stimulus range, but it breaks down toward the terminal stimulus values. The law also fails near the absolute threshold.

In considering the method of mean gradation, we noted the distinction between the psychological or perceived continuum and the physical or stimulus continuum. A weight that seems to us to lie midway between two standard stimuli is not ordinarily midway between them in number of grams. The relation between the subjective continuum S and the physical continuum R has been found experimentally to be logarithmic in shape, and hence the relation can be described by the empirical equation $S = k \log R$, where k is a parameter that varies with the nature of the stimuli and the experimental conditions. Although psychophysics is primarily concerned with measurement in the subjective continuum S, it deals also with the interesting relation between the subjective and the physical continua. This relation is expressed in Fechner's law. in the case of limen determinations, we are dealing with the relatively simple problem of expressing a just noticeable subjective difference in the corresponding physical continuum.

Two differences between these laws should be noted. The two laws are expressed as follows :

$$P_{R<kR} = C, \qquad \text{and} \qquad S = k \log R.$$

(Weber) (Fechner)

It can be seen by inspection that Fechner's law deals explicitly with the psychological continuum, whereas Weber's law says nothing explicitly about S. Another conspicuous differentiation is in the stimulus increments with which they deal. A difference that is barely perceptible is called a *liminal difference.* Large stimulus differences which are easily perceived are called *supraliminal differences.* Very small differences about which the subject would nearly always be in doubt are called *subliminal differences.* Now, with regard to the two psychophysical laws, note that Weber's law is always concerned with liminal and subliminal differences, whereas Fechner's law has no limitation in this regard. If the difference between two stimuli's supraliminal, then the subject can always distinguish them, and his proportion of correct discriminations is unity. Weber's law is concerned with stimulus differences that are small enough so that the subject has some difficulty in distinguishing them. Under certain conditions, to be described later, the two laws can be verified in the same set of experimental data, but under other conditions one of these laws can be satisfied when the other one fails [13, 24, p. 383].

The earlier statement of Weber's law—that we perceive

the ratios of stimulus magnitudes and not their absolute differences—can be interpretated as implying the logarithmic relation of Fechner's law directly, but experimental work on Weber's law has been universally restricted to the relation between the difference limen *t* and the stimulus magnitude *R*. It is thereby restricted to liminal differences. We shall see that there is good reason for separating these two problems, namely, (1) the functional relation between the subjective and the physical continua, and (2) the ease of discrimination between two stimuli. The first is the logarithmic relation that has become known as Fechner's law. The second problem is markedly affected by the stimulus ambiguities to be described later.

The Stimulus Error

In order to understand some problems in psychological measurement, it is essential to be able to observe one's own mental processes. This requires a psychological point of view which differs from that of judging the properties of physical objects. When the subject tries to guess whether a weight actually is midway between two standard weights, we say that he makes an *object judgment*. He tries to describe the physical properties of the object. When he reports whether a weight *seems* to lie midway between two standard weights, as experienced, and without reference to the number of grams or ounces, then we say that he makes a *sensory judgment*. He tries to describe his sensations. When the subject is asked to make a sensory judgment and yet reverts to the more naïve object judgment, he is said to commit the *stimulus error*. Then he pays attention to the physical stimulus, although he is asked to report sensory or perceptual intensities [1].

It has been found that the accuracy of object judgments can be improved with practice. For example, a grocery clerk may be so well practiced that he can estimate the weight of a piece of cheese with considerable accuracy. Similarly, a postal clerk may be able to judge the required postage for a letter by merely lifting it. Such individuals would probably find it difficult to serve as subjects in psychophysical experiments if they were required to make sensory judgments in the range of their experience. They have learned to describe perceptual intensities S in terms of the corresponding physical magnitudes R.

Method of Limits

One of the relatively simple methods of determining the limen is the *method of limits*, which is also called the *method of minimal change*. This method will be described separately for the determination of the absolute threshold and for the difference limen.

In the experimental procedure for the absolute threshold the subject is first presented with a single stimulus of very low intensity, so that he cannot identify it. The stimulus is augmented by the experimenter in successive steps until the subject reports that he does perceive it. This is the *ascending series of judgments*. Then the experimenter presents to the subject a stimulus which is definitely supraliminal, and the stimulus is altered by successive decrements until the subject reports that he no longer perceives it. The subject gives a report of presence or absence of the stimulus for each setting. This is the *descending series* of judgments.

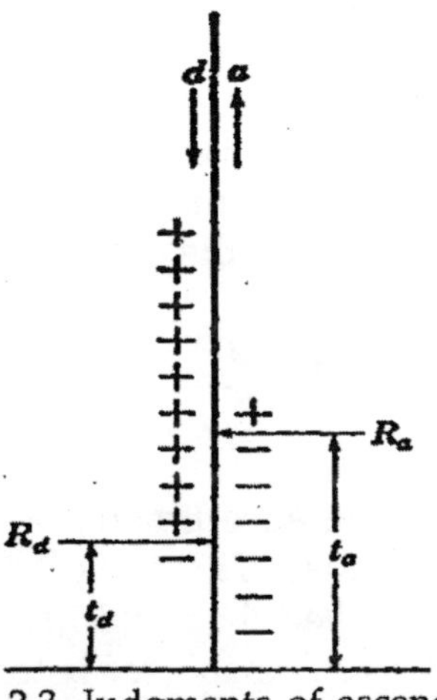

Fig. 2.3. Judgments of ascending and descending series for absolute thresholds.

In Fig. 2.3 we have a diagrammatic representation of the ascending and the descending series of judgments. The plus sign represents a positive judgment by the subject, and the minus sign represents failure to identify the stimulus. The ascending series starts with a low stimulus intensity, which the subject fails to identify. It is augmented in steps until the subject reports that he does perceive it. This stimulus is marked plus for the ascending series. Midway between the last two settings we have the *ascending threshold* intensity R_a, which is in this case identical with the *ascending limen* t_a as shown in the diagram.

A supraliminal stimulus which the subject definitely identifies is then presented. It is altered by successive decrements until the subject reports that he fails to perceive it. This last intensity is marked minus. The midpoint between the last two settings is recorded as the *descending threshold* R_a, and this is identical with the *descending limen* t_d. The absolute threshold t_0 is then taken as the average of the ascending and the descending limens. In practice, the experimenter presents a number of ascending and descending series, the average of which is taken as the absolute threshold. Formally, we have :

$$t_0 = \frac{R_a + R_d}{2} \quad \text{or} \quad t_0 = \frac{t_a + t_d}{2}$$

The difference limen is determined by this method in a similar manner. The subject is presented with two stimuli, which are called the *standard stimulus* and the *variable stimulus* respectively. The subject is told which of the two stimuli is the standard and which is the variable. He is told, further, that the variable stimulus will be altered in magnitude by the experimenter in successive increments, and that he is to judge for each setting of the variable whether it seems to be (1) lower than the standard, (2) equal to the standard, or (3) higher than the standard. These are called *three categories of judgment.* It is also explained to the subject that the initial setting of the variable will be quite low, so that it can be easily differentiated from the standard, and that the variable will then be augmented in successive steps until it exceeds the standard. This is called the ascending series of judgments.

In Fig. 2.4 we have a diagrammatic representation of the

method of limits for the determination of a difference limen. The low initial settings of the variable stimulus are marked minus because the variable is then easily seen to be lower than the standard. After several increments the subject reports that the two stimuli seem equal. The midpoint between these two settings is denoted R_{la} for the lower ascending threshold. After several increments during which the subject reports equality, he finds one stimulus which he reports as greater than the standard. This is marked plus. The midpoint between the last two settings is denoted R_{ua} for the upper ascending threshold. The standard stimulus magnitude is denoted R_s in the figure. The upper and lower difference limens are deviations from the standard and are denoted t_{ua} and t_{la} respectively. A similar diagrammatic representation is shown for the descending series.

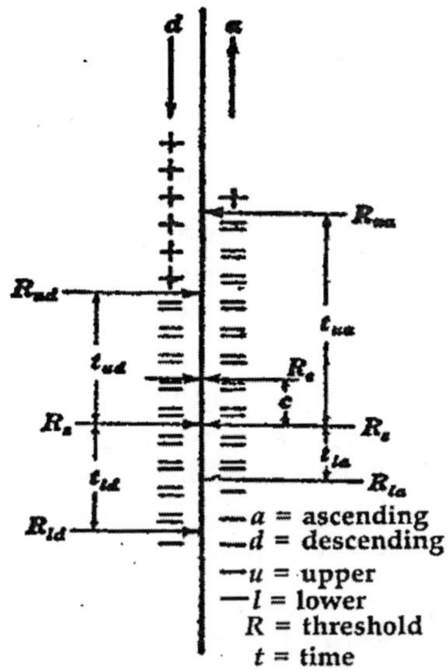

Fig. 2.4. Judgment of ascending and descending series for differential thresholds.

From data collected in this manner, three determinations are made. The *difference limen* is the average of the four limens, ascending and descending, upper and lower. We have then for the limen t :

$$t = \tfrac{1}{4} (t_{ud} + t_{ua} + t_{ld} + t_{la})$$

or

$$t = \tfrac{1}{4} (R_{ud} + R_{ua} - R_{ld} - R_{la})$$

The point of subjective equality R_e is that variable stimulus magnitude which seems, on the average, to be equal to the standard. This is taken as the average of the four thresholds, and we then have

$$R_e = \frac{1}{4}(R_{ud} + R_{ua} + R_{ld} + R_{la}).$$

The crude constant error c is the difference between the standard stimulus value and the point of subjective equality. We have then

$$c = R_e - R_g.$$

Both the figures for this method have been drawn so as to represent a usual effect in the method. The ascending thresholds are shown higher than the descending thresholds. The explanation is probably that the subject tends to retain the category of judgment which he has been giving until the conditions have been stretched somewhat beyond the true threshold. This effect is called *habituation*. The opposite effect is sometimes observed when the subject gives the next category of judgment sooner than is expected by his threshold. This effect is called *expectation*. The more common effect is habituation. It seems likely that individual differences in this effect have a temperamental origin. Psychophysical differences might be investigated in the search for objective indices of personality.

The Constant Method

For the purpose of making a limen determination the experimental procedure should preferably be such that the subject has no knowledge as to which stimulus is being increased or decreased. In most cases he should be unaware of any distinction between the standard and the variable stimulus because this distinction is largely a matter of book-keeping for the experimenter. As far as the subject is concerned, the two presented stimuli should be coordinate, and his task should be merely to judge which of them has more x-ness, where x is any stimulus attribute that is to be judged. The constant method satisfies these preferred conditions.

The subject is presented with a series of pairs of stimuli and is asked to specify for each pair whether a designated stimulus is the stronger or the weaker. For analytical purposes the two stimuli are called the standard and the variable. The subject may be allowed either two or three categories of judgment. If he has two categories of judgment, then he judges that the stimulus A is greater than B, or that it is less than B. If he has three categories of judgment, then he judges that stimulus A is greater than B, equal to B, or less than B. The stimuli A and B may be defined as right and left, or first and second. These two sets of instructions, for two or three categories of judgment, will be described separately.

When the subject has responded to a large series of comparisons of the standard R_g with different values of the variable R_v, then the results can be represented graphically in what is known as the *psychometric function*, which is illustrated in Fig. 2.5. Whenever the variable stimulus is much greater

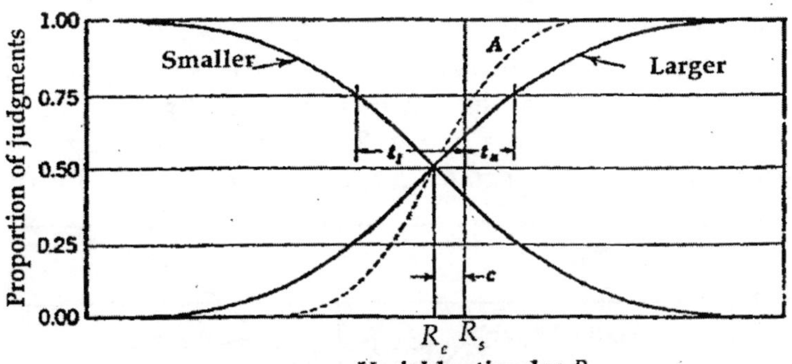

Fig. 2.5. The psychometric function (two categories of judgment).

than the standard, then the subject returns a large proportion of judgments $R_v > R_g$, and hence the curve "larger" rises with increasing values of the variable stimulus. The curve for judgments "smaller " is the complement of the curve for judgments " larger." The sum of the ordinates for these two curves equals unity for all values of the variable stimulus. The point of subjective equality R_e is that value of the variable stimulus which is defined by the intersection of the two curves at the level $P = 0.50$. The constant error c is the difference between the standard stimulus R_8 and the value R_e. The *sensitivity* is represented by the slope of the curve, and hence it may be measured by the standard deviation of the distribution of judgments "larger." Because of summetry, the two curves have the same dispersion. The dotted curve at A is steeper, and hence it would represent a subject with greater sensitivity and lower limen. One common measure of the sensitivity is the distance between the standard stimulus and that variable stimulus for which the psychometric curve has an ordinate of $p = 0.75$. This is the increment which must be added to the standard stimulus in order for the subject to make the correct discrimination in three-fourths of his attempts. This increment is denoted t_u in Fig. 2.5. In a similar way the lower limen t_l is defined as that decrement below the standard stimulus which the subject differentiates correctly in three-fourths of his attempts. This measure of the lower limen is also shown in the figure. Because of the constant error, the upper and lower limens are not necessarily equal.

If the subject has been allowed three categories of judgment, then the results can be represented graphically by the psychometric curves of Fig. 2.6. The equality judgments are called the *intermediate category of judgment.* The two

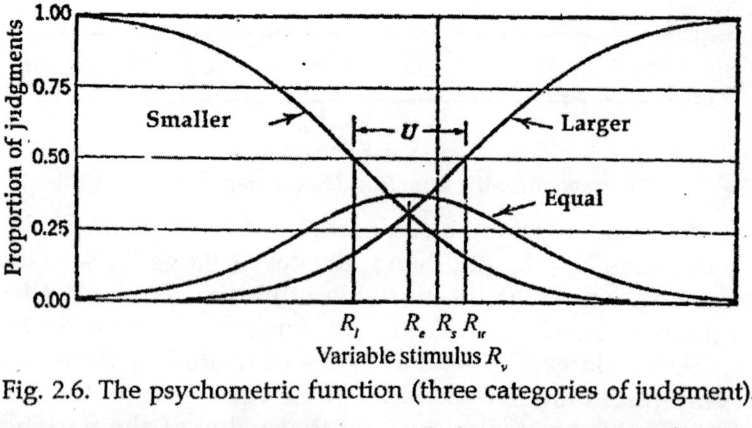

Fig. 2.6. The psychometric function (three categories of judgment).

psychometric curves then intersect below the median line. The upper threshold R_u is defined by the intersection of the curve for "larger" with the median line, as shown. The lower threshold is defined in a similar way from the psychometric curve for judgments "smaller." The midpoint between these two thresholds is taken as the point of subjective equality R_e, or this value may be defined by the intersection of the two curves. These determinations for R_e are nearly the same. The difference limen can be defined as the standard deviation of either curve, or it may be defined as half of the *interval of uncertainty* U, which is the difference between the upper and lower thresholds. Much has been written about the detailed methods for determining a limen from the psychometric curves, and the question has been the subject of more controversy than it is worth.

The question of whether to use two or three categories has also been much debated [4]. This question is quite easily resolved in terms of the purposes of the experimenter. If he wants to find the limen of a particular subject for a particular kind of sensory discrimination, then he should use only two categories of judgment. If he uses three categories, then the cautions subject will report equality when he is uncertain or when he does not give the necessary effort for a decision. A more confident subject will gi ve decisions with a minimum of equality judgments. Consider what happens to a limen

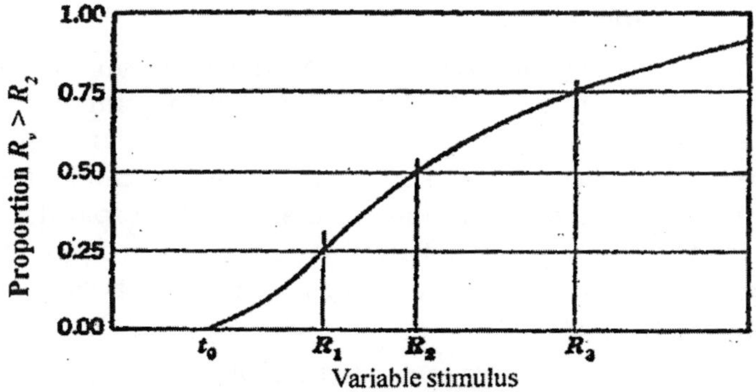

Fig. 2.7. Skewness of the psychometric function.

determination if the subject avoids the intermediate category altogether, either by intention or by temperament. The interval of uncertainty *U* in Fig 2.6 then disappears altogether, so that the curves look like those of Fig. 2.5. The upper and lower limens then vanish, and the interpretation is that the subject has infinite sensitivity, which is absurd. The determination is then markedly affected by temperamental characteristics which are irrelevant for the sensory limen. On the other hand, if the purpose of the investigator is to study the experience of equality, then he should use three categories of judgment. The result might give an objective index of some characteristic of temperament, or of the sensory tolerance of the subject, but not of his limen.

Because of the many hundreds of experimental studies with the constant method, there has been considerable interest in the shape of the psychometric curve. It has often been assumed that the curve is symmetric in the sense that the upper and lower limens are essentially equal, but this assumption has been shown to be erroneous on theoretical grounds [20]. The psychometric curve is positively skewed, as shown in fig. 2.7. The positive skewness of the psychometric curve varies with Weber's ratio. For keen discrimination where the ratio is, say, 1/100, the skewness is very slight, so that it can be ignored. For coarse discrimination, such as for loudness or smell, the skewness becomes conspicuous [5, 14].

Space and Time Errors

The preferred psychophysical methods usually involve the presentation of two stimuli for the subject to compare. The perception of two stimuli usually requires that they be separated in space over the sensitive surface of the receptor for simultaneous presentation, or that they be separated in time for successive presentation. Because of this circumstance, it is difficult, with two stimuli, to avoid the effects of spatial or temporal separation.

When two stimuli are presented visually with the constant method, they are displaced so that one of them is to the right and other to the left, or one is above the other. When the comparison is made, it happens not infrequently that the subject tends to overestimate, or underestimate, the stimulus to the right, or to the left. The result is a constant error which is then called a *space error*. Whenever the constant error is of considerable magnitude, one usually looks for an explanation in the experimental situation.

When the two stimuli are presented in succession, there is a frequent tendency for the subject to underestimate the first stimulus. Since the constant error is then due to the temporal displacement, it is called a *time error*. Much experimental work has been done on the nature of the time error [27, pp. 438-449]. When a subject makes a comparison between two successive stimuli, he is in effect comparing the second stimulus with the memory of the first one. There seems to be a tendency of his memory for the first stimulus to *regress toward the mean* of the whole set of stimuli in the experiment, or even toward the mean of the same general class of stimuli in the experience of the subject.

In some experiments the constant errors, either space errors or time errors, are irrelevant for the main purpose. They can be eliminated or ignored in some situations by presenting the same stimulus in some trials to the right and in some trials to the left, or sometimes first and sometimes second. This is called *counterbalanced order* of presentation. In other experiments the constant error is the main object of investigation, as in measuring the magnitude of an illusion. An illusion is an error in perceptual judgment. The cause is usually that the subject tries to judge one thing but is unwittingly affected by other things. If the object is to measure the size of the Muller-Lyer illusion, then the arrow of the figure may be to the right in half of the presentations and to the left in the other half. In analyzing the experimental results, one can determine separately the magnitude of the illusion for the experimental subject and his tendency to over-estimate the stimulus on the right or left side. In some experiments a constant error is introduced by differences in movement when the subject tends to make stronger movements toward the right or the left side. Such a constant error is called a *movement error*.

Method of Paired Comparison

In the constant method a single stimulus is chosen as a standard and is compared with all the stimuli in the experimental series. If there are n stimuli in the series, then there are n distinct comparisons to be made, or $(n-1)$ comparisons if the standard is not compared with itself. In the method of paired comparison every stimulus is compared with every other stimulus, and hence there are n^2 comparisons, or $n\ (n-1)$ comparisons if each stimulus is not compared with itself [24, 26]. As regards experimental procedure, the constant method is a special case of the method of paired comparison. The method of paired comparison can be used for the purpose of making limen determinations in which every stimulus serves in turn as a standard, but we shall consider it here for the more fundamental problem of establishing a metric for the psychological continuum.

When the subject has made a large number of comparisons for each pair of stimuli, the results can be arranged in a square table of experimentally observed proportions, like Table 2.1 The entry p_{32}, for example, shows the proportion of the subject's judgments $R_3 > R_2$ in the attribute that was judged. Such a table can be arranged for any attribute x about which the subject can say, " A is x'er than B." The general element in this table may be denoted p_{jk}. It shows the proportion of judgments in which j exceeds k in the specific attribute.

Table 2.1

Data Form for the Method of Paired Comparisons k

	1	2	3	—	n
1	0.50	p_{12}	p_{13}	—	p_{1n}
2	p_{21}	0.50	p_{23}	—	p_{2n}
3	p_{31}	p_{32}	0.50	—	p_{3n}
—	—	—	p_{jk}	0.50	—
n	p_{n1}	p_{n2}	p_{n3}	—	0.50

The problem is to allocate each of the n stimuli to a point on the linear subjective continuum which represents the differential experience of the attribute x [6]. Since only two categories of judgment are implied in this table, we have the restriction that $p_{jk} = 1 - p_{kj}$ and, in general the diagonal elements are 0.50, since we eliminate the constant error by counterbalanced order. Hence, there are $n(n-1)/2$ experimentally independent values which should be consistent with a set of n subjective scale values, one for each stimulus. For 20 stimuli, the problem is then to account for 190 experimentally independent proportions by 20 scale values.

In solving this problem it has been found necessary to distinguish between two kinds of stimulus series, namely, those in which the stimuli are *homogeneous* in that they differ only in a single attribute, and those in which the stimuli are *heterogeneous* in that they differ necessarily in attributes additional to the one which is being studied. In auditory experiments the attribute that is specified for comparison may be pitch. In a homogeneous stimulus series we should have pure tones that differ only in pitch. If we want to compare noises as to their pitch, however, then we are necessarily dealing with a heterogeneous stimulus series. It has been found that for homogeneous series a single parameter or scale value S_j can be assigned to each stimulus so that the observed proportions are accounted for. A heterogeneous stimulus series requires two parameters for each stimulus, namely, a mean scale value S_j and a measure of subjective dispersion σ_j.

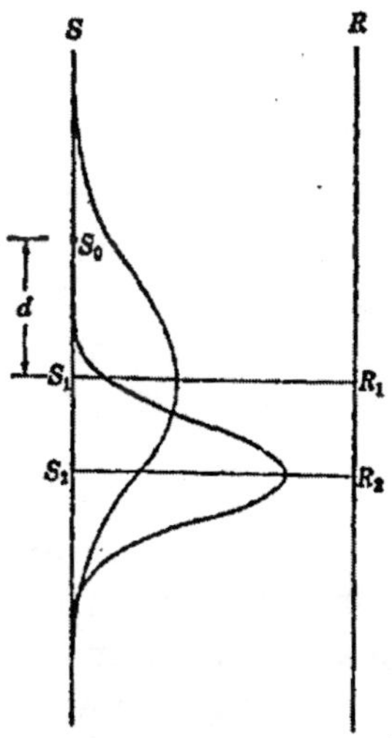

Fig. 2.8. Discriminal dispersions of two stimuli.

Consider the two continua, R and S, which are represented in Fig. 2.8. A particular stimulus R_1 is represented by a point on the R scale, determined by its physical magnitude.

The apparent or subjective magnitude of this stimulus on a particular occasion is represented at some point S_0 one the S scale. The stimulus R_1 is perceived with different apparent magnitudes S on different occasions. Let S_1 be the median apparent magnitude for the stimulus R_1. This apparent magnitude is medicated by a process of unknown nature which may be considered to be psychical or physiological or both, depending on philosophical preferences. We shall call this process the *modal discriminal* process for the stimulus R_1. The allocation of this discriminal process on the subjective continuum will be denoted S_1. On any particular occasion the stimulus R_1 may be perceived by other processes, such as the *discriminal process* denoted S_0. It will be assumed that each discriminal process is the modal process for some stimulus magnitude. The physical magnitudes and the corresponding average modal processes are covariant, and for every physical magnitude there is a corresponding modal discriminal process.

In order to introduce a subjective metric for the discriminal processes, we make the hypothesis that each stimulus projects a normal frequency distribution on the subjective continuum. By this we mean that the discriminal processes are so separated that the distribution of frequencies with which they are experienced in response to the stimulus R_1 is normal. We are free to define the S scale arbitrarily in this manner for any given stimulus, but it becomes an experimental fact whether the frequency distributions for other stimuli would then also be normal. Since the subjective quality of a single stimulus cannot be communicated, the experimental verification must be indirect.

Having defined the S scale in such a manner that the stimulus R_1 projects a Gaussian distribution, we next define the discriminal deviation d as the linear separation between S and the scale value S_1. This separation is determined by the relative frequency with which S is experienced when R_1 is perceived. The standard deviation of the S values is σ_1 .

We now introduce another stimulus magnitude R_2 as

shown in the figure. The modal discriminal process for this stimulus is denoted S_2, and it is again assumed that this stimulus projects a normal distribution on the subjective continuum, but not necessarily with the same dispersion. If the second stimulus is of such a nature that it is perceived more consistently as to its apparent magnitude on successive occasions, then it will project a smaller dispersion on the subjective continuum. It will be described as a stimulus of lower *ambiguity* or dispersion. The subjective dispersions are denoted σ_1 and σ_2 respectively. If one of the stimuli is chosen as a standard, its subjective dispersion may be defined as the *subjective unit of measurement* [8, 18].

It is assumed that, if the discriminal process for R_1 is higher on the S scale than the discriminal process for R_2 on the particular occasion when they are compared, then the subject will return the judgment $R_1 > R_2$. When this relation is reversed on the subjective continuum, then the subject returns the opposite judgment, namely, $R_2 > R_1$. If this pair of stimuli is presented, together with other stimulus pairs, for a large number of comparative judgments, then the proportions of judgments, p_{jk}, can be experimentally determine. It can be shown by statistical reasoning that

$$S_j - S_k = x_{jk} \sqrt{\sigma_j^2 + \sigma_k^2 - 2r_{jk}\sigma_j\sigma_k}$$

Where S_j and S_k are the scale values of the modal discriminal processes, x_{jk}, is the deviation from the mean of a normal distribution, determined by the proportion p_{jk} of judgments $R_j > R_k$, σ_j and σ_k are the discriminal dispersions of the two stimuli, and r_{jk} is the correlation between the scale values of the discriminal processes.

This equation is the *law of comparative judgment*, by which each stimulus can be allocated to the subjective continuum. The validity of this law is sustained if it is found that a set of consistent scale values S_j and subjective dispersions σ_j can be found by this equation such that they account for the experimentally observed proportions of comparative judgments. The number of stimuli in the experimental series must be long enough so that there is much larger number of experimentally determined proportion than there are parameters to be determined. In order to make the problem soluble, it is usually assumed that the correlational term vanishes. The correlations can be estimated separately by the method of successive intervals, but most experiments are so arranged that the correlations can be assumed to be negligible.

In the simplest case the discriminal dispersions are also assumed to be equal, so that the law of comparative judgment reduces to the simple form

$$S_j - S_k = x_{jk} \sqrt{2}$$

Which is known as Case V of this law [18, 24]. In this case it is assumed that the experimentally observed proportions can be accounted for by a single parameter S_j for each stimulus. This can frequently be done, but it is occasionally necessary to deal with two parameters for each stimulus, namely, the scale value S_j and the subjective dispersion σ_j.

Although the law of comparative judgment is easily applied to the stimuli of classical psychophysics, the more generally interesting applications are those which involve social, moral, and esthetic values, opinion polls, and consumer preferences. One example of the measurement of social distance and racial preferences will be given here. Several hundred students were presented with a schedule in which they were asked to check one of each pair of nationalities or races to indicate with which they would rather associate [19]. The resulting tabulations were analyzed by Case V of the law of comparative judgment. It must be recognized that the preferential values were determined, not only by the nationalities and races involved, but also by the particular groups of subjects, as well as the time at which their preferences were expressed. Students in other countries and at different times would return different subjective values. It is of interest that the average discrepancy between the experimentally obtained proportions and those which are implied by the computed scale values was only 0.03, even with the simplifying assumptions of Case V.

It has been assumed in some earlier psychophysical studies that "equally often noticed differences are equal," but it can be shown that the discriminal dispersion may have a serious effect on this assumption. In Fig. 2.9 we have represented the discriminal dispersions of three stimuli on the subjective continuum in which $S_A = S_B$. Hence p_{AB} =0.50. Stimulus a has a large dispersion, so that the subject perceives high values in it on some occasions, and low values on other occasions. The proportion of judgments *A*>C will be high but not unity, because these two subjective distributions overlap. The proportion of judgments *B*>*C* will be unity, because stimulus *B* is never perceived as below *C*. Here the scale separations (*A*−*C*) and (*B*−*C*) are equal, but their frequencies of discrimination are not equal. Hence we conclude that equally often noticed differences are not equal if the stimuli have different dispersions. The assumption is valid, however, when the dispersions are uniform.

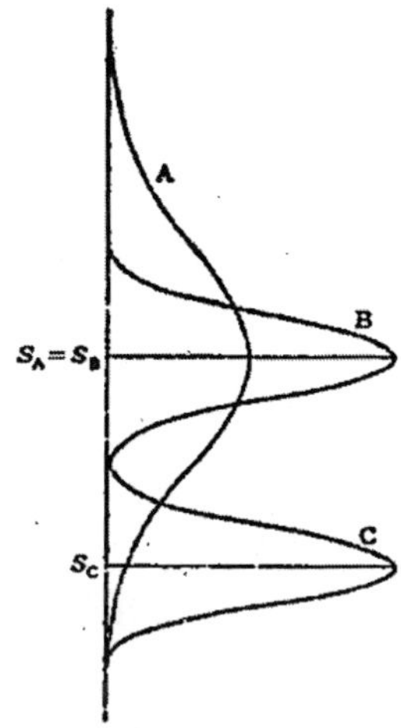

Fig. 2.9. Discriminal dispersions of three stimuli.

The law of comparative judgment takes no cognizance of the physical stimulus intensity or of any other physical measurement except relative frequency of comparative judgment. Hence it can be used to define the subjective continuum for a stimulus series which has no known physical measures to the designated attribute. A series of handwriting specimens, for example, can be compared as to their relative degrees of excellence without reference to the fact that this attribute has no known physical measure. One application is in semantic studies of cognitive and affective word meanings. The cognitive content of *famous and notorious* is practically the same, but they differ in affective connotation. These differences can be measured with the law of comparative judgment. For each experiment it is necessary, however, to verify the applicability of the law by showing that the scale values S and the discriminal dispersions σ actually do account for the much larger number of experimentally observed comparative judgments. This internal consistency must be demonstrated for each kind of application before we can speak of subjective measurement, as distinguished from mere rank order.

Method of Equal Appearing Intervals

In this method the subject deals directly with the psychological continuum, which is represented by a series of successive intervals. He is asked to assign each one of a series of stimuli to one of the intervals. If he does this a number of times, or if a group of subjects do the task with one complete sorting for each subject, then each stimulus will have a frequency distribution in the successive equal intervals. The scale value S_j of each stimulus is the mean of its distribution, and the standard deviation σ_j is called the *ambiguity* of the stimulus as regards the attribute that is being appraised.

A well-known example of this method is the Sanford weight experiment [7, p. 154]. Some envelopes are weighted so as to represent a fairly wide range. The subject is instructed to sort the envelopes into five piles, so that the successive piles seem to be equally spaced. When all the subjects have done this task, the mean scale position S_j can be determined for each envelope. Fechner's law can then be tested by plotting the scale positions S_j against the corresponding weights R_j in grams. The plot is usually logarithmic.

The method of equal appearing intervals has a methodological limitation in that it does not provide a test of internal consistency, as in the method of paired comparison. It has been found that, when the scale values obtained by the method of paired comparison are compared with those of the method of equal appearing intervals, these is a discrepancy, especially toward the ends of the scale, and this has been called the *end effect*. Since the method of paired comparison has a check of internal consistency, and since it agrees well with the method of rank order (to be described), it is assumed that the distortion of the end effect can be attributed to the method of equal appearing intervals [9]. The method is used in experiments where it is sufficient to have approximate estimates of subjective values. The subject easily understands this method, and the task for a long stimulus series can be completed in a relatively short time. The method of mean gradation, which has been described, is a special case of method of equal appearing intervals because the total subjective interval between two stimuli is there merely bisected.

For the purpose of appraising some types of educational results, there have been constructed a number of *product scales*. Such a scale consists of a graduated sequence of specimens which represents successive degrees of general excellence. Examples are appraisal of general excellence of handwriting [17], freehand lettering, English compositions [10], and some types of shop work. Although judgments of this kind are frequently made with some confidence and consistency, the judges usually find it difficult to identify the objective components that determined their total appraisal. The construction of a handwriting scale will be used as an example of this type of psychophysical problem.

In the construction of a handwriting scale, one starts with a large collections of handwriting specimens. The subjects who participate in the construction of the scale sort the specimens into a series of, say, ten subjectively equal intervals. On the basis of such experimental data, the mean scale value of each handwriting specimen can be readily determined. Those specimens which have usually large dispersions are eliminated because they are the ones about which the judges disagree as to general excellence. From the remainder, one can select an evenly graduated sequence of specimens to constitute a descriptive scale for judging general excellence of handwriting [17]. Each specimen that is to be appraised is then described by the number of the standard to which it is equated.

Method of Successive Intervals

In the method of equal appearing intervals, the subject is asked to sort the stimuli into intervals that are subjectively equal. Even though the subject does not realize it, this task is difficult. The intervals toward the ends of the scale tend to become subjectively larger than the intervals in the middle range. This end effect is caused partly by the fact that the total subjective range tends to shift during the sorting procedure. The method of successive intervals is experimentally similar to the method of equal appearing intervals. The subject is asked to make the intervals successive but not necessarily subjectively equal. The successive intervals may be denoted merely by successive numerals, or they may be defined by descriptive terms or phrases whose successive character is readily admitted by the subject at the start of the experiment. By this simple experimental method, the scale values S and the discriminal dispersions σ may be determined for the stimuli. The method is especially useful in studies of consumer preferences which involve judgments of a large number of forms of a product.

Method of Rank Order

When the subject has arranged a set of stimuli in rank order according to any designated attribute, we do not have enough information to transform the rank orders into psychological measurement. When the number of stimuli is quite large, the rank orders are sometimes transmuted into a scale, on the assumption that the group of stimuli represents a normal distribution in the designated attribute. For any given set of numbers, or rank orders, it is always possible to define a scale quite arbitrarily, so that the given set of numbers, or rank orders, represents a normal distribution on that scale. But nothing is proved by doing it.

When a group of subjects has placed a set of stimuli in rank order, we can determine, for each pair of stimuli, the proportion of judges who ranked one higher than the other. If a subject placed four stimuli in the rank order B, D, A, C, then we can extract for him six separate comparative judgments. In each of the six following judgments, the first is ranked higher than the second. We have then BD, BA, BC, DA, DC, AC. If these judgments are tabulated for all subjects, we can determine the proportion of judgments "*j* higher than *k*" for every pair of stimuli. With these data we can proceed with the method of paired comparison [21]. The method of paired comparison is theoretically superior to the method of rank order, but rank order is experimentally much easier for the subject and is general less fatiguing. Comparison has been made of these two methods when the same subjects rated handwriting specimens in pairs and also in rank order. The agreement was found by Kate Hevner to be very close[9].

Method of Single Stimuli

In most psychophysical methods there is preferences for the judgment of a stimulus in direct comparison with another stimulus or with a group of stimuli. In the method of single stimuli, however, the subject gives a descriptive rating of each presented stimulus [2, 25]. He is asked to say for each stimulus whether it seems large or small, or he is asked to apply one of several descriptive to each stimulus. In this method the subject must keep in mind his own standard. It has been found that this standard tends toward the average of the presented stimulus series. The method of single stimuli can be varied, and in one of its forms it becomes similar to the method of successive intervals. The method of single stimuli does not ordinarily imply the calculation of scale values and dispersions, as in the method of successive intervals. The method is sometimes called the method of *absolute judgment.*

Method of Judgment Time

In earlier psychophysical studies it was found that the time for discriminatory judgment was longest for the most difficult comparisons where the physical differences were smallest. If judgment time is plotted against physical stimulus difference, the result is a falling curve that approaches reaction time as an asymptote. It is possible to use this relation inversely, so that the psychological difference is inferred from the average response time [3,16]. The relation must be calibrated for each type of stimulus.

The negative relation between physical stimulus difference and response time is of some general interest. It is conceivable, for example, that individual differences in this curve may be of significance in judging the temperament of the subject. Some subjects retard conspicuously in judgment time when the physical difference becomes small and hence more difficult. This psychophysical relation may be characteristic of subjects who have difficulty in making up their minds.

In learning experiments it is customary to use the number of correct responses for each trial as a numerical index of learning. Complete learning is then indicated by a perfect score within the time limit allowed for each association. The method of response time can be used for measuring overlearning. If learning continues after perfect scores are obtained, the additional learning can be easily shown in terms of the continued reduction in response time, which becomes then an index of overlearning. It is to be expected that the rate of forgetting will be affected by the amount of overlearning beyond the first perfect response.

The development of psychological test theory has unfortunately been separate from that of psychophysics, in spite of the fact that many of the underlying concepts are similar or identical. This has been due to the fact that the two branches of psychological research have been carried out by different groups of men. In the psychophysical method of response time, we have one of many examples of the close relation between psychophysics and test theory. The ability of a subject to do a certain kind of task is frequently indicated by the speed with which he can do it, and the difficulty of a task is sometimes arbitrarily defined so that the distribution of ability in the population is normal. The power score of an individual as regards a certain kind of task is that degree of difficulty of task which he can do without pressure of time, but all experimental procedures must be finite in time allowances.

APPLICATIONS OF THE PSYCHOPHYSICAL METHODS

Measurement of Affective Attitudes

An attitude represents a restriction of some kind in the manner in which an object is regarded. In dealing with social attitudes we consider primarily the *affective attitudes* toward debatable issues. For the purposes of measuring affective social attitudes, we postulate an affective continuum with a neutral point. Positive affect represents appetition or favourable attitude toward a *psychological object*, which may be any object, person, or idea. Negative affect represents aversion or unfavourable attitude toward the psychological object in question. The purpose of attitude measurement is to assign each individual to this affective continuum, as regards his positive or negative attitude toward a specified psychological object X.

We limit ourselves in the present case to those psychological objects about which a person can express approval or disapproval in various degrees of intensity, which are represented by his position on the affective continuum. If we want to know how strongly a man feels for or against some psychological object X, we can proceed in several ways. We can ask him, and then note the strength of his free expression for or against X. We can watch his overt actions in relation to X, or we can present him with a list of statements of various degrees of intensity of affect for and against X to see which he endorses. Such a list is an attitude scale. The separate statements are called *opinions*, but our interest may be to determine the person's strength of approval or disapproval of X, which we call his attitude, rather than merely to tabulate endorsements and rejections of separate opinions.

The construction of an attitude scale starts with the name, phrase, or symbol which constitutes the psychological object. This object must be something about which people debate quite freely. A rather long list of opinions is then collected so as to include various degrees of both positive and negative affect about X, as well as neutral opinions. A group of readers sorts the opinions by the method of equal appearing intervals or the method of successive intervals. These readers are told merely to consider the question, "How strongly do you think somebody would feel for or against X if you heard him make this statement?" It should be specially noted that the opinions of the readers themselves have nothing is do with the case. They are asked merely to consider where somebody else who made these statements would be on the affective continuum. The main requirement for the readers is therefore that they be able to read English.

With data of this kind one can determine the scale value S_j and the dispersion σ_j for each opinion. The opinions with l large dispersion are eliminated because they contain some ambiguity as to affective meaning. From the remaining opinions, an equally graduated sequence is selected to constitute an attitude scale. The score of an individual who records his own responses on such a scale is intended to represent the strength of affective attitude toward the psychological object X. Within the limitations of the psychophysical method used, the intervals of such a scale can be regarded as roughly equal. With a schedule of this kind, it is possible to construct a frequency distribution of affective attitude toward a specified object for a given group of subjects. It is then legitimate to inquire about the shape of this distribution of affect. At the beginning of a political campaign this distribution may be unimodal, but during the course of the campaign it may be expected that the distribution of attitude becomes bimodal, especially if the issue are hotly debated. Psychophysical problems of general interest are involved here.

Many attitude scales have been constructed, and their interpretations have been frequently debated. One of the recurring issues is whether a man's overt behaviour is a better guide to his attitude than what he says on an attitude scale. It is sometimes supposed that overt conduct is the criterion against which an attitude scale must be validated, but this is erroneous. If we really want to know how a man feels about some debated question, then the best procedure is probably to learn what he says to his intimate friends when he is not publicly observed or quoted. His overt actions may be guided by administrative, social, or political expediency. What he says on an attitude schedule may, similarly, be determined by the personalities of the examiners and onlookers and those who might quote him. Both these indices are fallible if the issue is at all critical. Even when the verbal and overt indices agree, they may both be wrong. In general, it is probably easier for people to express their likes and dislikes verbally than to commit themselves to the corresponding overt acts. Attitude schedules can be used with confidence only in those situations where there is no strong pressure, explicit or implied, to influence verbal expression. Occasionally a man expresses himself with apparent freedom even when he is in a conspicuous minority, but all studies in this field must be interpreted with due regard to the social pressures that influence both verbal expression and overt conduct.

The question has been raised whether an attitude scale, considered as a psychological measuring device, is itself influenced by the opinions of the readers who determined the scale values of the opinions by sorting them. If this should be the case, then the interpretation of the resulting frequency distributions of attitude scores would be limited by the characteristics of the standardizing group of readers. A collection of opinions about the Negro was stored independently by three groups of subjects : a group of northern whites, a group of northern Negroes, and a group of southern Negroes. The three resulting attitude scales were linearly related, and they differed only in the allocation of the neutral point. An attitude which was considered by the northern whites to be neutral in affect was considered by the Negroes to be slightly negative. This displacement of the neutral point was predicted. The frequency distributions of attitude obtained from the three scales were the same except for the origin [11].

Measurement of Effects of Propaganda

For many problems in social attitudes it is sufficient merely

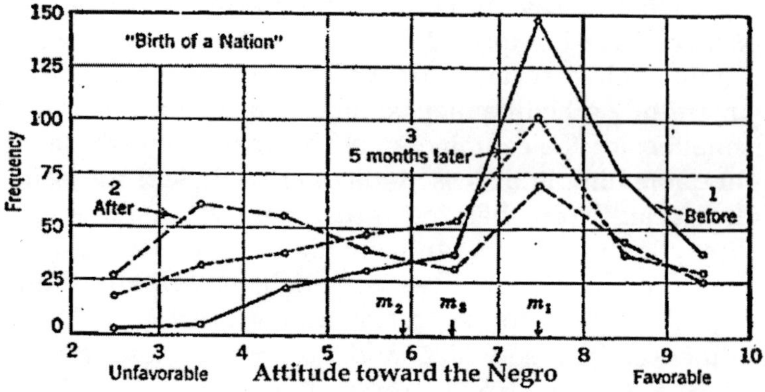

Fig. 2.10. Frequency distributions of scores on á measure of attitude toward the Negro.

to count the relative frequencies of endorsement of particular propositions or opinions before and after presentation of propaganda material. For such problems the sealing of attitudes is not necessary. On the other hand, if it is desired to describe the shift in a frequency distribution of attitudes which is caused by propaganda, a metric is required, and an attitude schedule is then indicated.

Many experiments have been made to study quantitatively the effects of propaganda. One experimental method is to compare the attitude scores on a schedule before and after presentation of propaganda material. Figure 2.10 shows the frequency distribution of scores on a schedule of attitude toward the Negro. The high school students who participated saw the film "Birth of a Nation" at a local theater. A few days after seeing the film, they were given a parallel form of the same schedule. After 5 months they were given a third schedule on the same issue. The figure shows the striking effect of this film in making the students less friendly toward Negroes. The third distribution shows that only half of the effect had worn off after 5 months. The three *m*'s refer to the means obtained. Experiments have demonstrated a summation effect with several films. When a single film was inadequate to demonstrate a statistically significant shift in attitude, a sequence of several such films showed a significant summation effect [23].

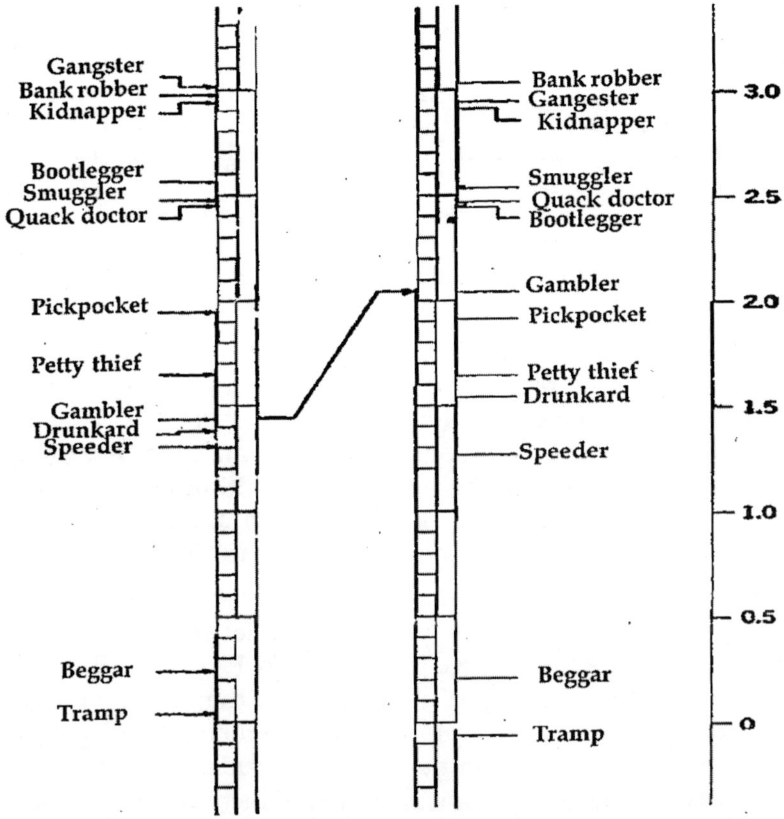

Fig. 2.11. Two sets of scale values for seriousness of offenses.

The paired-comparison method is probably more sensitive in measuring shifts in attitude than the attitude scales. Figure 2.11 shows two sets of scale values for seriousness of offenses. These offenses were presented in pairs, with instruction to check one of each pair to indicate which was the more serious. Two such schedules were presented, one before and one after the presentation of a film depicting the life of a gambler. The problem was to ascertain the effect of the film on the attitudes of school children toward gamblers. It can be

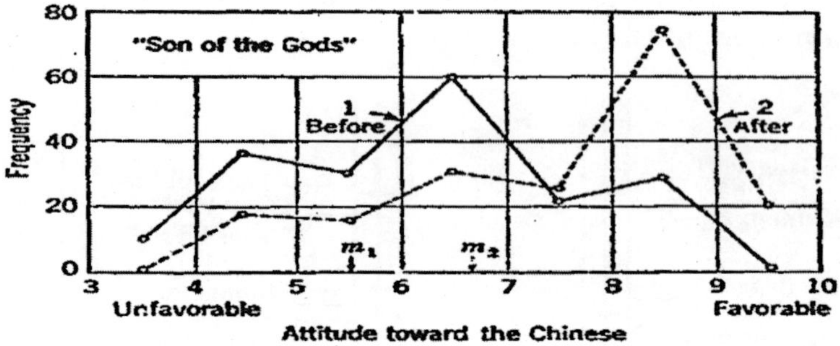

Fig. 2.12. Distributions of affective judgments toward Chinese, before and after seeing a moving picture.

seen in the figure that the only significant shift in scale value was that of "gambler." This experimental audience of school children considered gambling to be more serious after seeing the film. Similar experiments have been made to determine the effect of films on the international attitudes of student audiences. Figure 2.12 shows the effect of a film in making the student audience more friendly toward the Chinese.

The psychological methods can be adapted as a historical method. A tabulation was made of editorial comments about Germany and about France for the period 1910 to 1930. These were sorted by a group of readers, as in the construction of an attitude scale. Mean scale values were then plotted against time in order to ascertain the shift in attitude, as represented editorially, during the 20-year period, which included World War I. Figure 2.13 shows the shifting attitudes toward Germany and France before and during this war, as well as the gradual recovery of prewar attitudes after its conclusion. It has been suggested that such shifts in international attitudes be used as a sort of barometer of impending crises. A similar psychological study was made of Chinese editorial attitudes toward the Japanese, and vice versa, before those countries were at war [15].

The Prediction of Choice

So far we have been concerned with the problem of allocating

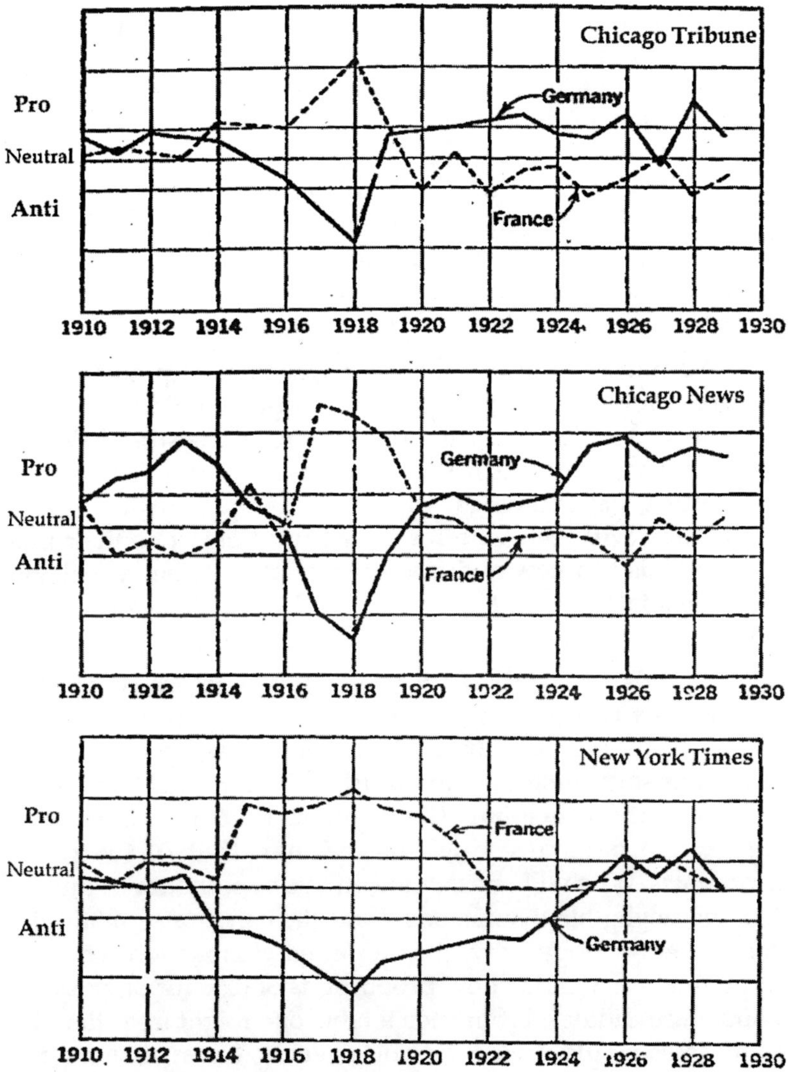

Fig. 2.13. Shifts in international attitudes by three newspapers during a period covering World War I.

each stimulus to the subjective continuum with regard to a specified attribute. In the simplest case, such as that of lifted weights, the physical measure of weight is easily ascertained for each stimulus. In more complex situations there is no known physical measure to represent the attribute completely. Such a case is that of handwriting excellence, which can be judged with some confidence but cannot be readily measured in physical terms. In still more complex cases, the attribute to be judged has no available physical measure. An example is affective or preferential judgments about moral and aesthetic values. The law of comparative judgment enables us to allocate a stimulus to the subjective continuum quite independently of whether there exists any physical measure at all.

We turn now to the obverse psychological problem. The obverse problem is to predict what people will do in terms of the affective scale values and dispersions of the stimuli. When the scale values and dispersions are known for several competing psychological objects, what proportion of the population will then vote for a particular object as their first choice? This is a new and fascinating field for theoretical and experimental inquiry. The obverse problem will be introduced with an example.

Consider a group of six candidates who are competing for elective office, and assume that their popularities are exactly the same, namely, S_j. Assume, further, that candidate A does or says something for which half of the electors dislike him, and the other half like him, so that his discriminal dispersion becomes much larger than that of the other candidates. Who will be assumed, in this hypothetical example, to have negligible dispersions. If all the candidates retain the same average popularity, then a paired comparison schedule of preferences would show proportions of 0.50 for all possible pairs of candidates. From such a table one might infer that the candidates would divide the votes evenly, but such is not the case. At election the more variable candidate would draw half of the votes, and the other candidates would draw only 10 per cent each. Hence the more variable candidate would get the plurality. When a tie threatens between two candidates who are equally popular, it can be shown that the more variable candidate can win the plurality by introducing a third candidate, even if the now candidate is less popular than either of the first two. It seems likely that this principle is known to practical politicians [22].

Fig. 2.14. Booth in psychophysical laboratory for taste experiments in the Quartermaster Food and Container Institute for the armed Forces in Chicago.

In the study of consumer preferences the manufacturer is interested in pleasing every consumer. If a number of commodities or designs are submitted to consumers for rating, the scale value and the dispersion can be determined for each commodity or design. If it is desired to select, say, ten designs for the market, it would be an error to select the designs with the ten highest scale values. To do so might please some people with several designs each, and leave the rest dissatisfied. The designs should be chosen so as to maximize the number of first choices, which are determines partly by the scale values and dispersions and also by the correlations of affective values among the designs. This psychophysical problem can be solved with the method of successive intervals.

In the manufacture of food products, it has been found that human subjects can identify and reject food by criteria that escape chemical and bacteriological tests. It is for this reason that the United States Army has established a food acceptance laboratory for making taste comparisons of food products. Figure 2.14 shows one of the booths in this psychophysical laboratory. The colour of the food specimens can be controlled by colour filters. Food products are here studied in formal taste comparisons to determine their relative acceptability for different ingredients, duration and temperature of storage, and various containers.

CONCLUSION

This chapter on psychophysical methods introduces the section of this book which is devoted to the methods of studying perceptual and sensory phenomena. In reading these later chapters the student will find many references to psychophysics, a discipline which is fundamental to the problem of measurement in psychology.

The basic concepts of measuring subjective phenomena have been treated with descriptions of the major and representative methods of classical psychophysics. In the section on *applications* it has been pointed out that the psychophysical methods transcend the older fields to which they have been applied, and that they have become powerful tools in the solution of important problems in political and social behaviour, as well as in merchandising and market research.

REFERENCES

1. Boring, E.G., The stimulus error. *Amer. J. Psychol.*, 1921, *32*, 449-471.
2. Bressler, J., Judgments in absolute units as a psychophysical method. *Arch. Psychol.*, 1933, *23*, No. 152.
3. Carlson, W.R., R.C. Driver, and M.G. Preston, Judgment times for the method of constant stimuli. *J. Exper. Psychol.*, 1934, *17*, 113-118.
4. Fernberger, S.W., The use of equality judgments in psychophysical procedures. *Psychol. Rev.*, 1930, *37*, 107-112.
5. Fritz, M. F., Experimental evidence in support of Professor Thurstone's criticism of the phi-gamma hypothesis. *J. Gen Psychol.*, 1930, *4*, 346-352.
6. Guilford, J.P., The method of paired comparisons as a

psychophysical method. *Psychol. Rev.*, 1928, *35*, 494-506.

7. Guilford, J.P., *Psychometric Methods*. New York : McGraw-Hill, 1936.
8. Gulliksen, H., Paired comparisons and the logic of measurement. *Psychol. Rev.*, 1946, *53*, 199-213.
9. Hevner, K., An empirical study of three psychophysical methods. *J. Gen. Psychol.*, 1930, *4*, 191-212.
10. Hillegas, M.B., A scale for the measurement of equality in English composition by young people. *Teach. Call. Rec.*, 1912, *13*, No.4.
11. Hinckley, E.D., The influence of individual opinion on construction of an attitude scale. *J. Soc. Psychol.*, 1932, *3*, 283-296.
12. Householder, A.S., and G. Young, Weber laws, the Weber law, and psychophysical analysis. *Psychometrika*, 1940, *5* 183-193.
13. Luckiesh, M., and F.K. Moss, A restricted extension of Fechner's law from sensation to behaviour. *Psychol. Rev.*, 1942, *49*, 135-142.
14. Lufkin, H.M., The best fitting frequency function for Urban's lifted-weight results. *Amer. J. Psychol.*, 1928, *40*, 75-82.
15. Russell, J.T., and Q. Wright, National attitudes on the Far Eastern controversy. *Amer. Polit. Sci. Rev.*, 1933, *27*, 555-576.
16. Steinman, A.R., Reaction time to change compared with other psychophysical methods. *Arch. Psychol.*, 1944, No. 292.
17. Thorndike, E.L., Handwriting. *Teach. Coll. Rec.*, 1910, *11*, No. 2.
18. Thurstone, L.L. A law of comparative judgment. *Psychol. Rev.*, 1927, *34*, 273-286.
19. Thurstone, L.L., An experimental study of nationality preferences. *J. Gen. Psychol.*, 1928, *1*, 405-424.
20. Thurstone, L.L., The phi-gamma hypothesis. *J. Exper. Psychol.*, 1928, *11*, 293-305.
21. Thurstone, L.L., Rank order as a psychophysical method. *J. Exper. Psychol.*, 1931, *14*, 187-201.
22. Thurstone, L.L., The prediction of choice. *Psychometrika*,

1945, *10,* 237-253.

23. Thurstone, L.L., and R.C. Peterson, *The Effect of Motion Pictures on the Social Attitudes of High School Children.* Ann Arbor, Michigan : Edwards Brothers, 1932.

24. Thurstone, L.L., Psychophysical analysis. *Amer. J. Psychol.,* 1927, *32,* 368-389.

25. Volkmann, J., The method of single stimuli. *Amer. J. Psychol.,* 1932, *44,* 808-809.

26. Wherry, R.J., Orders for the presentation of pairs in the method of paired comparisons. *J. Exper. Psychol.,* 1938, *23,* 651-656.

27. Woodworth, R.S., *Experimental Psychology.* New York : Henry Holt, 1938.

3

Studying Perceptual Phenomena

Every student of psychology knows that his awareness of the world is completely dependent on the activity of his sense organs, although sometimes he does not realize that this is a startling fact and not a commonplace one. He tends to take for granted the familiar world which he sees before him, not realizing that in all its aspects and in every detail it is apprehended only because his sense organs are functioning, and that if these functions failed for any reason, so also would his awareness of the world.

The succeeding chapters will describe the study of the sensory mechanisms which make possible this apprehension of the environment. It is obvious, however, that these mechanisms do not fully account for the experience of the concrete world. The world is a good deal more than a matter of colours and sounds, of warms and colds, of tastes and smells and feelings. It is also a matter of surfaces and shapes and distances and objects, not to mention friends and sunsets and symbols and nations. How does the organism come to be aware of these concrete and significant things, as distinguished from the more abstract and unfamiliar ones with which sensory psychology is concerned? Such features of the world are traditionally classified as perceptions rather than sensations, and it is with the investigation of these that the present chapter deals.

SENSATION AND PERCEPTION

A generation ago it was still possible to teach a fairly simple doctrine of the relation between sensation and perception. The experienced world was thought to be built up out of elementary sensations, supplemented by images of past elementary sensations. A perception, then, was a complex of elementary processes, combined or fused in some way not wholly understood, and logically distinct from the elements which made it up. This distinction has been overthrown in recent years. It has become clear to most psychologists that there is no way of deciding whether a given experience is elementary. The conception of elementary units of mind, therefore, has been abandoned for the more defensible notion of dimensions of variation of experience. In strict accuracy, one should no longer speak of sensations but of modes of discrimination, or variables with respect to which an experience is characterized and specified. These experience variables include perceptions as well as sensations. It thus becomes an arbitrary matter whether a given type of experience is classified as sensory or as perceptual, since the chief logical basis for the earlier meaning of these terms has disappeared. When the variable can be shown to correspond with a stimulus variation of physics, as hue and wave length can be shown to correspond, it is usually considered a sensory variable. When the variable in question corresponds with a complex variation of the physical stimulus, or when the stimulus is not measurable, it is apt to be considered perceptual.

Instead of the doctrine that the phenomenal world is built up out of sensations and images by a process of combination, Gestalt psychologists propose the theory that sensory processes organize themselves spontaneously into higher-order processes at the level of the cerebral cortex and produce physiological events which are fundamentally *like* the perceptions which it is necessary to explain. Perception results from neural organization in the brain. According to this theory also, the distinction between sensation and perceptions disappears and is replaced by levels of organization. The relation between sensory and perceptual phenomena, we may conclude, is very close, and the difference between them is not in *kind* of function but in *degree*.

Psychophysics and Psychophysiology

The explanation of how we perceive the world must ultimately include a physiological theory of perception, a theory of the correspondence between the experience and the neural process. The effort to find out what goes on in the nervous system has been called psychophysiology. It may be studied in two ways. One mode of approach is by working backward from the properties of experience to the probable properties of the underlying physiology, as the Gestalt psychologists have done. This is a speculative approach. Instead, one may study the neural events directly and experimentally.

The study of the correspondence between the experience and the stimulus, without reference to the intermediate physiological stage, is a much older and better established field of research. It is traditionally called psychophysics, and its methods have led to the accumulation of a vast amount of evidence about the sensory capacities of man and the dimensions with respect to which he can discriminate the world. The predominant methods of studying vision, hearing, and the other special senses are the *psychophysical* methods.

One might suppose that this concentration of sensory research on the correspondence between the experience and the stimulus would also be reflected in the study of perception, but such is not the case. Because of the complexity of the stimuli for perception, because of the difficulty of measuring and controlling them (the stimuli for the perception of distance are an example), and because they are in some cases not even identifiable in our present state of knowledge, experimental research on perception has been diverted from the psychophysical relationship in the direction of other problems. As a result there is a preponderance of experiments on the effect of learning on perception, the effect of attitude on perception, and on the question of whether perception can be accounted for by the theory of sensory organization. Now it will probably be readily admitted that the stimuli for perception, however complex they may be, must be identified before the further problem can be solved of what the organism "contributes to" these excitations. The organism may be imagined to organize the stimulus excitations, to transform them, or, in naïve terminology, to interpret them, but in any event the stimuli should first be discovered and specified. To the extent that a psychophysical correspondence can be established between the perception and some complex order of stimulus variable, it will not be necessary to postulate special processes of interpretation or transformation or special laws of sensory organization. If it is no longer believed that sensations are the elements or the data of experience and that perception is the result merely of combining or interpreting these data, then the first problem in perception is to look for the stimuli.

For these reasons attention will be devoted in this chapter primarily to the study of the psychophysical relationship in perception. Experiments of this type should be understood by the student because, in the judgment of the writer, they promise the greatest immediate advancement of our knowledge of how we perceive the world.

The Major Perceptual Problems

If we assume that the psychophysical relationship is the primary one in the study of perception, the task of the experimenter is straight-forward. *He must first describe the perceptions to be studied, then identify their stimulus correlates, and finally set up a relationship between the two.* As we shall see, he may not be able fully to complete this programme. What, for example, is the stimulus correlate for the perception of beautiful versus ugly? It would be a bold investigator who would undertake to answer this question. But if he should do so, there are ways in which he can proceed. Even though he cannot identify the stimulus correlate, he can systematically obtain descriptions of the experience, he can vary the objects which carry the stimulus, *e.g.*, drawings or abstract patterns, in as many ways as he can invent, and he may then be able to guess what the stimulus correlate might be, *e.g.,* the ratio of "order" to "complexity" in the drawing. Such a ratio has been proposed by Birkhoff [2] as the essential "stimulus" for esthetic quality.

Some of the principle classes or types of perception which may be experimentally treated in this way are listed below. The list is chosen almost entirely from the field of visual perception, and the classification in tentative. It will, however, exemplify the writer's opinion of what the primary problems of perception are, and will serve as a list of the fields from which experiments will be selected to illustrate the important methods of studying perception.

1. The perception of visual form in two dimensions : lines, contours, and objects.
2. The perception of a three-dimensional world : distance and depth.
3. The perception of objective colour, size, and shape in relation to their retinal counterparts, *i.e.,* constancy of object perception.
4. The perception of visual motion and locomotion.
5. The perception of meaning and of symbols.
6. Social perception.

METHODS FOR THE STUDY OF PERCEPTION

The primary method of studying experience, like the method of studying behaviour, is systematic observation. In the study of experience, observation is called *introspection.* Although the proposition has sometimes been denied, the observation of experience is not basically different from the observation of objective events, as Boring has shown. [3]. Introspection is a necessary preliminary step to the setting up of psychophysical relationships ; it defines the perception to be studied and may lead to the identification of its stimulus correlate.

The classical *psychophysical* methods are another fundamental procedure in studying perceptual experience. The experiment is usually more formalized than in simple introspection, and two persons are generally involved, the experimenter and the subject or observer. The experimenter manipulates the stimuli, and the subject makes discriminative judgment or reports. As we shall see, however, the more exact psychophysical methods are not applicable if the perception to be studied, *e.g.*, geometrical shape, cannot be arranged on a scale or dimension. Forms, patterns, or *Gestalten* can be judged in various ways, but the triangularity of a triangle does not vary from more to less in the way that size or brightness does. Consequently, another discriminative method, such as the *method of reproduction* or of *non-serial matching*, must be employed in the study of such perception. The three kinds of methods will be discussed in order.

Systematic Observation or Introspection

There is nothing in the least erudite or mysterious in the examination of one's own experiences, despite the popular belief to the contrary, and introspection is as valuable to the contemporary student as it ever was. Like other forms of scientific observation, it may be formalized in an experimental situation or performed in natural or semicontrolled situations. There are a least five different types of observation which may be classified as introspection.

1. **Analyzing the Stimulus Situation.** Introspection may consist of looking for psychophysical correspondence in the course of ordinary experience. Some of the most acute observations in psychology have been of this type. Leonardo da Vinci, for example, discovered that "aerial perspective" was a cue for the perceptions of distance by noting that buildings of the same objective colour appeared successively bluer as their distance increased, particularly on a hazy day.

2. **Listing the Attributes of an Experience.** Introspection may involve the sorting and arranging of stimulus objects; according to their discriminable features. The intention is to discover the attributes of an experience or its different modes of variation. For example, the colours of the visual world may be serially arranged on the dimensions (scales) of hue,

brightness, and saturation. Quality and intensity in the various senses have long since been schematized in this way, the colour cone being a familiar example. Perceptual qualities may also be classified and serially arranged, but they seldom fall into quite such neat schemata as these.

3. **Observing the Effect of Systematic Variation of the Stimulus.** When an experimenter suspects that he can isolate an unfamiliar perceptual property, he may use whatever means are at hand to vary the stimulus object or situations systematically and then observe whether there results a variation in the perception. He may try it on himself or bring in another observer. He may use only the simplest technique of varying the stimulus, or he may build an elaborate apparatus for controlling it experimentally. In any event he is seeking to correlate a property of the perception with some feature of the stimulus. Up to this point his method would be called introspection, but if he observes a relationship, the same procedure can be turned into a psychophysical experiment. An example may be found in studying the property which objects possess of being visually *upright*. More specifically, any elongated object is oriented in the visual field; *i.e.*, it has the quality of being vertical or horizontal or tilted. So far, the introspection is scarcely above the commonsense level. The experimenter may now draw a vertical visual line and rotate it about its midpoint. He observes a perceptual variable which he calls "tilt quality" or, more accurately, two opposed qualities denotable as inclination-to-the-right and inclination-to -the - left. Both qualities vanish into a unique quality when the line is vertical, and both increase with deviation from the vertical. When the line is rotated more than 45 degrees, a new set of qualities emerges, analogous to that described but based on deviations from the *horizontal*. The experimenter now can construct an apparatus and carry out a full-fledged psychophysical experiment to investigate the series of interrelated qualities.

4. **Analysis of the Content of Consciousness.** Introspection of still another type may consist of the analysis

of a single, usually momentary, perception into its discriminable features. The aim is to describe them exhaustively. The familiar example is reporting the experience of tasting lemonade. This experience consists mainly of the qualities of sour, sweet, cold, and touch, with the addition of smell and other minor accompaniments. Such introspection requires the observer to report in terms of accepted sensory variables, which are then likely to be thought of as elements. It aims to describe the content of consciousness, without reference to the stimulus correlate (the "stimulus error"), and is in method unlike a psychophysical experiment. It is no longer in such common use as it was in the laboratory of E.B. Titchener.

5. **Description of "Organized" Experiences.** The type of introspection favoured by Gestalt psychologists is also concerned with the content of consciousness rather than its correspondence to stimuli, but the description is not given in terms of orthodox sensory attributes or qualities. It is sometimes said to be observation on a "phenomenological" level. The important feature of a form or a melody is lost if the perception is analyzed : observation should therefore be directed to the form or organization of a perception rather than its elements or dimensions of variation. This type of introspection has led to the description of a number of types of perception which had been neglected by the older introspectionists and which now constitute some of the chief problems in perceptual psychology. Examples are contour, shape, and surface quality. The fact to be noted about these perceptions is that they are similar to things or entities rather than to variables or dimensions. Experimental variation of their stimulus correlates cannot be a continuous variation, and the judgment of more or less on a scale of quality or intensity is not possible. The experimental methods of studying these phenomena are therefore somewhat different from those by which one studies dimensional perceptions.

The Psychophysical Methods

Introspective observation, as we have seen, may lead directly into a psychophysical experiment. The classical methods of psychophysics, although invented for the study of sensory discriminations, are equally applicable to discriminations called perceptual. One may study the "tilt-quality" of a line or the speed of visual movement or the apparent intelligence of persons are represented by photographs in the same way that he may study the intensity or quality of colour. The only requirement for the application of these methods is that the phenomenon to which they are applied must exist in some magnitude, or be such that it can be scaled on a dimension. As we have seen, some of the phenomena of perception do not fulfill this condition, or at least cannot at present be shown to do so. Although it has been said that "everything which exists, exists in some quantity," the triangularity of a triangle has as yet not been qualified.

The psychophysical methods of dealing with sensory or perceptual variables are discussed. It is therefore necessary in this chapter to emphasize the experimental methods employed when the critical aspect of the stimulus being studied is patterned or configurationally. These methods are of course *psychophysical* in the sense that what is investigated is the relation between the stimulus pattern and the perception, but they are not based upon the logic of continuous variables.

Non-quantitative and Semiquantitative Psychophysical Methods

Suppose that an experimenter has isolated and presented some configurational stimulus to an observer. What response can the observer make (other than describing it in words) if we exclude judging it as more or less than its variations? The response must be such as to prove that he can discriminate it. The possibilities seem to be as follows. He can (*a*) report the having or not having of a perception; (*b*) reproduced or construct or represent it (*e.g.*, with a pencil and paper); or finally (*c*) judge it as "same" or "different" in comparison with another stimulus (although he cannot specify what the difference is), *i.e.*, he can match it with another stimulus.

For example, if a visual pattern is shown to the observer

under one of a number of conditions which reduce its "visibility," as is done in visual-acuity experiments or experiments with very brief exposures, the observer may report either, "I see only a blur" or "I see a striped figure." If the stimulus object actually was a striped figure, the experimenter has evidence of discrimination. Such reports may consist of any response which will server to identify to the experimenter the perception by the observer. This simple procedure might be called the *method of identification*. If, however, the visual pattern to be investigated is such that it cannot be readily named, the experimenter may employ other criteria as evidence of discrimination. The observer can draw the pattern, or he can attempt to match it with one of a group (not a series) of two or more patterns. The former is a variant of the *method of reproduction;* the latter is the *method of non-serial matching*. By all three of these methods the experimenter is enabled, first, to distinguish between "correct" perceptions and "errors" and, second, to count or otherwise evaluate the "errors."

Not-dimensional Modification of Patterned Stimuli

The methods described above are the available modes of response of the *observer* to configurationally stimuli. What expedients does the *experimenter* have for studying the relation between the stimulus pattern and the perception? When he cannot vary the stimulus in a serial fashion, he can modify the stimulus "situation"—the total complex of stimulation—in a number of ways. The common methods of doing so when the aspect of the situation being studied is patterned are as follows.

1. **The Experiment of Reducing or "Impoverishing" the Stimulus Pattern.** This is probably the method most frequently employed in studying visual perception. It may involve any of several techniques. The pattern may be exposed for only a short time interval; the brightness difference between the figure and its background may be reduced to a barely noticeable one; the figure may be reduced in size; or it may be presented to peripheral vision, where form perception is weak as compared with that produced by direct fixation of the eyes.

By all four of these methods a *threshold* is discoverable below which the observer cannot identify the figures. Moreover, it is found that, even when the figure is identifiable, it is seen (or reproduced or matched) more or less incorrectly and is experienced as more or less indefinite or unstable. Experiments on brightness discrimination and on visual acuity are of this type, depending as they do upon the seeing of some kind of a figure in the visual field, although the problems involved are conventionally classified as sensory rather than perceptual. When nonsense figures or meaningful forms are presented to an observer under reduced stimulation, interest is usually centered on the analysis of the errors made by the observer and the trends of these errors. The attempt is generally made to interpret these trends in terms of some special perceptual process of assimilation or organization. More recently, interest in the fundamental problem of visual *contour* has arisen in connection with reduced stimulus experiments, and studies of the problem give promise of linking together the evidence regarding brightness perception, visual acuity, and form perception [15].

By far the most frequently used device in this type of experiment is the tachistoscope, which gets its name from the Greek words for "very rapid" and "view". Its purpose is to present an exposure field for a brief controllable duration; the technique of using it and the requirements of a good apparatus are discussed by Woodworth [17, p. 688]. The difference in brightness between a stimulus pattern and its background may be reduced by various devices for controlling illumination or for projecting an image of the stimulus through a rotating sectored disk. The method of reducing the stimulus pattern in size (or presenting it at a distance) and the method of exposing the stimulus in the periphery of the observer's visual field, although less used, are valuable and have the advantage of presenting fewer difficulties in the construction of apparatus.

2. **The Experiment of Presenting Indefinite or Ambiguous Stimulus Patterns.** It is possible to devise stimulus

fields which, for reasons not thoroughly understood, are only partially patterned or configured. Natural stimuli of this sort occur in cloud patterns and on the inhomogeneous surfaces of plastered walls. The commonest artificial stimuli are ink blots possessing irregular contours and a random distribution of texture. As everyone knows, the onlooker tends to see "pictures" in these objects. Since the stimulus conditions for the perception of pattern or contour are present in such fields but ambiguous and unspecific, the patterns, shapes, objects, and meanings which do appear in perception may take any of a variety of directions. Many different shapes may arise from a single field of stimuli, depending on the observer, or may arise for the same observer on different occasions. The responses which are made in this type of experiment obviously cannot be treated as correct or incorrect, and the experiment itself does not seek to establish a psychophysical correspondence. As applied, the method presupposes a *non-relationship* between the stimulus pattern and the perception; it is used instead to study individual differences among observers, since the attitudes and interests of the individual are assumed to determine what he perceives. This kind of perception is said to be "projective."

The shapes seen in ink blots are nevertheless not entirely free from the influence of the ink blot itself. It is possible that further study of the indefinite and heterogeneous kind of stimulation which ink blots exemplify may reveal some of the stimulus conditions for the perception of pattern and contour.

3. **The Experiment of Devising Reversible or Equivocal Stimulus Patterns.** It is possible to construct visual stimulus fields which can be seen in only two ways instead of in many ways. These stimuli are not indefinite; they are clearly patterned, but the patterning yields either one kind of perceived object or a wholly different kind usually incompatible with the first. Three examples are given in Fig. 3.1. In these illustrations the stimulus conditions, whatever they may be, for the perception of contour and solidity are balanced or pitted against one another. In the first, the "thing quality"

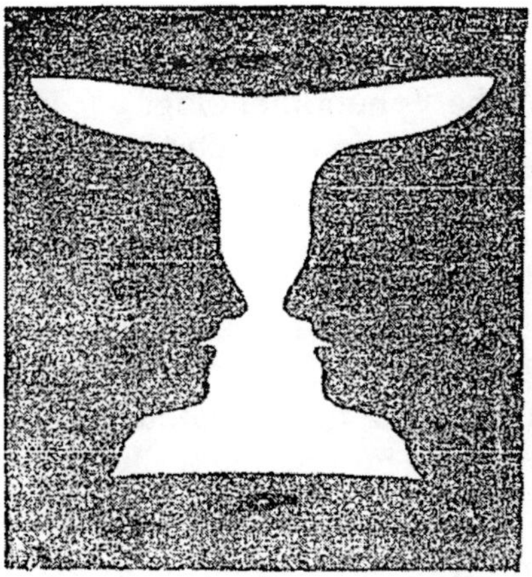

A

B

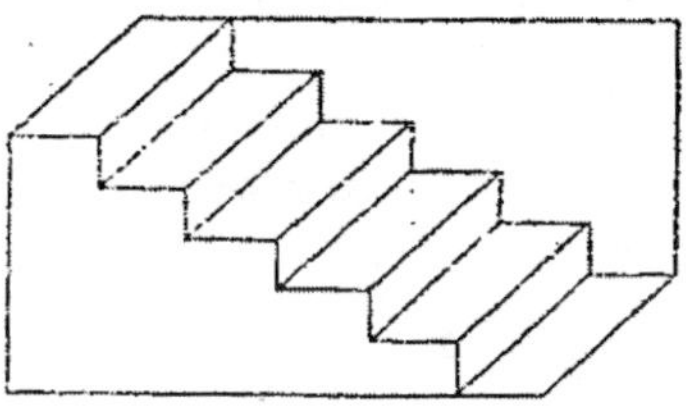

C

Fig. 3.1. Equivocal stimulus patterns.

In A either a goblet or a pair of faces may be seen. When either object is formed in perception, the remaining area of the picture recedes and becomes background. The latter is "formless," *i.e.*, seems to extend behind the object (Rubin [11].) In B the "shaping" function of contour is again brought out; the ear of one face becomes the eye of the other, the jaw and cheek of one become the nose of the other, etc. The artist entitled this picture "my wife and my mother-in-law." (By courtesy of E.G. Boring.) In C the solid surfaces represented in the picture may be shaped in either of two ways; the solid portion of one staircase becomes empty space in the reversed staircase.

may emerge either on one side of a line or on the other in the third, the solidity may be visible in one part of the figure or in the other. In the second, the contours are such that they can produce either of two quite different shapes : the one being a young face looking away from the observer, and the other being an old face seen in profile.

Are such figures merely psychological curiosities or simply demonstrations that attention may fluctuate or that perception cannot be explained by the stimulus pattern? Although they are often interpreted in this way, they are more properly to be considered perceptual experiments which facilitate introspection, particularly of the "phenomenological" kind. They are also the nearest approximation an experimenter can make to an experimental isolation of such properties as contour, "thing quality," and the other differences between an object and its background. Reversible figure-ground patterns do, in a sense, *isolate* such properties. In the first place the properties become evident to observation, and in the second place the conditions or variables which underlie them, although at first obscure, become susceptible to study by systematically varying the equivocal figure.

More generally, the method of devising artificial constellations of stimuli has proved extremely fruitful for the description of visual pattern phenomena. It has been widely used by the Gestalt psychologists both for that purpose and for the development of a theory of sensory organization considered as a physiological process. Like the method of ambiguous stimulus fields previously described, equivocal stimuli *seem* to imply a *lack* of relationship between stimulus and perception. If they are considered experiments rather than curiosities, however, this conclusion need not follow, and the abstruse conditions which give rise to the perception of form and shape may be clarified by studying them.

4. **The Experiment of Rotating or Distorting the Retinal Projection.** Physical objects and surfaces are projected as an image on the retina, in accordance with the laws of optics. From the neural processes initiated by this retinal image the organism discriminates the physical object successfully and obtains his visual world of objects and surfaces. This projection on the retina may be changed in several ways by placing optical devices in front of the eyes, where upon the visual world is changed accordingly. The projection may be inverted, *i.e.*, rotated 180 degrees, by a lens system; it may be tilted, *i.e.*, rotated to a lesser degree, by totally reflecting right-angle prisms; or it may be displaced and differentially distorted by optometrists' trial prisms [13, 7, 4].

Most of these experiments have not proved to be highly illuminating with respect to our phenomenal experience of space, since, as a rule, the phenomenal world simply appears to be modified in the expected fashion and to remain that way. The psychophysical correspondence between the retina and the visual appearance of space does not seem to be affected by the changed projection of objects on the retina. The inverted world, for example, does not shift around in experience and look "right side up," even after many hours of seeing it inverted. With respect to motor adjustments and orientations, however, a learning process occurs, and responses of localization and locomotion become adjusted to the new environment fairly rapidly. Along with this adjustment goes a decrease in the feeling of strangeness and unfamiliarity [13, 7].

There are some indications, however, that if the retinal projection is changed, not by being rotated or translated, but by being *distorted,* as it is to some extent when prisms are worn like glasses in front of the eyes, the psychophysical correspondence between retina and visual space is modified and shifts so as to make the distorted retinal image correspond more nearly to the normal undistorted space. This shift is verified by the fact that there occurs an *opposite* distortion in the appearance of normal space when the prisms are removed—a distortion which itself wears off after a lapse of time [4]. It is possible that other types of optical distortion, *e.g.,* those produced by cylindrical lenses, would yield the same type of effects, but such experiments have not been reported.

5. **The Experiment of Maintaining a Stimulus Image on the Same Retinal Area for a Prolonged Interval.** The eyes are normally never at rest except for momentary periods of fixation. The retinal image of the environment is constantly changing, the total pattern being shifted on the retina by extremely rapid movements of translation which correspond to the movements of the eyes from one fixation point to another. Pattern stimulation of the retina is therefore of short

duration in ordinary perception. It may be prolonged experimentally, however, by requiring the observer to fixate a stimulus field and to maintain fixation for a certain period of time.

The results of this experiment, with respect to colour and brightness stimulation in the fixated field, are well known. When illuminated surfaces are used a coloured form on a gray background slowly becomes less saturated; a black form becomes lighter and a white form darker. The relation between stimulus and perception has changed with respect to the colour variable. The change is such that in the stimulated area of the retina any new stimulation now evokes a colour which is shifted in the direction of the complementary. This shift appears in perception as a negative afterimage.

It is less well known, and only recently established, that in this fixation experiment there may be shifts other than that of colour value in the psychophysical correspondence between the retinal pattern of stimulation and the perceived field. Forms do not, it is true, change shape in any noticeable degree, but single lines or contours appear to have the effect of modifying, within the localized area where the retinal image was made to persist, the perception of subsequent lines and contours. The writer discovered that a curved line appeared less curved in the course of continuous prolonged perception and that, when another line was substituted for it, *i.e.*, projected on the same retinal area, the shape of the second line was modified with respect to curvature, a straight line, for example, looking curved in the opposite direction [5]. An analogous effect occurred if the lines of the experiment were, respectively, a tilted line and a vertical line; the negative aftereffect was one of tilt in the opposite direction. Kohler and Wallach [9] subsequently demonstrated certain aftereffects of fixating both line patterns and closed contour figures. The principle aftereffect of a fixated figure seemed to be to displace the contour of *another* figure away from its own (no longer present) contour when the second figure was not congruent with the first but when its lines were not too far distant. An example is shown in Fig. 3.2. Both these experiments demonstrate that the relation between retinal shape and seen shape may be modified under the influence of prolonged stimulation. The exploration of this influence, however, has only commenced, and the method needs to be pursued by other investigators.

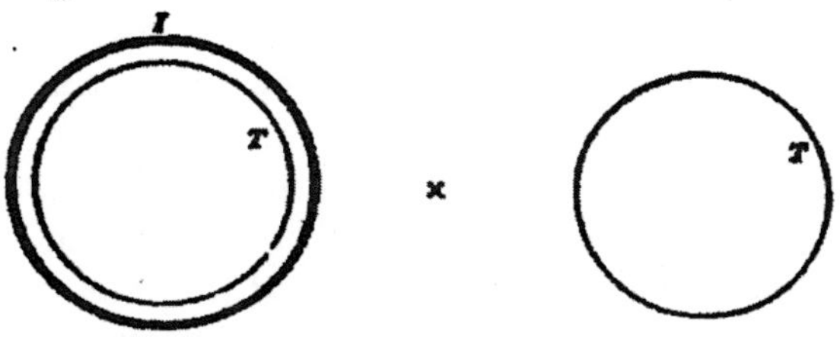

Fig. 3.2. Displacement of a contour after fixation.

The large circle labelled *I* is the "inspected figure"; the pair of circles labelled *T* is the "test figure". Each is drawn on a separate chart, the two being superimposed in this illustration. The small cross is the fixation mark, which is common to both charts. The *I*-figure is fixated by an observer for several minutes, and then the *T*-figure is substituted for it. The left-hand circle now appears smaller than the right-hand circle, although they are of identical size.

The experiment of fixating printing words for long intervals at one time attracted the interest of experimenters. The reports indicated that the meaning of the word receded from the pattern and also that the word tended to fall apart into letters or letter groups. The study of meaning by this method, using a variety of objects as stimuli, for the most part remains to be carried out.

APPLICATION TO SPECIFIC PROBLEMS IN THE PERCEIVING OF THE VISUAL WORLD

The outstanding problems of perception, already listed tentatively may now be taken up. The first three will be discussed from the point of view of the psychophysics of perception. Each of the remaining problems will be exemplified by a single experiment illustrating one of the methods already discussed.

The perception of Visual Form in Two Dimensions

The environmental world, as perceived, consist in large part of objects or things. How, then, do we perceive them—why do things look as they do? This is a psychological problem of the first importance, although its formulation has been historically delayed by the theory that objects could be explained in experience as bundles of colour sensations. Introspection directed toward the perception of objects as *such* reveals a set of properties which they possess independently of their colour qualities. Such properties are *line, contour, shape, emergence from the background, solidity, surface quality, and distance.* For convenience, perceptions (or sensations) of line, contour, shape, and surface may be treated as two dimensional, the three-dimensional qualities being deferred for later consideration. Actually, as the Gestalt psychologists have emphasized, all these properties of the visual object are interdependent. The best systematic description of them is to be found in Koffka's *Principles of Gestalt Psychology* [8].

The fundamental experiments on *outline or contour* are those of Rubin [11]. His method was simply observation and description of the phenomena. A typical experiment consisted of presenting the observer with an ingenious combination of two figures which shared a common contour. An example is the "goblet-faces" pattern already shown in fig. 3.1. Rubin could not isolate the role of the contour by *varying it* independently of other properties of objects; what he could do was to isolate it by using the same line for the contours of two alternative figures, the appearance of one figure obliterating the other. He could show that a visual object which is clearly seen at one moment may become non-existent a moment later when its contour is used by or attached to another visual object which was formerly merely the background. The functions of a contour in always possessing an "inside" and an "outside," of acting in only one of these directions (inward) to produce a shape, and of making the shaped figure "stand out" from the unshaped background thus became open to observation. These phenomena may all be observed in Fig. 3.3. This apparently simple type of experiment, involving the balancing of visual conditions against one another, has been widely used in perceptual research.

Werner [15] has pushed the study of contour formation one step further. His results appear to demonstrate that even a black disk on a white ground can be made invisible, the whole black area being obliterated and the colour stimulation being nullified, it its *contour* is not given enough time to develop in perception. The disk was presented tachistoscopically for a brief interval. If, then, a black ring was presented immediately afterward, whose inner contour registered exactly with the contour of the circular disk, nothing was seen but the ring. Presumable the loss of its contour to the ring inhibited the perception of the disk both as a *figure and as an area of colour stimulation.*

Presumably the stimulus correlate for the perception of an outline or a contour is an abrupt change of stimulation

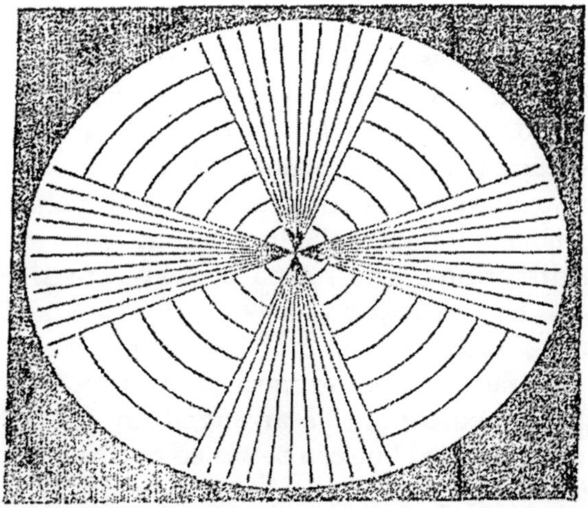

Fig. 3.3. Balanced alternatives of figure and ground.

Note how the areas of the circle which constitute the ground seem to extend continuously behind the areas which constitute the figure. This is what is meant by saying that the gound is not "shaped," whereas the figure is.

between adjacent retinal areas. A *gradual* change of stimulation along the retinal surface may occur, but such a continuous gradient does not apparently produce a contour. As a hypothesis the suggestion may be made that retinal gradients of this continuous sort have the function of producing three-dimensional perceptions, which are to be discussed in the next section. The *abrupt* change of stimulation may be studied not only by the experiment of equivocal forms and the experiment of brief intervals of exposure but also by the psychophysical method of a just noticeable brightness difference. The study of brightness discrimination and visual acuity employs this experimental method. All the evidence is consistent with the conclusion that the discrimination of brightness and colour, which involves the perception of area and shape, is dependent on the formation of a contour in experience. Since it is also probable that the formation of a contour depends on an abrupt change in areal stimulation on the retina, such a change would seem to be the fundamental stimulus condition.

The visual *line*, which may be produced artificially on man-made surfaces, can be used to represent the kind of contour which makes possible object perception in the natural visual field. If the visual line does not return on itself—is not "closed"—it becomes an isolated stimulus element, separated from its shape-producing function as a contour. Its stimulus is a *double* change in retinal stimulation, the two changes being adjacent to one another, if the line is sufficiently thin, and in opposite directions. The retina is very sensitive to such changes, as the research on visual acuity shows. The visual line, as such, has received some investigation and deserves more. In contradistinction to most of the properties of form and shape, which cannot be arranged on dimensions, the qualities of an isolated line can be scaled and therefore studied by quantitative psychophysical methods. Every student of calculus knows that a line (or a curve) can be analyzed mathematically, *i.e.*, measured. The perceptual qualities of a line, or any chosen segment of it, are its direction (upright, tilted, or horizontal) and its quality of being straight, concave, or convex. The latter property might be called "curvature quality." The mathematician speaks correspondingly of the *slope* and *the rate of change of slope* of the curve. The writer has shown [5] that these two qualitative dimensions are akin to other kinds of sensory dimensions. Not only are they introspectively simple, they also manifest adaptation with negative aftereffect, which is characteristic of supposedly more "elementary" qualities of the world, like temperature and colour. It seems possible that further introspective and psychophysical study of simple lines may help to explain how the contour produces the visual shape of objects and things.

Experiments on the perception of surface, or surface quality, have gone no farther than to establish the existence of this property of visual objects and to determine that it probably depends on the sensing of the "microstructure" or texture of the object surface. According to Metzger [10], whenever a surface is seen, it is seen because the area in question is characterized by "grain" or spots or other irregularities of brightness. The terms available to describe this quality are not definite; it needs to be observed and described further. Visual texture, as it will be called here, is nevertheless evident to introspection, and its stimulus correlate is definable as inhomogeneity of retinal stimulation. When an area of perfectly homogeneous light stimulation is presented to the retina, as occurs when one looks at clear sky or certain artificial setups, no surface is seen, and the area appears at an indefinite distance. The area is said to possess film colour instead of surface colour.

The results of the experiments on line, contour, shape, and surface do not enable us as yet to account for the perception of objects in their two-dimensional aspect. They do suggest, however, the direction which future experiments should take and the methods experimenters should follow to reach this goal. There have been a large number of other experiments dealing with the perception not of objects, *i.e.*, forms with contours, but of visual order and grouping among *constellations* of stimuli. They have received their impetus from the classical experiments of Wertheimer [16]. The stimuli used were abstract dots or lines. These elements, when seen, tend to become organized into groups or units in accordance with certain laws which Wertheimer formulated. Proximity, similarity, or "good continuation" of the elements, for example, all make for unit formation. Wertheimer's method was the balancing of one factor against another or others, with observation of the units which emerged from the constellation; *i.e.*, he studied the factors which made an equivocal constellation less so. These units, however, are not like the objects or forms of the ordinary visual world. Wertheimer's laws are not so relevant to that problem as they are to an even more difficult one—that of the order and interrelations among elements within the visual fields, and especially within artificial visual fields. Wertheimer's laws are of special interest to abstract artists and others who are concerned with the problem of visual arrangement, composition, design, and esthetic unity.

A great many studies have also been performed on the perception of *nonsense* forms and patterns, by the method of requiring the observer to draw them (or recognize or match them) immediately after presentation or after an interval of time. The data available for study are the errors which the observer makes, the discrepancy in each case between the shape of the reproduced or matched figure and that of the original stimulus figure. The former shape is assumed to be indicative of the perception or the memory image. These are qualitative errors and are distinct from the quantitative errors of a regular psychophysical experiment. The discrepancies will be of many different varieties. The experimenter must classify and evaluate them on the basis of his subjective opinion instead of scaling them on a dimension of variation. As a substitute for mathematical averaging of the errors, however, he may utilize the method of composite drawings to obtain a kind of "mean shape" and thereby secure evidence of any general trend among the discrepancies of shape. Trends towards symmetry, toward closure of the contour, and toward resemblance to meaningful shapes have been found. This experiment, as a type, is methodologically appropriate for exploratory studies, but inexact. Future experiments in this field might benefit by first adopting a hypothesis as to the trend of the discrepancies for a given form, then *scaling* a series of forms showing increasing discrepancy from the original (if this is possible), and finally measuring the errors.

This type of experiment may be criticized on other grounds in so far as it purports to study the perception or memory of visual forms. It neglects the main problem and concentrates on a secondary issue. We need to know primarily why there is a *correspondence* between the shape of the stimulus and the shape of the experience, not why there are discrepancies between them. There is small use in studying the errors in form perception when so little is known about the reasons for the psychophysical correlation. Why is the percept (or the memory image) shaped like the stimulus object? To say that it is *organized* is only to say that it is shaped and is not a mosaic of point sensations. To say that it is shaped by memory images of past experience with similar objects is to say even less. The question is, Why is it shaped like the stimulus object? Either a tendency toward precise organization (symmetry, closure of contour) or a tendency toward the standard shape of a meaningful object will account for *errors* in the perception of nonsense forms, but neither will account for the fact of their *correct perception.*

The Perception of a Three-dimensional World : the Problem of Distance and Depth

The properties of visual objects include not only contour, shape, and surface; in addition, things emerge from the background, possess solidity, and appear at a distance. The problem of how these additional characteristics can arise from nothing more than a pair of two-dimensional retinal images is a problem which is older than psychology itself. It is still not adequately solved. If there are three experimental stages to any sensory or perceptual problem, *i.e.*, describing the perception, identifying the stimulus correlate, and setting up a relationship between them, then it may be suggested that the problem of three-dimensional vision exists only in the first stages. Psychologists have not yet succeeded even in identifying the stimulus correlates, presumably complex, for all types of distance perception. Hence they are unable to vary or otherwise modify the stimuli presented to observer in the effort to establish a psychophysical relationship.

There is, however, one retinal correlate of the depth and solidity of objects which has been identified and experimentally studied. It is the disparity of the images from a single object on the two retinas which is produced by "parallax," *i.e.*, by the fact that the two eyes get their images from slightly different positions in space. Since the two images jointly are the stimulus correlate of a single perceived object, it is easy to suppose that their disparity might be the correlate of a third-dimensional quality of the perceived object. If the disparity can be measured, reproduced, and optically presented to an observer, with systematic variations, the hypothesis can be verified. It was actually verified by Wheatstone over a hundred years ago. He was able to do so because he invented an ingenious instrument, the stereoscope, which enable him to reproduce and manipulate artificially varying degrees of retinal disparity. As the discrepancy between images increased in certain regular ways, the depth quality of the perception increased correspondingly (Fig. 3.4).

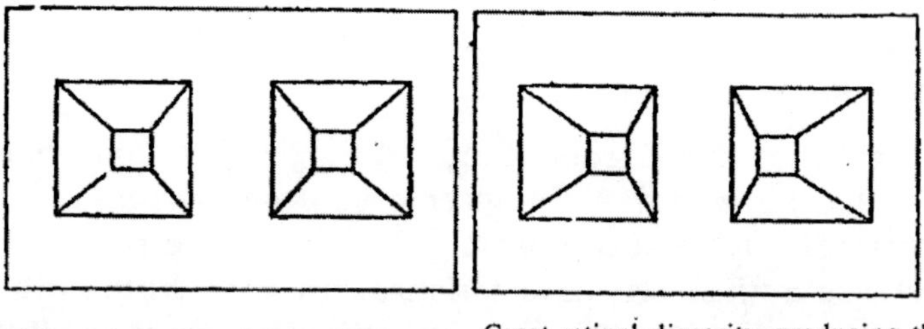

Slight retinal disparity, producing the perception of a low pyramid.

Great retinal disparity, producing the perception of a high, steep pyramid.

Fig. 3.4. Amount of retinal disparity and degree of perceived depth.

The stereoscope is an example of the way in which the development of apparatus can affect the progress of a branch of perceptual psychology. A major difficulty in studying certain kinds of perception is the constructing of artificial counterparts of the natural physical stimuli. Even though the stimulus correlate may be suspected, it cannot be fully verified, and the correlation cannot be established until it has been "synthesized," as it were, and subjected to experimental control. Synthetic retinal disparity can be produced and modified at will in the stereoscope, but visual texture, for example, has not yet been reproduced in a systematic manner for experimentation. Artists have of course "experimented" with texture in paintings for many centuries, but without use of the method of control and isolation of the "independent variable" which constitutes a scientific experiment.

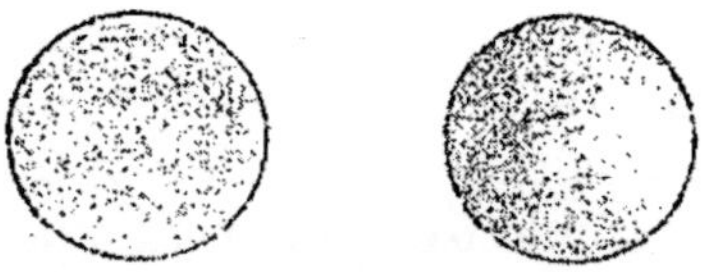

Fig. 3.5. The perception of solidity in relation to a retinal gradient of brightness.

The binocular stimulus correlate accounts in part for the phenomena of solidity, emergence from the background, and depth, but it cannot wholly account for them, since it is a fact that one-eyed persons also see depth and distance. There exist monocular cues for these three-dimensional properties, as well as the binocular cue. These monocular cues are, however, only imperfectly identified in our present state of knowledge and have in almost no degree been brought under experimental control. The accepted view is to say that they are "secondary" cues for the perception of space, which have been learned in the course of experience. It does not solve the problem, however, to conclude that these cues are learned. Even if they are, which is probable, the question still remains of exactly what complex stimulus correlate it is to which the experienced observer has learned to react. We come around to face the same question which is asked of supposedly unlearned sensation : What is the psychophysical relationship?

It is a possibility that the monocular cues for distance, depth, and solidity, when considered as stimulus correlates, will be definable as *gradients* of retinal stimulation. A gradient is a continuous, transitional change of stimulation over a retinal area and is to be contrasted with the abrupt change of stimulation between two adjacent retinal areas which is related to a contour. Two examples of retinal gradients will be given, one being a gradient of brightness and the other a gradient of texture. The first produces a quality of three dimensionality in a form; *i.e.,* it yields solidity. The second produces three dimensionality on the ground and yields the impression of continuous distance.

The "modelling of surfaces by light and shade" implies that there is a psychophysical relationship between specific gradients of bright and dark stimulation on the retina and specific perceptions of the "depth shape" of objects, *i.e.,* their shape in the third dimension as distinguished from their shape in two dimensions. The relation between "depth shape" and gradients (or levels) of brightness could be established if the experimenter proceeded systematically to isolate the variables and devise a method of controlling the stimulus.

Gradients of size, linear perspective, aerial perspective, and retinal motion might also be studied by this procedure. Since they are all capable of being scaled, the ordinary psychophysical methods should be applicable. If a satisfactory experimental analysis can be made of the so-called "cues" for space perception, an age-long puzzle will be on its way to a solution.

The Perception of Objective Color, Size, and Shape in Relation to Their Retinal Counterparts : the Problem of Constancy

Some of the properties of visual objects as perceived do not correlate very well with what we shall call their retinal *counterparts.* They correlate instead with the objects themselves. Since the perception must be mediated by the retinal stimulation, we are faced with a contradiction. How can our perceptions correlate so well with their objects when the retinal counterparts do not apparently correlate with either? This is the problem of perceptual constancy or, as it might better be called perceptual objectively.

There is no doubt that the retinal image, considered as a counterpart, is not a reliable indicator of objective shape, for instance. When the face of a flat object is inclined to the line of sight, the shape of the image changes from what it was when the face was perpendicular to the line of sight. As the object is turned, the retinal counterpart changes radically (Fig. 3.7), but nevertheless we continue to see the same object (not quite the same object, to be precise, for the slant of its surface is part of what we see). The percept, like the object, is said to be "constant," whereas the shape of the retinal counterpart changes. Does this imply that the principle of psychophysical correlation does not hold true for perceptions as it does for "sensations"? If retinal shape does not correspond with seen

Fig. 3.6. Perspective drawing of an object in different orientations.

shape, neither the basic assumption nor the methods of psychophysics are applicable to the problem. It will have to be studied in terms of mental transformation, interpretation, intuition, or, at best, a process of spontaneous sensory organization.

The difficulty can be resolved if we distinguish between the retinal *counterpart* of objective shape and the retinal *correlate,* which remains to be discovered. We tend to assume, in studying space perception, that the retinal "image" is a counterpart of the object and of the percept. But the retinal image *considered as a complex of stimulation* need not be, and seldom is, such a counterpart. We are misled by the fact that such objects as a circle drawn on paper, viewed head-on, projects a circular retinal image. This is actually a rare situation, except in form-perception experiments in psychological laboratories. In ordinary perception the shape of the retinal image is seldom a counterpart of the object. A genuinely three-dimensional shape could not in the nature of things have a retinal counterpart, since the retina extends only in two dimensions. The phenomenon called depth shape—the "modeling" of a surface—has no retinal counterpart, although it probably has a retinal correlate in the form of gradients or steps of brightness and texture. Objective shape does not need to be copied on the retina to be perceived; it needs only to have specific correlates there for all its objective properties. The contour of the retinal image is only one of these correlates.

If the foregoing argument can be generalized, the objective nature of perception is a subject for psychophysical investigation rather than for theories of epistemology. The so-called constancy of shape, *i.e.*, the fact that a shape is three-dimensional and is located and oriented in space, requires a complex stimulus correlate. The shape is not experienced in isolation; it is always shape in a given orientation. At least two isolated stimulus variables might be tentatively identified within the total correlate : the retinal contour on the one hand, and the cues for slant and orientation on the other. When the object is rotated on a vertical axis, the retinal contours change their horizontal dimensions; at the same time the cues for the slant of the object surface change horizontally. These changes in stimulation are *reciprocal*. It might be supposed therefore that one aspect of the total stimulus correlate remains constant despite rotation of the object—the sum or product of these reciprocal stimulus variables. This would provide a basis *in stimulation* for an unchanging percept.

The perceived size and colour of objects are similarly out of correspondence with the retinal stimuli to which they have been found to correspond in the unique situations where distance and illumination are held constant. Retinal size is a poor indicator of perceived size when the distance of the object varies. The brightness of the retinal image is likewise not indicative of the physical nature of the surface of the object when the illumination changes. Nevertheless the size and the colour of objects are not much modified by these changes. The object size is seen at the *different distance,* and the coloured surface is seen in the *changed illumination.* A summary of the experimental evidence on these types of constancy may be found in Koffka [8] and in Woodworth [17].

Constancy experiments in general consist of demonstrations that the observer perceive the shape, size, or whiteness of an object, with a discrepancy from what would be expected of the retinal counterpart. The procedure is to introduce a variation in orientation, distance, or illumination between the standard and the variable stimulus-objects. Otherwise the procedure is that of a regular psychophysical experiment. The discrepancy between the perceived property and its retinal counterpart is computed and is sometimes called an index of phenomenal regression toward the real object [14]. The chief emphasis is placed on the amount of constancy revealed by the experiment.

The difficulty in these experiments is not in the techniques, but in the preliminary introspection and the definition of the problem. There is dissatisfaction with the term constancy. In the view just presented, is not so much the shape, size, or colour of the object which remains constant under varying circumstances as it is the *object itself.* Its shape and orientation, its size and distance, its colour and illumination are all features of the object in its environment. The stimulus correlates of *all* these features are necessary to make the perceived object look like what it is. The interaction between the members of these pairs of stimulus correlates provides the basis for a consistently identifiable, or constant, object in perception. The experimenter, therefore, needs to define a two-variable stimulus complex, *e.g., both* size and distance, when he is setting up a constancy experiment. He can then discover whether the two-variable stimulus is in correspondence with the perceived object.

The Perception of Visual Motion and Locomotion

We turn now to a more specific consideration of the experimental methods of perceptual research. A single experiment only will be described in each field, exemplifying one or another aspect of these methods.

A practical problem in motion perception arises in learning to fly an airplane. How does the pilot sense the exact direction in which he is going, particularly when he is landing? By looking at the ground, obviously, but what does he look for and how can he judge his direction? An airplane cannot be "aimed" like an automobile by pointing its nose toward a distant point ; the cue for the guidance of flight has to be looked for in the visual scene ahead. This is a problem requiring the *analysis of a complex stimulus situation*—not an analysis of the content of consciousness but a "phenomenal" analysis—and the *identification of the cues for judgment*. This identification must then be *verified* by an experiment which establishes the correspondence between the stimulus and the judgment. The writer and others [6] undertook a study of this problem, the methods and the results of which may be in part described.

Observation and the facts of optics both suggested that the visual basis of the perception of one's own locomotion is retinal motion, not of an isolated image but over the whole retina. The ground and the objects on the ground are all projected on the retina. When the observer moves, this image is *deformed,* near objects of the visual world corresponding with points which flow rapidly over the retina, farther objects with points which flow more slowly. The only points at which the retinal image is not flowing, during motion of the observer, are those corresponding to extremely distant points in the visual world—the horizon—and the *point toward which one is moving*. If the observer "looks where he is going," his retinal image is expanding radially from a center, and this center corresponds to the point in the physical world toward which he is going. Figure 3.7 represents the retinal pattern of expansion during an approach glide to an airfield. The arrows are vectors indicating the amount and direction of retinal flow at the given point. Their direction, no matter where one may look, is always *away from* the point toward which the observer is going at the moment. This expansion pattern would appear to be the cue for the pilot's sense of his direction of flight.

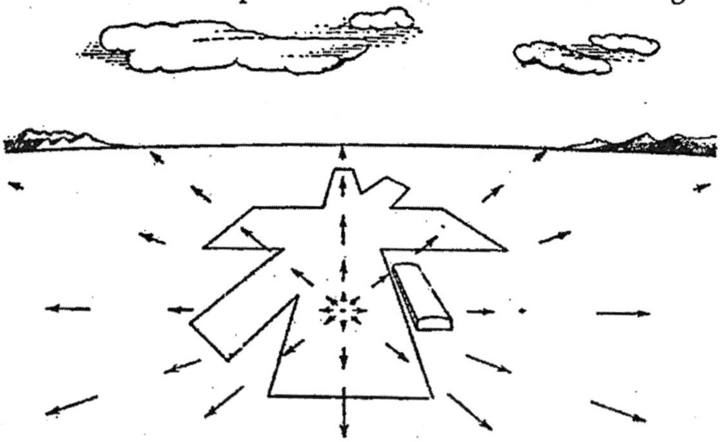

Fig. 3.7. Retinal motion perspective in the scene viewed while landing an airplane.

The experiment to verify this conclusion was based on a motion-picture sequence of a scene similar to that shown in Fig. 3.7. The scene was photographed in miniature so as to permit control of the conditions, with the camera moving as the observer would move in that situation. When the film was projected the velocities and directions of expansion could be plotted on the screen. They proved to be similar to those illustrated. Furthermore, when an observer looked at the screen, he obtained a compelling experience of moving through space in a specific direction. This direction could be judged with some accuracy even in the early portions of the sequence when the expansion was slow, and it could be judged with greater accuracy as the expansion became more rapid.

An experiment of this sort raises many more questions than it answers, but it illustrates a procedure for the study of complex perceptual patterns.

The Perception of Meaning and of Symbols

The problem of meaning and the nature of symbolic perception present a variety of problems for psychology. Most, if not all, meanings are *learned* by the individual. As determiners of behaviour, the meanings of objects have been studied in learning experiments. But meanings are also perceptual experiences, and in this aspect they are difficult to study by experimental methods. The meanings of situations, objects, pictures, and words are difficult or impossible to arrange in accordance with their modes of variation, as colours can be arranged, because of their seeming uniqueness and their almost infinite variety.

The method of "impoverishing" the stimulus may be used, however, and the apprehension of printed words exposed in a tachistoscope has been investigated in many experiments. A meaningful word can be apprehended under exposure conditions where an equivalent, but less meaningful, group of letters is scarcely perceived at all. Words and symbols can also be subjected to prolonged optical fixation. The meaning is reported to recede eventually from the visual pattern, and the letters of a word appear to "break up" into subunits.

Symbolic meaning can always be identified and described by introspection, although it cannot be scaled and measured by classical psychophysical methods. There exist certain complex types of meaning, however, which apparently cannot be described adequately, *i.e.*, in such a way as to make other observers of the same phenomenon agree with the one who described it. The study of esthetics and of personality is hampered by this difficulty. Is there, for example, meaning in the handwriting of individual persons? Does the quality of "style," which is almost indescribable, indicate or express the person whose handwriting is examined? Graphologists maintain that such meanings exist, but their claim is doubted. Problems of this sort can be investigated by the method of non-serial matching.

Allport and Vernon report an experiment on the expressive quality of handwriting in which this method was used. Ten sketches of personality were written, describing the traits and characteristics of ten individuals. Samples of their handwriting were obtained. The samples and sketches were then submitted to a group of judges, some of whom were professional graphologists. Each judge examined a given sample of handwriting and, from the qualities he saw in it, attempted to select the personality sketch with which it matched. He would be correct by chance only once in ten tries. He then repeated his attempt for the remaining samples. The *perceptual basis* of the selections did not have to be described, not did it enter into the experiment. The mean number of correct identifications out of ten attempts was approximately two instead of one. The graphologists were somewhat more successful than were those who disclaimed any special ability to interpret handwriting, but both types of judges were more successful than the hypothesis of chance guessing would predict.

Social Perception

A whole realm of perception has scarcely been touched upon in this chapter. The methods and experiments discussed have to do primarily with the perception of the world of objects—the physical world. The methodological problems are difficult enough in that realm, but they become even more complex when we come to deal, as scientists, with the world of values, customs, stereotypes, and fashions. We then have to study the perception of such objects as food, clothing, and articles of daily use; of the actions of other people; of social situations and problems; and of races, classes, and nations. There is one very important difference between space perception, for example, and social perception. It is always possible, subject only to the ingenuity of the experimenter, to establish, in the first case, whether a perception is "correct" or "incorrect." It is a very complex and often controversial matter, however, to establish whether a given social perception is "veridical." Since the realities behind social values and judgments are at best subtle and obscure (some social scientists deny that there are any realities), these properties of things are studied by the method used to investigate indefinite or ambiguous stimulus patterns that is to say, the experimenter studies the perception not as a function of the stimulus but as a function of variables within the subject—his past experience, his motivations, his prejudices, and his personality.

An experiment of this sort is that of Sherif on the determination of perception by a "social norm" [12]. The stimulus situation he employed was even more ambiguous and "unstructured" than are inkblots or nonsense patterns; it consisted of a single stationary pinpoint of light in an absolutely dark room. Under these conditions the "autokinetic phenomenon" occurs. Sooner or later in this situation the point of light, being unlocalized on any spatial surface and divorced from any visible frame of reference, begins to drift or change position erratically. This purely illusory impression of movement is variable and indefinite, as one would expect. The judgment which Sherif required of his observers was an estimation of the *amount* of this movement in inches during a certain time interval after the light appeared. The instructions were such as to suggest that the light would *really* move, although it never did.

After a number of repeated judgments, a standard or normal amount of movement began to characterize the estimates of an observer. One individual would report 1 or 2 inches of displacement, while another reported 9 or 10 inches. If at this stage a pair of observers, or a group of three, were given a repetition of the experiment *together*, so that they could hear each other's judgments, the established individual norms of judgment began to be modified, and a *group norm* emerged, to which the individual norms gradually conformed. At the end of three sittings (100 judgments each) all the individuals in a group had standards to guide their estimates, which were very close together. The majority of observers were not aware that their judgments were being influenced by others. The standards were by no means the same in different groups of individuals, one group tending to see 1 inch of movement as the normal amount, whereas another saw as much as 4 inches.

If an individual observer faced the situation *alone*, after first observing as a member of a group, the socially determined norm continued to affect his judgments, although the influence of the group was no longer physically present. Although he did not realize it, the amount of movement which he expected to see was now the result of his interaction with the group. An elementary social custom had been established, both in the group and in the individuals who composed the group.

CONCLUSIONS FOR THE STUDENT OF PERCEPTION

It has been implied throughout this chapter that the first necessity in setting up an experiment on perception is to formulate its aim. Formerly the aim of perceptual experiments was to establish the *differences* between a percept and its presumed stimulus correlate, analyzing the latter in terms of those stimuli which were known to yield "sensations," and then to account for these differences by some hypothesis. Recently, with the breaking down of the logical distinction between sensation and perception, it appears possible in many cases to establish a psychophysical *correspondence* between a percept and its own stimulus correlate. The latter may be a ratio, a gradient, or an integration of stimuli of a more complex order than are the accepted correlates of so-called sensory experience. Whenever such a correspondence is conceivable, the experimenter should first devote his attention to it, on the grounds that, if established, it will reduce the necessity for extra hypotheses. The methodology of such research has been the principal concern of this chapter.

There are, of course, many aspects of human perception for which the corresponding stimulus complexes are unknown. They are presumably based on intricate and subtle discriminations of the physical properties of things, persons, and events, but they are so far from being identifiable by the ordinary procedures of the physical sciences that they can scarcely be guessed at. The meanings, the "dynamic" and "physiognomic" qualities, and the social significances which make up a great part of human experience are all of this type. Although they are perceptions and depend on the functioning of the sense organs for their development, they require hypotheses concerning the organization of experience and the process of learning in order to account for them. They are so much dependent on the concepts, attitudes, and prejudices of the observer that the methods of studying them become indistinguishable from the methods of studying thought processes.

The phenomena of object perception, space perception, and perceptual constancy, on the other hand, are probably more nearly akin to sensory processes than they are to concepts. If this is true, they should be studied after the fashion of psychophysical experiments. Evidence is needed on the perceptual resultants of complex stimulation. This evidence can be obtained by introspective analysis, by isolating and controlling the relevant variables in the total stimulus situation or at least by systematically varying the situation, by obtaining discriminative judgments from an observer, and by applying the techniques of psychophysical measurement to the results.

REFERENCES

1. Allport, G.W., and P.E. Vernon, *Studies in Expressive Movement.* New York : Macmillan, 1933.
2. Birkhoff, G.D., *Aesthetic Measure.* Cambridge : Harvard University Press, 1933.
3. Boring, E.G., *The Physical Dimensions of Consciousness.* New York : Century, 1933.
4. Gibson, J.J., Adaptation, after-effect, and contrast in the perception of curved lines. *J. Exper. Psychol.*, 1933, *16*, 1-31.
5. Gibson, J.J., Adaptation with negative after-effect. *Psychol. Rev.*, 1937. *44*, 222-243.
6. Gibson, J.J., Ed. *Motion Picture Testing and Research.* Washington : Government Printing Office, 1947.
7. Gibson, J.J., and O.H. Mowrer. Determinants of the perceived vertical and horizontol. *Psychol. Rev.*, 1938, *4*, 300-323.
8. Koffka, K., *Principles of Gestalt Psychology.* New York : Harcourt, Brace, 1935.
9. Kohler, W., and H. Wallach. Figural after-effects. *Proc. Amer.*

Philos. Soc., 1944, *88*, No. 4, 269-357.

10. Metzger, W., Optische Untersuchungen am Gangzfeld. II. Zur Phanomecnologie des homogenen Ganzfelds. *Psychol. Forsch*, 1930, *13*, 6-29.
11. Rubin, E., *Visuell wahrgenomene figuren*. Copenhagen : Gyldendalske Boghandel, 1921.
12. Sherrif, M., *The Psychology of Social Norms*. New York : Harper, 1936.
13. Stratton, G. M., Vision without inversion of the retinal image. *Psychol. Rev.*, 1897, *4*, 341-360 and 463-481.
14. Thouless, R.H., Phenomenal regression to the real object, I. *Brit. J. Psychol.*, 1931, *21*, 339-359.
15. Werner, H., Studies on contour. I. Qualitative analyses. *Amer. J. Psychol.*, 1935, *47*, 40-64.
16. Wertheimer, M., Untersuchungen zur Lehre von der Gestalt, II. *Psychol. Forsch*, 1923, *4*, 301-350.
17. Woodworth, R.S., *Experimental Psychology*. New York : Henry Holt, 1938.

4

Studying Vision

The present chapter is devoted to the major and most representative methods of studying vision *as such*, independent of the more perceptual qualities related to the field. The student should carry over the material of the previous two chapters and relate it to the methods to be described in the next several pages.

In order to accomplish the most within the boundaries of a single chapter on the complicated methodology in vision, a number of economies are necessary. The first is the reduction of certain of the broader aspects of method to ideas that can be presented in general statements. Accordingly, a number of these statements precede the description of the phenomena of vision and the specific experimental conditions under which they are included.

FIELDS OF VISUAL INVESTIGATION

One of the major ways in which visual studies differ is in terms of their objectives. These differences are quite marked and are reflected not only in the types of questions for which answers are sought, but also in the procedures involved in the process of experimentation. The different aspects in which attention is directed may be called *areas of investigation*, each of which may be subdivided into several *types of inquiry*. One of the first areas of investigation pertains to the nature of what is perceived. It deals with the problems of how the visual field is organized, what is in it, and similar questions. The study of the most general and basic structure (organization) of the visual field is the first type of inquiry. It so happens that the first differentiable feature of visual-field organization is the separation into figure and ground (see Figs. 4.1 and 4.2). Thus figure-ground relations and all similar studies belong in our first type of inquiry.

Studies of the second type of inquiry deal with *objects* as such. Questions of their identification, location, etc., are pertinent here. Size, shape, and similar characteristics are involved only in a secondary way and are of concern only as they distinguish one object from another or help determine

Fig. 4.1.

Fig. 4.2.

Figs. 4.1 and 4.2. These drawings indicate the fact that differentiated visual fields are structured into two parts—the figure and the ground.

In fig. 4.1 the lines becomes figure. Not only are they figures (objects) but also they cluster so as to enclose portions of the field which becomes part of the figure—representing the surface of parts, boards, etc. Fig. 4.2 can be seen in two ways—the figure and ground mutually alternate.

object character or position. A third type of inquiry is the investigation of visual properties, such as colour. Although colour, for example, is often studied as a property of object surfaces, it may be abstracted from the object itself and dealt with under conditions in which it has a minimum of relation to specific objects.

It is obvious from the foregoing that the study of vision necessitates certain amounts of arbitrariness, as do all psychological investigations. As was pointed out such arbitrariness is a matter of abstraction which is involved in all our techniques of analysis. We must recognize that the kind of abstraction used plays an important part in our end results. In a certain sense experimental phenomena are products of sensory abstraction.

A second area of visual investigation deals with the functional characteristics of the organism. It is not directed toward descriptions of visual phenomena, but toward understanding visual capacities. For instance, brightness discrimination, adaptation, and visual acuity are terms that refer to a capacity of the organism rather than to its experience. Brightness discrimination and adaptation refer to what the organism does visually. Visual acuity refers to a discriminatory capacity the organism possesses.

A third area of investigation involves study of the organic mechanisms and anatomical relations which underlie the properties just mentioned. These mechanisms may be chemical, motor, or neural. Visual studies in this third area are concerned with inquiry into retinal structure and function, the structure and activities of the remaining stations in the visual pathway of the nervous system, and ultimately the nervous system as a whole. Photochemical activity in the receptor cells and neural interaction in the retina are two very common objects of study in this area of visual investigation.

Still a fourth area of investigation is the study of the role that vision plays in the behaviour of organisms. One type of inquiry in this direction seeks to find how vision participates in the general behaviour of the individual. A second type is concerned with particularizing the relations of vision and the other senses. Much of what is included in this area is conventionally dealt with in perception.

In the present chapter we shall limit ourselves to several well-recognized and thus formalized categories in which vision is studied. The categories of adaptations, visual acuity, brightness discrimination, colour discrimination, spatial localization, and response to intermittent stimulation (flicker, etc.) have each arisen from observations in everyday human experience. Now, when one speaks of a visual phenomenon, he tends to put it into one of these major categories. Before we take these categories up in detail, we shall survey some of the more important psychophysical relations necessary to an understanding of visual methodology.

PSYCHOPHYSICAL RELATIONS IN VISION

Visual experiences are both quantitative and qualitative. To the extent that they are qualitative, they have properties which cannot be directly described in numerical terms. As a series, however, a series of qualitative changes may be related to some numerical order. This order lies outside the qualities themselves and applies to stimulus or internal physiological conditions. The properties of visual experience which appear to be quantitative pertain to time (duration), space (size, direction, etc.), and intensity (brightness, etc.). The stimulus conditions involve time, space, and intensity. Procedures for studying visual processes are those which manipulate these factors precisely to discover new types of phenomena, to make clear the relations between already known phenomena, or to discover the mechanisms underlying the phenomena themselves. This involves relating the visual outcomes to stimulus conditions (psychophysics), although it is recognized that certain conditions lying within the organism are often as crucial in determining the literal outcome in a specific case as are external stimulus conditions (psychophysiology).

One of the most basic and widely employed concepts in the study of biological phenomena is the *threshold* or *limen*. The notion of threshold arises out of the discrepancy between physical conditions which are considered to be potential stimuli and the responses themselves. The smallest amount of stimulation which will produce a given result is spoken of as the threshold amount. The threshold is not absolute, but instead is statistical, because of the unavoidable instability of both the stimulus and the organism. Hence all threshold definitions are couched in statistical terms. Part of what has just been called "a given result" is defined by the numerical probability of detecting a given target or a difference between two of its parts. In vision, for instance, there are amounts of radiant energy which fail to elicit visual experience. A room may be so dark that no objects are visible in it, but if the illumination is increased sufficiently, a point will be reached at which certain objects will just be discernible. The level of illumination will then be just threshold for the objects in question.

If, in a fairly well lighted room, two sheets of paper are put before an observer, he may be able to detect that they are not equally white. The difference may be so slight as just to be perceptible. This means that had the physical difference been any less, the two sheets would have looked alike.

Form this description it will be evident that thresholds are of two general types. There are "absolute" thresholds and "relative" ("difference") thresholds, as indicated respectively by the two illustrations.

The subject of thresholds brings us to the consideration of what is new and what is old, what is an enduring object (or experience) some what changed, and what is a new (different and discrete) object with some resemblance to an earlier one. When conditions are shifted in such a way as to provide for just barely seeing something in the dark, the something is a new object of experience. With added light it changes in various ways. Were each of these kinds of change to be examined, a series of difference thresholds could be established by simply manipulating conditions step by step, so that notations of the amount of stimulus change necessary to produce each perceivable increment of change could be obtained. In a sense, when an object changes, it is a new object. In another sense, it is not. When the experiential emphasis lies in the continuity between what was and what is, the difference constitutes a change. Without this, the present object is new relative to any other one in the past. Whereas difference thresholds pertain to just perceivable changes, absolute thresholds pertain to situations in which something new emerges. When thresholds pertain to differences, a series of differences are generally obtainable by incremental or decremental changes in physical dimension. Steps from one threshold to the next are called "just noticeable differences" (JND's).

A number of trials (observations) are necessary for determining threshold, for a very weak stimulus will not always evoke a sensory end result. A target seen on one attempt will not necessarily be seen on another. A statistical relation exists between the strength of the stimulus and the seeing of an object.

It is possible to define threshold in any one of a number of ways. If the target is an object to be seen only in one place and in a single orientation about the axis of regard, the observer has only one of two responses to make. He either reports seeing the target, or he fails to report. If he is apprised of each time the target is presented, he reports either that he does or that he does not see it. Hence, by pure chance, he will be able to be correct half of the time. In such cases threshold is sometimes defined as the stimulus strength which evokes a response in 75 per cent of the trials. In many experiments the number of possible reports is increased by rotating the target into several positions in chance order or by placing it in various predetermined positions eccentric to the fixation point. This reduces the chances of being correct by mere guessing.

In actual experimentation, standardization and short cuts in procedure are necessary. These tend to modify response, making for some predetermination of result. Scoring procedures cannot therefore be constructed on the assumption that only two factors, actual sensitivity and pure chance, operate. They must take into account certain biases of the observer resulting form his ability to predict to some degree from what he has learned of the experimenter's procedure. In what way these biases reduce chance factors has to be determined for the particular method used.

Although a threshold stimulus is one which just succeeds in producing a response, less intense physical conditions are not without their effects. Hence they are called *subthreshold stimuli*, even though such terminology is paradoxical. Literally, that which does not stimulate can hardly be a stimulus.

Subthreshold stimuli can be considered effective in bringing about certain chemical conditions, and these effects, when added to more of the same, will end in a response of the same category as that produced by a single threshold or suprathreshold stimulus. There is no such thing, however, as a subthreshold experiential response. The effect produced, if ever to be called a physiological response, is in a category other than the response which was originally meant and which originally determined the definition of the threshold.

Scientific measurement may either be direct, the response itself being measured, or indirect, the measurement being of the stimulus used to obtain a specified response. It is seldom that a visual response can be measured by the first method. Direct measurement is possible only in the case of pupil reflexes and other visuo-motor activity.

The indirect method is necessitated by the fact that the response is something for which there are no physical units, such as length, distance, or volume. This method takes advantage of the fact that response is generally a comparison. Two things are compared : either they are matched and are thus biologically equivalent in some respect, or they are differentiated. In the latter case, the least stimulus difference which enables a differentiation is the threshold or limen which we have just discussed. When, of course, the response in question is not a comparison, the stimulus conditions required to elicit the response are the only measurables. To the extent that a responses cannot be predicted by defining stimulus conditions, the experiment moves away from the conventional psychophysical one to a kind in which the organism, rather than the physical surrounds, is the reference point. Methodology for such experimentation is as yet poorly developed, but there is a growing recognition for need of it.

Differentiation is only fully meaningful when conditions are so adjusted as to produce a JND. Discernible differences, when they are larger than JND's, are less definite and are therefore often more poorly measured. For example, one area cannot be as well judged to be twice as bright as another as the two can be judged equally bright or just different in brightness.

FUNDAMENTAL CONSIDERATIONS AND VISUAL PHENOMENA

The Eye

All the precise work on and understanding of vision presupposes a knowledge of the structure of the eye as an energy-receptor system and a translator of this energy into suitable neurophysiological patterns for conduction to the central nervous system. Likewise knowledge of the visual pathway is also becoming more and more necessary in the understanding of visual phenomena.

The outstanding facts regarding the eye are the following: (1) It contains a mosaic of two kinds of sensitive cells, the cones and the rods, each of which is sensitive to radiant energy and capable of transforming it into a series of discrete impulses appropriate to activate in turn the next structural unit in line, the bipolar cell. (2) These receptor cells (the rods and cones) are not alike in their range of sensitivities, and all visual functions on this account are affected by which set of cells participates or in what proportions the two sets participate. (3) These two sets for receptors are unlike in their distribution across the retinal mosaic from center to periphery. The central portion of the retina is populated only with cones, the paracentral (parafoveal) region is populated with both rods and cones. The farther toward the periphery, the greater is the relative number of rods and the smaller the relative number of cones. (4) The neural connections of the rods and cones differ. Each foveal cone has a one-to-one connection with its succeeding unit in the visual pathway. In contrast to this, the fiber processes from several rods converge on a single succeeding neural unit, and cones outside the fovea do not have "private line" connections. (5) Where the bundles of afferent fibers constituting the optic nerve leave the eye, a total absence of receptor cells is assumed. This region is called the optic disk, and the corresponding area in the visual field which is "blind" under some conditions is called the blind - spot [1].

Important Units of Measurement

Since the optical system of the human eye involves the focusing of light through a nodal point, the *visual angle* is one of the vehicles of spatial measurement. The visual angle is the angle subtended by the observed object when the nodal point of the eye is the apex. If absolute size of an object (test object or target) is known, the distance of the object from the eye must be known, so as to calculate the area of the retina involved in the image of the object.

A unit of sensitivity which takes into account the light actually reaching the retina should be employed. The *photon* is a unit of retinal illumination which takes into account the size of the pupil and is the conventional unit which most nearly satisfies this demand. Although the reader will have to resort to the proper handbooks [27] to acquaint himself with the various light units and their conversion factors, it is not likely that he will find the definition of the photon among them. When the eye is confronted with a surface intensity ("apparent brightness") of 1 candle per square meter, the illumination on the retinal is 1 photon if the papillary area is 1 square millimeter. Three avenues of procedure are open in applying the photon. One is to use an artificial pupil to limit the effective pupillary aperture to a known area. The second is to measure the natural pupillary area existing at the time, and the third is to calculate pupillary area from graphs or tables providing the standard pupillary aperture for the various intensity levels of target and for given states of retinal adaptation [35].

Adaptation

Adaptation is the adjustment in the visual mechanism underlying improvement in seeing after sudden shifts in stimulus intensity. Adaptation may proceed in either of two directions : progressive improvement in vision after illumination has been suddenly lowered (dark adaptation), and improvement after illumination has been raised (light adaptation). Light adaptation progresses much more rapidly than dark adaptation.

All adjustments toward improved functioning of the visual pathway with reference to the intensity of stimulation might well be called adaptation [1]. The initial tissue process in the receiving of light is chemical and is very influential in setting the quantitative pattern of the processes that follow. That adaptation is confined to the photochemical processes of the receptor cells in the retina has often been taken for granted [4]. Nevertheless it has more recently been shown that all the adjustment phenomena which would naturally be given the label of adaptation are not photochemical [36]. Some of them are neural.

The usual method of studying dark adaptation consists in subjecting the eyes to total darkness and, at regular intervals, testing the ability to see (determining absolute thresholds) [37]. The threshold progressively drops, at first rapidly and then more slowly, till finally no further drop occurs. The series of thresholds are plotted against time in the dark, and the result is called an adaptation curve. One customary target is a figure which can be rotated from trial to trial into any one of a number of fixed positions. For example, a letter C (Landolt broken circle) is often employed (see fig. 4.3). The open side of the circle may be placed in any one of four or more positions, and the observer is asked to tell in which position the opening is, either by expressing the position in terms of the hour designation on a clock dial, or by pressing the appropriate key on a panel wired to designate the various positions. A plain figure, such as Fig. 4.4, may also be used. To insure that the observer is looking in the right direction to see the target, a fixation point is customarily provided. This is a very small red light just strong enough to be seen. The target bears a fixed spatial relation to the fixation point, providing the observer does not move his head. If measurement of various precisely known parts of the retina is required, the precaution of a "biting board" or other head-stabilizing device is used. Biting boards are of many degrees of stability, the best being a horizontal plate bearing a wax impression of the observer's teeth. Each time that the observer "bites" into this impression, his head is certain to be placed in the same position with reference to the target as before, if the plate is stable.

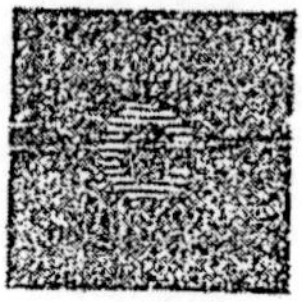

Fig. 4.3.

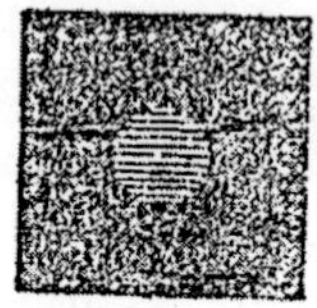

Fig. 4.4.

Trials are made at set intervals. Since dark adaptation progresses much more rapidly at first than it does later on, the readings must be closer during this time than later. It is objectionable from the observer's standpoint to make readings quite close together. A number of readings for every desired interval of time elapsing in the dark are necessary to obtain a reliable set of readings for a dark-adaptation curve. Routine clinical examinations, however, follow a shortened procedure [23].

Further to insure the meaningfulness of the results acquired in obtaining a dark-adaptation curve, a preadaptation period of subjection to a known level of illumination is used. Generally a uniformly lighted opal-glass screen large enough to cover most of the angular visual field is employed. The screen may be illuminated at any level of intensity, depending upon the purpose of the investigation, just so the level is known and specified in describing results.

The process of adaptation can be measured for various parts of the retina and for various levels of preadaptation [4]. It has been found that the rods and cones adapt at different levels and at different rates [4]. This is evidenced in the irregular shape of the adaptation curve, it being composed of two parts. The one is an early drop, which reaches virtually its full extent in a very few minutes, and the other is a later greater drop, which continues for a far longer time.

By the use of dark-adaptation curves it has been shown that vitamin A deficiency affects the process of adaptation

[23]. It has also been shown that insulin hypoglycemia and anoxia affect dark adaptation. In vitamin A deficiency, the difficulty has its primary origin in the eye, whereas in hypoglycemia and anoxia, the difficulty is further along in the visual pathway [36].

Brightness Discrimination

Adaptation is the process whereby sensitivity to retinal illumination changes after a more or less abrupt shift in illumination level. Although it has been implied that various parts of the retina can adapt more or less independently, the more usual studies of adaptation have not been limited to localized regions. Brightness discrimination as a process differs form adaptation only in certain arbitrary ways. As the eyes are moved to and for, the images of dark and light objects move across the retinas. The intensity differences between the various images may be quite great, and therefore it can be said that the areas of the retina just newly stimulated by images differing greatly from their predecessors are not fully adapted to the new levels of intensity. Brightness discrimination is a set of complicated, short, and relatively mild processes of adaptation.

The standard concept of brightness has been reached through use of the photometer, in which the two target area (standard and test) to be matched are contiguous and appear on an unilluminated field, either lying side by side or the one target surrounding the other. Adjusting for equal brightness involves, as much as anything else, obliterating the boundary between the areas. Under conditions of contiguity the relative size of the two areas is not critical, and the match in brightness is most nearly a physical match in intensity. Hence the standard definition of brightness used by those interested in light from the stand-point of physics follows : *Brightness is the luminous intensity per unit of area.* The term luminous is a recognition of the fact than an observer is involved and that he is not equally sensitive to all wavelengths within the visible spectrum.

Most methods used in studying brightness discrimination differ essentially from the purely photometric in one or more particulars. Whereas the photometric technique, through its simplification, is taken as an absolute one, other setups actually emphasize the fact of relativity in the perception of brightness and must be looked upon form this standpoint. Even when we employ setups apparently similar to those used in photometry, we are investigating brightness discrimination as a biological function, rather than presuming to match two physical quantities.

That brightness depends at times upon total flux (total light emitted or reflected from the target to the eye) rather than flux density (light emitted or reflected by each unit of target surface) is demonstrated in the following illustrations.

Let two surfaces reflecting equal flux per unit area be observed. In the first case let the two surfaces be equal in area and equally distant from the eye. In the second case let their areas be equal, but their distances from the eye be unequal. In the third case let their areas be unequal, but their distances from the eye be equal.

When, in all three cases, the paired surfaces are seen to match in brightness, it may be said that flux per unit area is the crucial factor, for in cases two and three the total flux reaching the eye from each of the surfaces is not equal. But when the paired surfaces in cases two and three are seen as unequal in brightness, total flux may be the crucial factor.

If, for example, the paired surfaces are the sole objects in the field to receive illumination, and one does not focus well upon them but looks beyond them, the surface subtending the greater visual angle of the two will then tend to become the more effective and appear the brighter. In case *two* it will be the surface nearer to the eye; in case *three* it will be the larger surface. In such cases the total flux determines the brightness. Total flux operates in many everyday situations as well.

Methods used to study brightness discrimination are aimed at taking into accounts (1) the relations between area of total target, or its parts, and threshold, (2) the relation between intensity level of target and surround, and threshold, (3) the relation between time of target exposure and threshold, and (4) the relation of target movement and threshold.

The simplest arrangement of the visual field for the study of brightness discrimination is similar to that for dark adaptation (Fig. 4.3 and 4.4). From what we know about retinal anatomy, the angle that the target subtends is an important matter. For central vision the target should be about 1 degree or less (about 1 inch at a distance of 55 inches). The amount by which a target must be either greater or less in intensity than its surrounds so as just to be perceived is a measure of brightness discrimination. This threshold is generally called ΔI, and its relation to the intensity I of the surrounds has often been studied. The ration $\Delta I/I$, called the Weber fraction, is another measure common in the study of brightness discrimination. This fraction becomes smaller as I increases. The reciprocal of this fraction ($I/\Delta I$) is also a common measure.

It is possible to vary the area of the target and determine the relation of threshold to area. It is also possible to apply the small-area target to various parts of the retina by using a fixation-point whose relation to the target is manipulated systematically.

Another and very definite step is taken when the target is made of two parts of unequal intensity. The particular threshold measured in this case is that of the difference between the two parts of the target. The ratio $\Delta I/I$ in such cases pertains to the difference in intensity between the two parts of the target divided by the intensity of one of the parts.

Under these conditions, as with simple targets, the intensity level of the background or general field cannot be ignored. It has been found to be and important factor in determining the absolute value of the threshold. The level of the background (surrounds) is sometimes put at an intensity somewhere between levels of the two parts of the target. By a few preliminary trials a point almost halfway between the two parts of the target may be found. The surrounds may also be set definitely below or above the two parts of the target in intensity.

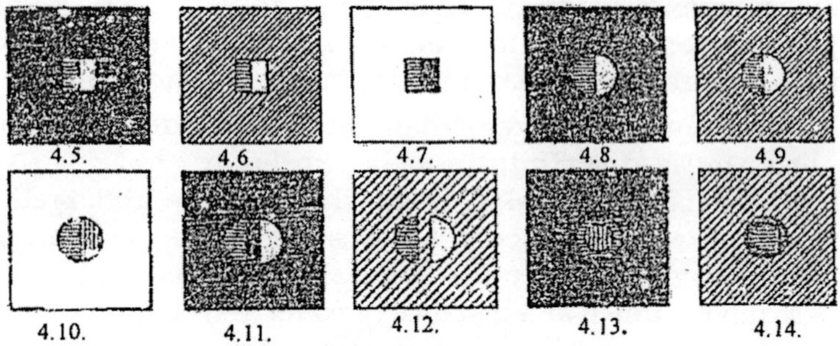

Fig. 4.5 to 4.14.

The complex target may be anyone of several shapes. In general, there are bisected targets, such as in Figs. 4.5, 4.6, 4.7, 4.8, 4.9, 4.10, 4.11, and 4.12, and disk-annulus targets, such as in Figs. 4.13 and 4.14. Bisected targets consist of a square, rectangle, or circle divided equally into two parts. At times the two halves are separated, as in Figs. 4.11 and 4.12. When separation is employed, the effect of width of separation is studied. The disk-annulus targets do not give thresholds of the same value as the bisected targets. The existence of a difference is a demonstration of a very important matter in visual function, the effect of border-building processes on each other [16]. As another variation in technique, the two halves of the complex target may be held constant in their intensity relation to each other while being varied in relation to the surround.

A totally dark field surrounding a test object (target) could be expected to function one way, and a fairly well illuminated field another way. While black is a sensation, the absence of retinal stimulation is functionally different from the presence of any amount of it. One of the problems that has arisen in connection with surrounds, especially the illuminated ones, is whether a portion of the visual field illuminated at a given level might function as a substitute for the whole field. If so, how many degrees must a surround subtend to be substantially equivalent to having the whole field illuminated at the same level? Some investigators have come to the conclusion that a surround subtending 30 degrees of visual angle is this equivalent, at least for certain purposes. (An ordinary doorway—32 inches—subtends a visual angle of 30 degrees when the eye is about 2 yards from it.)

There is a fundamental phenomenon regarding the behaviour of light in the eye that may account for this virtual equivalence. It is the existence of internal stray light, called *entoptic stray light* [10]. The eye as a hollow sphere acts, in principle, like an integrating sphere. In solving certain problems in photometry, a source of light is placed inside a hollow sphere whose walls are coated a matte white. A photometer pointed through a peephole in the sphere measures the "mean spherical candle power" of the light source, because of the fact that light is evenly reflected in all directions from the walls of the sphere. No matter toward which portion of the inside wall the photometer is pointed, the reading will be the same. In the eye the bright image on the retina forms the light source, and although the ocular walls absorb a considerable part of the light, the portions of the retina not involved in the bright image are receiving reflected light. The amount of this depends upon the size and intensity of the image acting as source. As the image increases in size, the differential between its intensity and that of the rest of the eye materially lessens. As the image increases in size, it of course occupies more and more of the total sensitive retina. For these reasons a stimulus covering somewhat less than the whole visual field will substitute for illumination of the whole field.

Certain findings incidental to the study of brightness discrimination have led to the use of figures even more complex than the bisected targets [1]. It appears that the presence of borders in the visual field has an influence on the differential thresholds. For example, if a target such as is found in Fig. 4.15 is used, the differential brightness threshold decreases as the width of the annulus 2 is increased. Originally this was attributed to a summation process. This hypothesis is tested by use of a pattern, as indicated in Fig 4.16. By surrounding the inner disk 1 by an annular field 2, between which and an annular outer area 3 is ring *R*, the combined area of 2 plus 3 can be kept constant while the diameter of the ring is varied

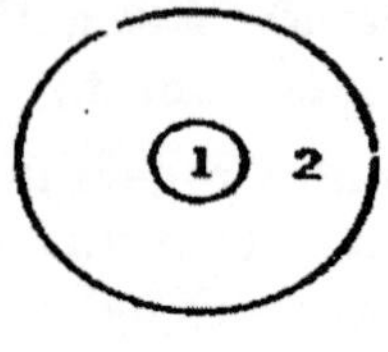

Fig. 4.15.

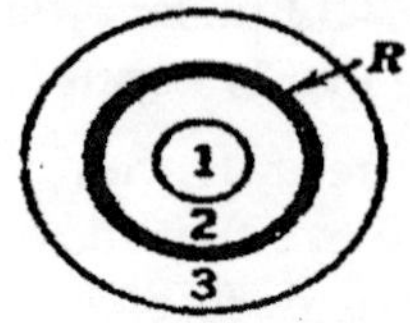

Fig. 4.16.

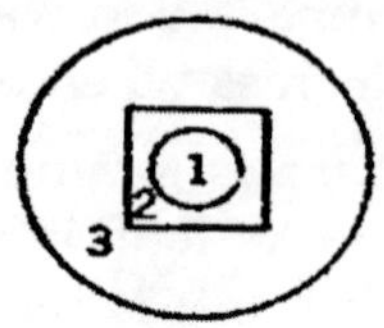

Fig. 4.17.

to manipulate the distance of the ring from area 1. The inner border of the ring is thus varied in its distance from area 1 without changing total illumination. As the ring is moved farther from area 1, the differential threshold between 1 and 2 decreases. Since the variable is the distance of the inner border of the ring form area 1 and not the total flux, the distance of the border must be the crucial factor.

Figure 4.17 involves the same kind of border (contour) phenomenon. The effect of varying the intensity of 3 on the differential threshold between 1 and 2 is the object of study. Area 1 is made either brighter or less bright than 2. The lowest thresholds are found when 2 and 3 are equally intense. The threshold becomes greater when 3 is either more intense or less intense than 2. When 3 is either more or less intense than 2, the "contrast" border is thought to interfere with the formation of a border at the outer edge of 1. By this means the differential threshold between 1 and 2 is raised. Additional patterns have also been used to test the assumption that borders in the visual field influence each other, and that it makes a difference whether one border acts on the end of another border or on the side of it.

Whereas the targets just mentioned are those characteristic of academic studies of brightness perception, several other types of targets are dictated by more practical considerations. For instance, the question of detection of targets in actual outdoor situations often involves land and sky divisions of the visual field : *i.e.*, a horizon or boundary between unequally illuminated upper and lower parts of the visual field in involved. Targets may appear fully within the lower part of the field, fully within the upper part of the field, or across the horizon. A target placed on the horizon is shown in Fig. 4.18. Were the square somewhat below the horizon, it would, in this case, be invisible. The target may be of a different intensity from either the upper (sky) or lower (land) parts of the field.

Practical considerations in "detecting" targets introduce the factor of target motion. It would be expected that angular motion could not become very great before an otherwise visible target would become ineffective. The factor of "blurring out" at weak illuminations easily becomes great enough to offset any "attention-getting" advantage a moving target may have.

The term *brightness contrast* is often used in the study of brightness discrimination. It is not always kept clear whether the subjective phenomenon, the underlying physiological mechanism for the experience, or the intensity differences in two parts of the stimulus field are begin referred to. Simple brightness-discrimination studies become the conventional studies of "contrast" when a number of levels of surround are employed to study the Weber fraction.

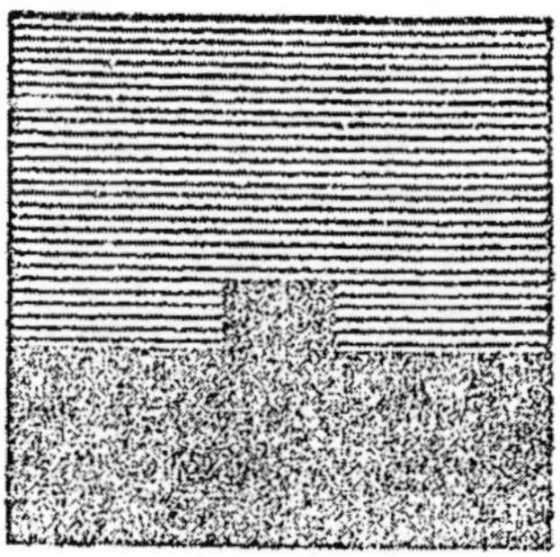

Fig. 4.18.

Visual experience and the ability to make discriminations are studied sometimes when two eyes are used, and at other times when only one eye is employed. In these two cases certain very decided differences pertaining to adaptation, brightness discrimination, visual acuity, and space perception have been brought out. Targets may be used successively with one and with two eyes, or simultaneous comparisons may be made, part of a target being seen by tow eyes and the other part with one. Figure 4.19 illustrates the latter form of setup [12]. Two disks or other areas form the comparison fields of the target. One eye is allowed to see both comparison fields, and the other eye is prevented from seeing one of them. The obstacle to the one eye may be a solid (opaque) black shield, or it may be a revolving disk (episcotister) with open sectors. This sort of obstruction is only partial ; it merely *reduces* the light flux from the one comparison field. By such a method the efficacy of various partial reductions can be tested. By reducing the intensity of the opposite comparison field, which is seen by both eyes, the quantitative effect of the two eyes working together (binocular summation or subtraction) can be studied.

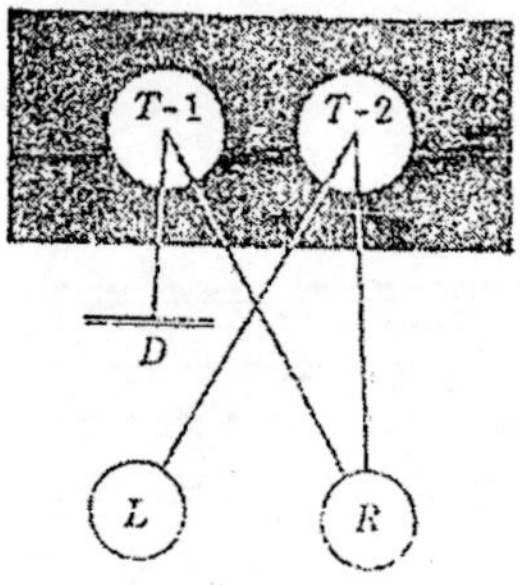

Fig. 4.19.

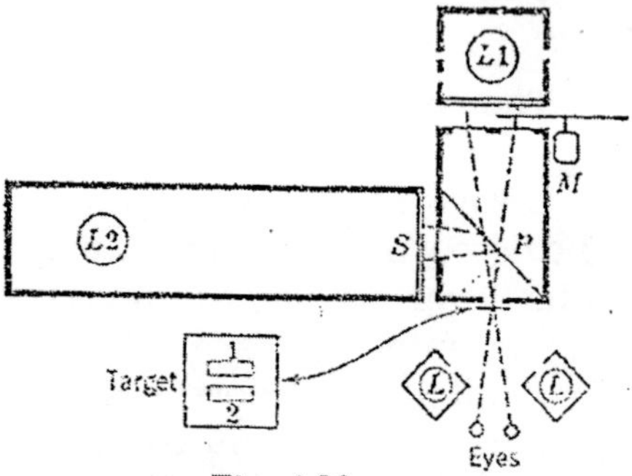

Fig. 4.20.

Figs. 4.19 and 4.20. Setups to indicate arrangements for studying binoculor vision.

In Fig. 4.19, *L* and *R* represent the two eyes; *T*-1 and *T*-2 the two test objects, light from both of which reaches the right eye. Light from *T*-1 to the left eye may be partially or totally obstructed by an episcotister wedge (*D*). In Fig. 4.20, *L*1 and *L*2 are light sources whose effective intensity is determined by their positions in their elongated housings. *L* and *L* provide for the illumination of the surrounds of 1 and 2 in the target. The light form *L*1 to part 2 of the target is obstructed by a blind in the lower half of glass *P*. Light from *L*2 is reflected by the upper half of *P*. *S* and *M* represent any controlling screens or motors to be placed in the apparatus.

If a setup in which the two eyes can be stimulated independently is employed, the image of a bright disk can be placed on one retina, and the image of a dim disk on the corresponding area of the other retina. The observer will thus be made to see them as a single disk, since their images fall on corresponding retinal areas. It would be expected that adding to the total stimulation by placing an image on the second retina would brighten the surface of the originally bright disk, but such is not the case. The resulting brightness is less than with a single eye stimulated and lies somewhere between the brightness of the two disks seen individually. This is known a Fechner's paradox. If, however, the two stimuli are equally or nearly equally intense, the resulting disk is brighter than the disk occasioned by only one of the stimuli [9].

Binocular interaction has also been studied with such a setup, as suggested in fig. 4.20 [17]. By use of this arrangement not only the two comparison areas but also the field surrounding them can be varied, and by the episcotister *M*, light to one eye can be either partially or totally obstructed. In addition, the factor of Fechner's paradox and that of the effects of one border upon another can be studied.

The effect of the use of two, as compared to one, eye on adaptation has also been studied [14]. It has been found that binocular preadaptation on monocular vision is more prolonged than monocular preadaptation on monocular vision. The time required just to be able to discern an object on its background has been studied under the several possible combinations of preadaptation and test. The longer the time, the slower is the adaptation.

Visual Acuity

Whereas brightness discrimination has to do with the factors of stimulus area, flux per unit area, total flux, duration of exposure to light, etc., in relation to the grosser areal aspects of experience, visual acuity, a form of brightness discrimination, is concerned with the finer spatial aspects of stimulation and resulting experience. Whereas in studies of brightness discrimination *intensity differences* are the primary objects of attention, in visual acuity finer *spatial features* are the central object of study. The aim is usually to discover how small the visual angle between two objects in the visual field may become without the objects still being seen as touching each other. To be able to see close-lying objects or areas as spatially separate is to *resolve* them. The study of visual acuity is the study of the fineness of resolution under various sets of conditions. Resolution depends upon many factors, such as general level of illumination, difference in intensity between the areas involved, pattern of the field, and duration of exposure to stimulation, as well as upon fineness of the retinal mosaic, etc.

Of primary consideration in the usual study of visual acuity is the resolving power of the eye, as dependent upon its relative ability to form a sharp image and upon the fineness of the retinal mosaic. Image formation is by no means a mathematically sharp affair. Such factors as blur circles provide for a tapering illumination, rather than perfectly steep gradients as boundaries between light and dark. Methods for studying visual acuity have had to recognize this fact in more and more ways [1, 18]. The retinal mosaic is the grid formed by the ends (cross-sections) of the receptor cells and intercellular spaces. It is upon this grid that the retinal image is placed; hence "fineness of grain" in the retinal mosaic plays a determining role in visual acuity. Methods in the study of visual acuity pertain to the systematic manipulation of physical conditions to indicate the factors which control visual resolution.

Visual acuity is measured clinically by the use of black letters of standard sizes or of the Landolt broken circle (Fig. 4.3) in a series of sizes and positions. Letters which subtend 1 minute of are when viewed at a distance of 20 feet are taken as the normally resolvable size. These letters are placed in rows, successive rows subtending smaller and smaller visual angles. The ability to read the letters of the small rows indicates better than normal vision. The ability to discern only the large letters at a distance of 20 feet indicates less than normal vision. If an individual can read at 20 feet only the letters which should be read at 40 feet, his vision is 20/40 or subnormal according to such crude charts.

In the laboratory the Landolt broken circle is occasionally employed, but the usual target is a pair of bars of different widths, such as Figs. 4.21 to 4.23, or gratings, as in Fig. 4.24.

Even very fine single lines, as in Fig. 4.25, have been used.

Fig. 4.21

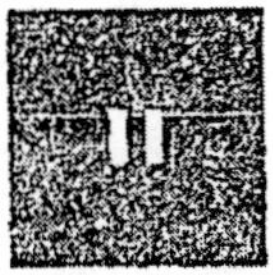

Fig. 4.22

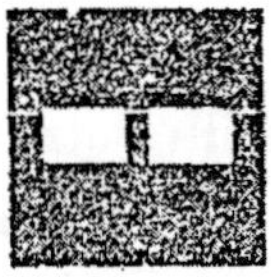

Fig. 4.23

Fig. 4.24

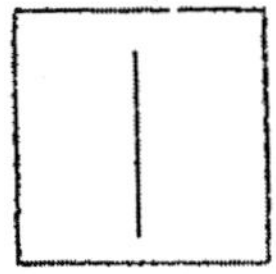

Fig. 4.25

The factors to consider in the formal measurement of visual acuity by bars or lines are : (1) the luminous-intensity relation of bars or lines and field, (2) size of field, and (3) with of bars. The experiment may consist in using lights bars on a dark field, or dark bars on the light field. The use of the two procedures has turned out to be more than precautionary, for the results are quite unlike. As in the study of brightness discrimination, the size of the filed when it is illuminated is important. It is obvious that these arrangements (Figs. 4.22 and 4.23) produce what can be called a glare situation, if the bars are at all intense. For some purposes this objectionable, but the results of a setup of this sort are nevertheless important to know.

Visual acuity, defined as *the reciprocal of the just resolvable visual angle measured in minutes of arc*, becomes progressively greater as the field illuminated is increased, regardless of whether broken circles or gratings are used. The absolute results, however, are not equivalent. At low illuminations the broken circle provides for a lower visual acuity than the grating. At high illumination the broken circle provides for a higher visual acuity. Somewhere the curves representing the two functions cross. Light bars on a dark field provide for an increasing visual acuity only until a certain level of intensity is reached (in some experiments, between 0 and +1 log photons), beyond which a reversal sets in [40].

Although it might be thought that resolution depends almost if not exclusively upon the magnitude of the interspaced and the related intensity features involved, this is not the case. The width of the bars, as well as their separation, is an effective factor in determining resolution. Broad and narrow bars (Figs.

4.22 and 4.23) do not yield the same result [18]. As the intensity of light bars on a dark field is raised, visual acuity first rises rapidly. With wide bars the rise slowly continues after the initial rapid onset, but with narrow bars visual acuity falls again very slowly. This might be explained on the assumption that borders interfere with each other. The highest visual acuity of all has been recorded with the single lines. Resolution of lines which subtended only 0.5 minutes of are has been recorded.

It is important in methodology to note that the subjective width of bright bars undergoes striking variations during manipulations of intensity. The shift in contours of the bars has been attributed to a form of irradiation. How this irradiation operates has been the subject of study by a number of individuals [40].

Colour Discrimination

There are three ways of discriminating colour : through its hue, distinguishing red, yellow, green, etc.; through its brightness (brilliance, tint); and through its saturation, the amount of the hue present (deep blue as against a blue-gray). These attributes of colour have connections with two aspects of radiant energy, namely, wavelength and flux density. Colour may be experienced in several ways in accordance with the conditions under which it appears. There are surface colours, film colours, and volume colours. In looking through a spectroscope, for example, the observed colour has a completely different kind of appearance from the same hue on the surface of objects. The former is a film colour; the latter is a surface colour. Again, the colour of some fluids has a certain voluminousness that is absent in the other two cases; the colour seen in looking through a clear fluid is a volume colour.

The human eye is not equally sensitive to all wavelengths within the visible band. One of the fundamental procedures in the study of vision has been the examination of this differential sensitivity. The findings are represented in a graph called a visibility curve, or a luminosity curve. In obtaining data for this curve, a form of matching is employed. The various wavelengths are adjusted in intensity so as to give equal brightness. The reciprocals of these values are plotted

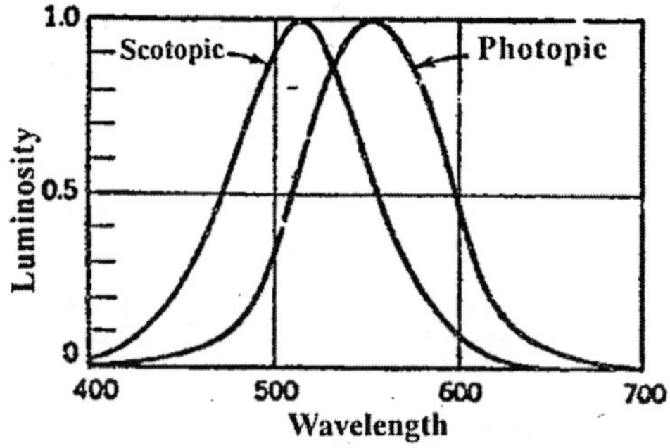

Fig. 4.26. Luminosity curves.

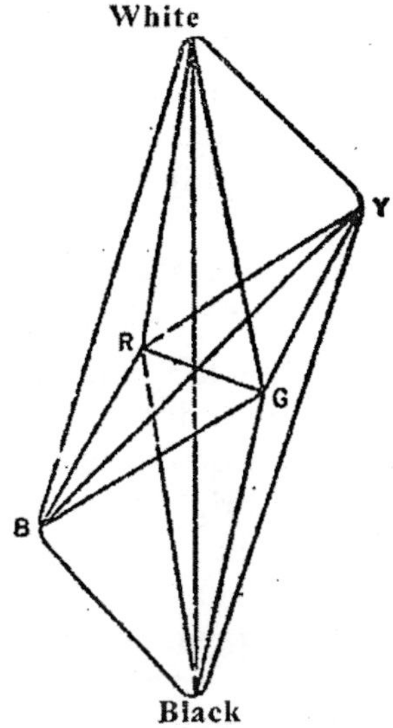

Fig. 4.27. An example of the colour solid.

on a scale of 10 to 0, the wavelength with the lowest intensity having a value of 1.0. Figure 4.26 indicates separately the luminosity values for scotopic and photopic vision. The scotopic curve is obtained by using only enough light to activate the rod-receptors, and the photopic by using enough light to activate the cone-receptors. The actual values are not equivalent in the two curves. The curves show only relative values for the different parts of the spectrum, the actual values having been converted to a common scale.

The next consideration in understanding colour perception is the ascertainment of the total number of colours, perceptible. This is done by finding out how many JND's of hue, brightness, and saturation can be discerned.

Since there are three variables to colour experience, an orderly representation of colours can be handled by a geometrical solid. Colour solids of various sorts have been made. One of the oldest was a double pyramid, base to base (Fig. 4.27). The axis from apex to apex represented the brightness scale (achromatic axis). The complementaries, red-green and blue-yellow, occupied the opposing corners. Distance from the axis outward to the pyramidal rim represented degrees of colour saturation. Such a solid was an oversimplification. Although it represented the most general relationship between the colour variables, it by no means approximated quantitative relations.

One of the latest colour solids is that of Nickerson and Newhall [33] (Fig. 4.28). It consists of nine irregular segments of a "cylinder" placed one on top of the other. Nine segments were chosen so as to make the cylinder compare to the divisions in the brightness (value) dimension of the Munsell system, one of the most used classification of colour. Each of these value segments is different in shape and size. The rims of each represent the hues of the spectrum, and the segments are quite eccentric to the value axis. This eccentricity varies progressively from one segment to the other, as can be seen in the figure.

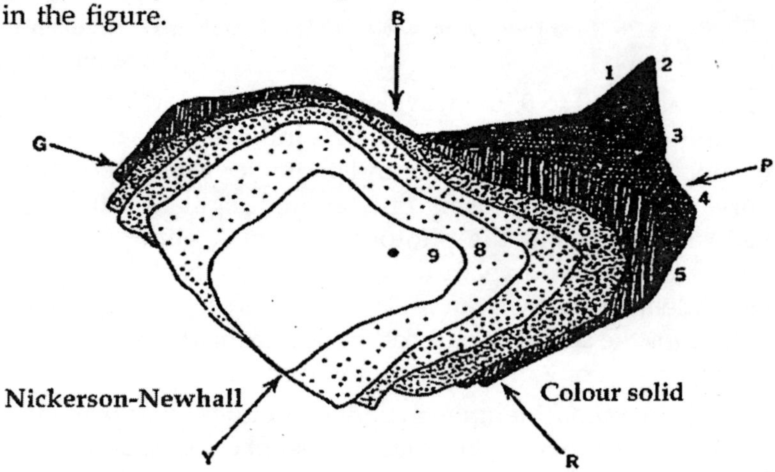

Fig. 4.28. A colour solid ("cylinder") as seen from the top of the cylinder.

The segments from top to bottom are numbered. The letters surrounding the solid indicate the locations of the hues.

The two basic facts of colour which stand out in the colour solid and in colour systems such as the Munsell are that not all hues may reach the same saturation, as measured in JND steps (or multiples thereof) and that the maximum possible degree of saturation varies from one level of brightness to another for almost all colours.

The Munsell colour system uses the three dimensions of colour in the following way. In it there are forty subjectively equi-spaced hues, and chips (specimens) of them are arranged on twenty charts, each with a hue and its complement. In each chart the chips are arranged on a value (brightness) scale of nine subjectively equally spaced steps. Horizontally the steps are of subjectively equal chroma (saturation). All chips having the same position on the several charts presumably posses the same chroma. Red, for instance, will have more steps in the chroma dimension than will the unsaturated hues, such as yellow.

One of the fundamental procedures in colour study has been to determine the experiential (sensory) results from combining selected portions of the spectrum. This has been done by means of the colour wheel, on which different colours occupy various radial segments. When the wheel is revolved, the separate fraction "fuse" and become a new colour. This procedure has been called colour-mixing. Although this is simple as a procedure, it involves complexities not under control. The use of surfaces as colour sources involves uncontrolled reflectances, uncontrolled qualities of illuminants for the surfaces, etc.

The best analytical way of studying colour is with the spectrometer, an instrument by which controlled separation of white light into its spectral components (wavelengths) and recombination of them can be accomplished. One form of the spectrometer is the Helmholtz colour mixer, the essentials of which are indicated in Fig. 4.29 [24].

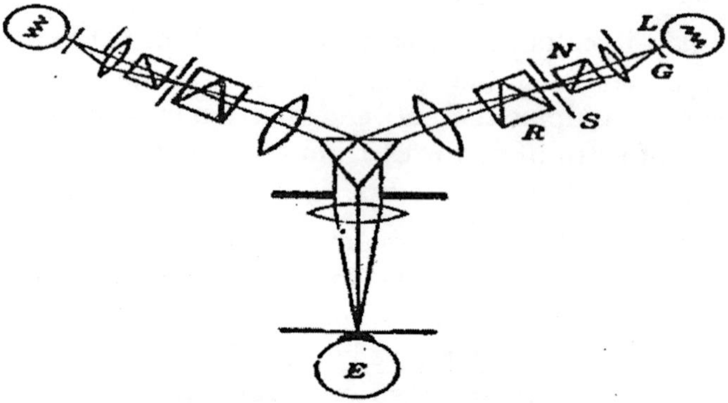

Helmholtz colour mixer

Fig. 4.29. The optical system of a Helmholtz colour mixer, such as was used by Hecht.

G = ground glass, L = light source, N = a Nichol prism, S = slit off a collimator, R = Rochan prism, and E = the eye at the exit pupil of the telescope. Portions of the faces of the prism are visible and are seen as contiguous semicurcular fields. The whole field has a visual angel of less than 1.5°, thus stimulating whithin the rod-free area of the eye. For an explanation of the action of the prisms see [24].

It has been found that normal colour vision is trichromatic. Any part of the spectrum may be matched by a field whose radiation is composed of three properly chosen other parts of the spectrum. By the matching technique, defects in colour perception have been found in certain individuals [28]. Some defects are called colour weakness; others, colour blindness. These defects consist in confusing various parts of the spectrum with each other. The individuals with defective colour vision are roughly as follows : (1) persons who confuse parts of the spectrum but who nevertheless require three primary wavelengths to make a spectral match (anomalous trichromats); (2) persons who confuse large portions of the spectrum and can match any part of it with a mixture of only two primaries (dichromats); and (3) persons who are fully colour-blind (monochromats).

Dichromats are of three kinds· (*a*) protanopse, who confuse green, yellow, and red and match blue-green with white; (*b*) deuteranopes, who also confuse these colours but have a distribution of brightness perception much like normal persons; and (*c*) tritanopes, who match a point in the yellow with white.

Monochromats are of two kinds : (*a*) the scotopic monochromats, those whose brightness sensitivity follows the visibility curve for rod vision; and (*b*) the photopic monochromats, those whose brightness vision follows the visibility curve for cone vision.

Colour weakness consists in a reduction in the number of distinctions (JND's) that can be made when tested with spectral stimulation. Colour blindness is the total absence of ability to discriminate on the basis of wavelength. In such cases only intensity discriminations are possible.

Since the eye (the observer) cannot analyze radiation into its spectral components, colour experience represents an over-all effect. There are many different stimuli (coloured surfaces, etc.) of complex wavelength composition which will elicit the same colour sensation. Instrumentally, however, the difference in actual spectral composition can be detected.

A usable connection between colour sensation and the spectral reflectance of surfaces has been worked out. The technique of obtaining these relations between the spectral stimulus and colour experience is called colour specification. Instrumental colour analysis by either a spectroradiometer or a spectrophotometer is first necessary. The information obtained from these instruments is transformed by means of standard data from colour-matching experiments. The most used system for colour specification is based on the supposition that the chromaticity (hue and saturation) of the stimulus can be specified by the quantities representing the proportions of three primary light distributions needed to match the colour experience induced by a given stimulus. The primaries stated in terms of their intensities are called the tri-stimulus values.

Intermittent Stimulation

Any portion of the visual field may be illuminated by radiation which fluctuates in intensity. If the one phase of the fluctuation reaches zero, the stimulation is intermittent. The most common experimental setup employs a disk target as the fluctuating field, while the surrounding field is left unilluminated [1]. Among the more complex targets is the disk-annulus pattern, in which the disk alternates in intensity [8]. The intensity level of fthe annulus may be set at any fixed level or may be systematically varied step by step. The annulus level is often halfway between the high-intensity and the zero-intensity phases of the cycle. The name of the experience of rapidly fluctuating light is flicker.

In general, the objectives involved in the study of fluctuating and intermittent stimulation are the following : (1) to discover the experiences elicited by intermittencies of different rates, when intensities and spatial features are also systematically varied; (2) to relate these experiences to quantitative features of the stimulus situation; and (3) to relate these features to neural events in the visual pathway.

The salient feature of intermittent stimulation is that the series of discrete flashes interrupting darkness gives way to a series of different phenomena as the rate of stimulus intermittency is raised. (1) The flashes cease to be fully discrete; absolutely dark intervals disappear light begins to fill them in. finally the experience the experience is one of a continuously lighted field. (2) Superimposed on this is an undulating or flicker component. As the stimulus rate increases, flicker becomes less extreme and more rapid in its undulations; it is said to become "finer." Finally a stimulus rate is reached at which a uniformly bright field is seen; all flicker disappears. The "fusion point" has been reached. The lowest stimulus rate responsible for this is the critical flicker frequency (CFF).

Strangely, little attention has been paid to the experiential phenomena below the fusion point [8]. Most of the work on intermittent light stimulation has been directed toward determining and measuring the various factors involved in the production of fusion, *i.e.*, measurements of CFF. It has been found that area of the intermittent field, intensity of light, and ratio of the stimulus duration to interval between stimuli are the major factors. Various parts of the spectrum do not elicit like responses at all intensities. The intensity level of the surround also plays a part.

It has been possible to study response to intermittent light in sub-human species by the use of certain specific motor reactions of animals while on a stationary floor inside a horizontally revolving drum composed of vertical black and white bands [12].

The study of intermittent stimulation has been instrumental in many ways in disclosing the nature of the photoreceptor process and the nature of the neural processes in the retina and elsewhere along the visual pathway [12]. The fundamental feature of *time* as well as intensity can be studied to best advantage by variously spacing the components in a series of stimuli. Recovery, in addition to excitation, can be examined. With intermittent stimulation the onset and the waxing and waning of brightness sensation in relation to stimulus characteristics can also be studied to advantage.

One of the oldest generalizations which has come out of the use of intermittent light stimulation is Talbot's law, which

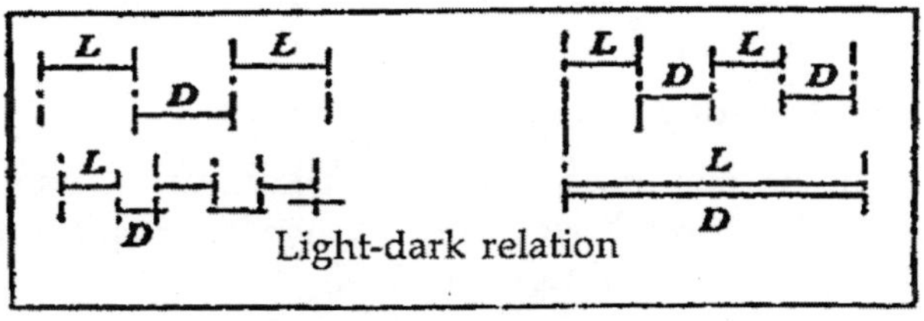

Fig. 4.30. This figure shows results of varying flash rate with ring annulus target.

Upper left diagram indicates subjective alternation of light and dark phases. Upper right diagram shows the same phenomenon. Lower left diagram shows the beginning of overlapping. Lower right diagram shows the subjective stimultaneity of phases, the dark phase seen through the light phase. At still greater flash rates simultaneity is lost and fusion approaches.

pertains to the brightness resulting from such stimulation. It states, in effect, that the resulting brightness level is to the brightness level induced by continuous stimulation a the fractional time occupied by the intermittent stimulus is to the continuous stimulation; *i.e.*, if the photic pulse and the "dark" period are of equal lengths, brightness is one-half that expected from continuous stimulation. This reduced brightness is often called the Talbot brightness. Thought of as a level, it often called the Tablet level.

Single pulses of light are seen as brighter than continuous light of the same physical intensity. This greater effect also pertains, within certain rate limits, to repeated pulses and has been called brightness enhancement [1, 21].

Aside from brightness enhancement, one of the outstanding phenomena resulting from subfusion stimulus rates is the existence of the dark and light phases of the cycle simultaneously [1]. This occurs only when the intermittently illuminated surface is surrounded by a steadily illuminated field, *e.g.*, an annulus. With slowly increasing rates of stimulus repetition, the two phases (*L* and *D*) can be seen to shift from alternation to simultaneity (Fig. 4.30). If the rate is further increased, this phenomenon (*L* and *D* simultaneity) disappears. While the two phases are still seen concurrently, the light phase is a glary translucent film through which the dark phase can be seen lying behind.

The Perception of Motion

Studies on the perception of motion involve various senses and are of many kinds. Those that involve the visual perception of motion may be divided into three kinds : (1) the use of moving stimuli with the observer stationary, (2) the use of successive stationary stimuli to give the impression of motion (apparent movement), and (3) the use of a moving observer (not necessarily in aviation, but in special laboratory experiments) whose relations to well-known objects (earth, horizontality, etc.) are changed. Whereas many investigations of the first two general kinds have been performed, study in the third category (outside of rotation experiments and aviation) is only in its beginning. At the present time the most common procedures in studying visual movement involve two general sets of conditions, those in which the stimuli move and those in which they do not.

It is of fundamental importance to recognize that a necessary requisite in eliciting the visual experience of movement is a certain kind of differential stimulation of receptor mosaic and that this may be accomplished by difference in intensity of stimulation, as well as in time. For example, a homogeneously illuminated field, suddenly increasing or decreasing in intensity, induces the visual experience of movement. When it is remembered that the retina is graded in its sensitivity from fovea to periphery, and when it is assumed from certain neuropsychological facts that conduction to the cerebral centers varies in accordance with strength of peripheral excitation, the necessary temporal factors exist to account for the kinds of visual movement experienced.

Gamma movement, the expansive movement seen as illumination suddenly increases (Fig. 4.31), can be reversed if the proper target is used (see Fig. 4.32). If the field is illuminated more intensely at the periphery than in the center, the movement will be centripetal, rather than centrifugal, when illumination is suddenly increased [1].

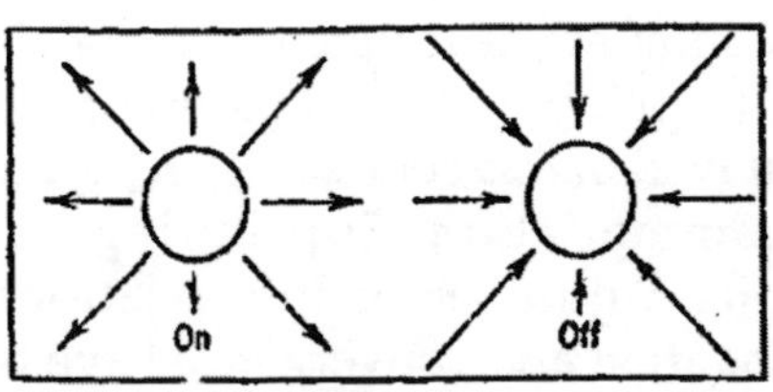

Fig. 4.31.

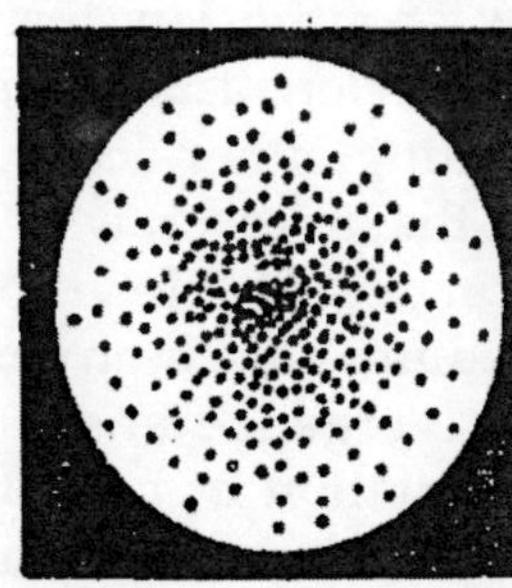

Fig. 4.32. This diagram indicates a visual field of wide angle and of greater intensity toward the periphery than at the center.

There are many phenomena to be considered in studying

the perception of motion, but they, like a number of other visual phenomena.

Motor Aspects of Visual Behaviour

Vision as a mode of contact between the organism and its physical surrounds is not fully understood until its motor aspects are considered. These motor aspects include the adjustments of the eyes so as to be optically adequate and the exploratory and "manipulatory" movements of the eyes themselves, as well as body posture and, at times, appropriate movements.

Eye-movements cameras of various sorts have been employed to record the action to the two eyes in reading and in other situations, such as observing apparent movement, or the autokinetic movement (Charpentier's illusion, etc.). These situations generally involve the projection of a spot of light onto the eye, from which it is reflected onto a recording film and moves in accordance with eye motion.

By other instrumental setups various measurements of convergence and accommodation and their interrelations have been made. Although most of these measurements have not been made in psychological laboratories, they form an important part of what the experimental psychologist should know about vision. Instruments for this purpose are varies, but characteristically employ lenses and prisms for the purpose of putting either accommodative or convergence demands upon the observer, who is, in effect, instructed to resist either blurring or double vision (dipolopia). So-called ergographic procedures have been employed in this connection in the study of convergence and accommodation [26]. By ingenious manipulation of conditions a number of interrelations in function between accommodation and convergence have been worked out.

Pupillary behaviour has also been studied. Papillary diameter has been measured by several devices. One is an optical arrangement which can be adjusted so that, when the second of two points of light can just be seen, a scale is read and the measurement transformed into a known pupi diameter. Other devices include instruments for sighting upon the eye. A final and much better method is photography. This may be either flash photography to determine papillary diameter at given instants, or ultraviolet or infrared motion-picture photography, which enables one to follow the variations in papillary diameter from instant to instant [9]. It is only by this method that the most precise knowledge of pupillary behaviour can be obtained. One of the problems in pupillary behaviour is the question of what parts of the retina are effective, when stimulated by light, in inducing a papillary reaction (pupillo-motor response, or light reflex).

Another problem, as was implied, consists in determining the speed of papillary reaction to abrupt changes in illumination level and to transient illumination of various durations. It has been found that the pupil responds by a change in diameter to a transient dark interval and that this response is mediated, at least in part, by nervous paths different form the light reflex to transient light stimulation.

Photographic techniques have indicated that the pupilllary light reflex is quite highly differentiated [9]. In many respects it parallels perceptual behaviour in quantitative aspects of complexity. For example, it parallels the already described

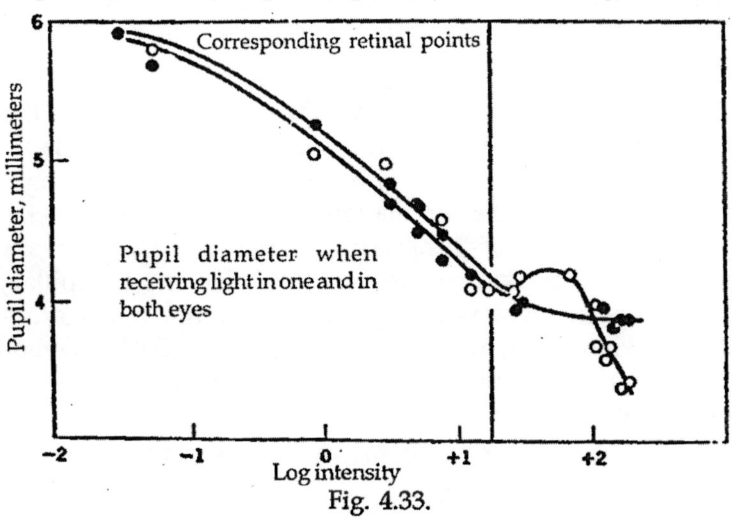

Fig. 4.33.

Fechner's paradox in its reactions, as can be demonstrated by using the very same experimental target arrangement already described to demonstrate Fechner's paradox. If the pupils are photographed in infrared radiation, pupillary behaviour under the low, as well as the high, level of visual stimulation can be recorded. As the light falling on one retina is increased, the pupils of both eyes constrict. If, after reaching a high level, the light in one retina is held constant, and weak light is cast on the corresponding area of the second retina, the pupils "paradoxically" begin to dilate instead of continuing to constrict. With increasing intensity of light on the second retina, the dilatation becomes still greater. After a certain point in intensity is reached, however, constriction sets in, and by the time that the illumination of the second retina is equal to that of the first, both pupils have constricted to a point beyond that reached before the second retina was stimulated. This constriction is greater than that occurring when all of the same total amount of light is cast on one retina. These results are shown in Fig. 4.33. The curve with solid circles pictures the results when a given quantity of stimulating light is gradually increased by casting it on one retina. The curve indicated by the open circles pictures the outcome when the same amount of light is used, part being applied to one eye, and part to the other. The vertical line indicates the point at which the second eye became involved.

The parallel to Fechner's paradox consists in the fact that increasing the total stimulation by adding stimulation via the second retina fails to increase constriction, decreasing it instead. Only when the stimulation of the two eyes approaches equality does the brightness of the perceived area or the pupillary constriction become greater. This same pupillary behaviour occurs when using non-corresponding retinal areas, and even when using two areas of a single retina. Such a method holds promise for further comparisons between sensations and reflexes.

THE STUDY OF VISUAL MECHANISMS

Among the objectives of the study of vision is accounting

for the phenomena that are known to occur. The means involved are generally spoken of as mechanisms. The mechanisms responsible for the phenomena are of interest and significance. For our purposes, these mechanisms lie within the organism itself.

Interest in visual mechanisms leads the investigator to the study of the basis for the phenomena in the several categories already described. It directs him to physiology and anatomy, and to chemistry and physics.

It is evident that, for the most part, adaptation is to be accounted for in terms of the photochemistry of the receptors. Differences between adaptation in binocular and monocular vision have made it evident that the nervous system is also responsible for adaptation.

The knowledge gained from studies of the discharges of single receptor organs [3, 22], as well as studies which disclose how photoreceptor systems operate [4], have helped to account for brightness discrimination.

Processes underlying colour vision have possible received more attention as mechanisms than have those underlying any other aspect of vision [15]. Theorization regarding colour vision has been persistent over many decades. Only recently, with neuropsychological techniques which record retinal activity, is new progress beginning to be made in answering some of the fundamental questions upon which any understanding of colour vision must rest [20].

It has been shown that the primary ocular mechanisms upon which space perception rests is the differential nature of the images in the two retinas [34]. With every eye movement or change in position between the object and the observer, the relations between the shapes and sizes of the images in the two retinas change and form a basis for the experience of object position. What role the innervation of the extrinsic eye muscles plays is not yet certain, although it is apparent that this role is secondary. As was already pointed out, the perception of motion is dependent upon some sort of temporally differentiated excitation reaching the central nervous system, and this can be induced by either stationary or physically moving objects.

Visual phenomena pose molar as well as molecular problems. This is to say that explanations aimed at accounting for such problems must tell how various parts of the retina, or how the two retinas, or even how other parts of the nervous system work together. Theories developed to solve such problems are often what are called field theories [11]. Field theories are those which describe the system that is known to be involved as a complex unit, the activities of the parts of which are controlled by laws of the system as a whole. There are many phenomena that demonstrate the need for such explanation, but as yet little headway has been made in deriving fundamental field laws.

The phenomena that accrue form casting light on the optic disk or, more inclusively, from casting unequal intensities of light on the optic disk or, disk and the rest of the retina, lead quite immediately to questions of underlying mechanisms. It is generally taken for granted that the optic disk contains no receptor elements or photically sensitive tissue, but certain phenomena still pose questions of optic-disk sensitivity in the minds of some investigators. Blind-spot phenomena seem to be dependent on spatial features of stimulation in such a way as to come into the category of field phenomena. Hence, to study blind-spot phenomena is either to study them as examples of field phenomena or to study them for their own sake and to attempt to discover the mechanisms underlying them.

Kohler and Wallah [29] have studied "figural aftereffects" as basic explanatory phenomena or as illustrative of some basic mechanism or mechanisms in the organism. Although they use perceptual phenomena, the ones they select are particularly appropriate for investigating aftereffects which provide for theoretical speculation on physiochemical mechanisms in the central nervous system.

METHODOLOGICAL SUMMARY

In spite of its brevity, the foregoing presentation of methods in vision should lead the reader to develop some such ideas as the following.

1. That visual sensation is capable of measurement when the experimental setup is properly planned.

2. That the measurements pertain to the relations between experience and physical conditions in the individual's surrounds.

3. That such measurements are possible because instruction given the subject rule out, or at least greatly minimize, individual differences in criteria and other contributive features involved in observation.

4. That the phenomena dealt with in the various classes of visual experiments are products of the specific sets of conditions involved. To understand results, the conditions under which the data were obtained must be known.

5. That usable forms of visual observations are comparisons in which two features are matched through manipulation of stimulus conditions, or one is differentiated from the other by manipulating conditions until a just perceivable difference arises.

6. That the measures obtained (thresholds, etc.) are statistical because of the fact that idea precision is never obtainable. In a series of observations aimed at determining a relationship between stimulus conditions and experiential outcome, both the stimulus an observer change at least enough to provide a series of data differing numerically.

7. That, because of the fact that the observer is a contributor to the experiential end result, not all relations which are important to discover lie solely between stimulus conditions and experience, but lie in part between discoverable features of the individual's organization (alignment, attitude, etc.) and the experiential end results. This leads us to the study of "peception" as such and to the frequent use, in that study,

of the organism rather than the physical world as a primary reference.

8. That vision is not fully understood until the mechanisms underlying it are determined and comprehended.

9. Last, but not least in importance, that there is much yet to be discovered about the basic features of the contact between the individual and the physical world.

REFERENCES

1. Bartley, S.H., Some effects of intermittent photic stimulation. *J. Exper. Psychol.*, 1939, *25*, 462-480.
2. Bartley, S.H., Some parallels between pupillary "reflexes" and brightness discrimination. *J.Exper. Psychol.*, 1943, *32*, 110-122.
3. Bartley, S.H., The comparative distribution of the light in the stimulus and on the retina. *J. Comp. Psychol.*, 1935, *19*, 149-154.
4. Brown, J.F., and A.C. Voth, The path of seen movement as a function of the vector field. *Amer. J. Psychol.*, 1937, *49*, 543-563.
5. Crozier, W.J., E. Wolf, and G. Zerrahn-Wolf, Intensity and critical flicker frequently for visual flicker. *J. Gen. Psychol.*, 1937, *21*, 203-222.
6. De Silva, H. R., and S.H. Bartley, Summation and subtraction of brightness in binocular perception. *Brit. J. Psychol.*, 1930, *20*, 241-250.
7. Elsberg, C.A., and H. Spotnitz, Some neural components of the visual response. *Amer. J. Psychol.*, 1937, *118*, 792-797.
8. Fry, G.A., A photo-receptor mechanism for the modulation theory of colour vision. *J. Opt. Soc. Amer.*, 1945, *35*, 114-135.
9. Fry, G.A., and S.H. Bartley, The effect of one border in the visual field upon the threshold of another. *Amer. J. Physiol.*, 1935, *112*, 414-421.
10. Fry, G.A., and S.H. Bartley, The brilliance of an object seen binocularly. *Amer. J. Ophthal.*, 1933, *16*, 687-693.
11. Fry, G.A., and P. Cobb, Anew method for determining the blurredness of the retinal image. *Trans. Acad. Ophthal.*

Otolaryng., 1935.

12. Geldard, F.A., Measurement of retinal fatigue to achromatic stimulation, I and II. *J. Gen. Psychol.*, 1928, *1*, 123-135, 578-590.

13. Granit, R., The colour receptors of the mammalian retina. *J., Neurophysiol.*, 1945, 8, 195-210.

14. Halstead, W.C., A note on the Bartley effect in the estimation of equivalent brightness. *J. Exper. Psychol.*, 1941, *28*, 524-528.

15. Hartline, H.K., Nerve messages in the fibres of the visual pathway. *J. Opt. Soc. Amer.*, 1940, *30*, 339-347.

16. Hecht. S., and J. Mandelbaum, The relation between vitamin A and dark adaptation. *J. Amer. Med. Assoc.*, 1939, *112*, 1910-1916.

17. Hecht S., and H. Shlaer, Colour vision of dichromats. *J. Gen. Physiol.*, 1936, *20*, 57-93.

18. Helson, H., Some facts and implications of colour constancy. *J. Opt. Soc. Amer.*, 1943, *33*, 555-567.

19. Hofstetter, H.W., An ergographic analysis of fatigue of accommodation. *Amer. J. Optom.*, 1943, *20*, 115-135.

20. *Illuminating Engineering Nomenclature and Photometric Standards.* Illuminating Engineering Society, 51 Madison Ave., New York.

21. Judd, D.B., facts of colour-blindness. *J. Opt. Soc. Amer.*, 1943, *33*, 294-307.

22. Kohler, W., and H. Wallach, Figural after-effects. *Proc. Amer. Philos. Soc.*, 1944, *38*, 269-357.

23. Kluver, H., The functional significance of the geniculo-striate system. *Biol. Symp., VII*, pp. 253-300. Lancaster, Pa .: Jaques Cattell Press, 1942.

24. Lashley, K.S., The problem of cerebral organization in vision. *Biol. Symp., VII*, pp. 301-322. Lancaster, Pa.: Jaques Cattell Press, 1942.

25. Marshall, W.H., and S. A. Talbot, Recent evidence for neural mechanisms in vision leading to a general theory of sensory activity. *Biol., Symp., VII*, pp. 117-164. Lancaster, Pa.: Jaques Cattell Press, 1942.

26. Nickerson, D., and S.M. Newhall, A psychological colou solid. *J. Opt. Soc. Amer.*, 1943, *33*, 419-422.

27. Ogle, K.N., Theory of the space eikonometer. *J. Opt. Soc. Amer.*, 1946, *36*, 20-32.

28. Reeves, P., The response of the average pupil to various intensities of light. *J. Opt. Soc. Amer.*, 1920, *4*, 35-43.

29. Schouten, J.F., and L.S. Ornstein, Measurements on direct and indirect adaptation by means of a binocular method. *J. Opt. Soc. Amer.*, 1939, *29*, 168-182.

30. Sheard, C., Dark adaptation : some physical, physiological, clinical, and aeromedical considerations. *J. Opt. Soc. Amer.*, 1944, *34*, 464-508.

31. Wald, G., Area and visual threshold. *J. Gen. Physiol.*, 1937, *21*, 269-287.

32. Walls, G., Factors in human visual resolution. *J. Opt. Soc. Amer.*, 1945, *33*, 487-505.

33. Wilcox, W.W., The basis of the dependence of visual acuity on illumination. *Proc. Nat. Acad. Sci.*, 1932, *18*, 47-56.

5

Studying Hearing

In our study of hearing we employ a variety of method : physical, anatomical, physiological, clinical, and psychological. Most problems must be approached from several directions at once, with all the techniques available. Recent years have seen notable developments of the methodology in this field. Particularly significant is the growth of electronics, which has put in out hands new tools for the production, control, and measurement of tones and thereby has stimulated a re-exploration of auditory phenomena. Also the development of high-gain amplification has given birth to a new physiological approach, the method of electrophysiology, in which acoustic processes are studied in terms of their electrical manifestations. These two types of methodology, the electrophysiological and the phenomenological, are the ones with which we shall be especially concerned.

THE ELECTROPHYSIOLOGICAL METHOD [5]

The electrophysiological method makes use of the fact that al living processes have an electrical aspect, and the activities c tissues are reflected in a changed of electrical state. B recording the electrical changes we obtain information on th nature of the organic processes.

In hearing there are a number of levels at which th electrical responses can be studied. They can be observed a the cochlea the auditory nerve, and in any of the nuclei and fiber tracts of the acoustic system of the brain, up to the temporal cortex. At any level we discover the form of the activity, as determined by the initiating stimulus and the various transformations that have taken place up to that point. The study is practically limited to experimental animals, although in a few instances the effects have been demonstrated in human subjects.

The technical procedure consists of anesthetizing the animal, operating upon it to gain access to the tissues

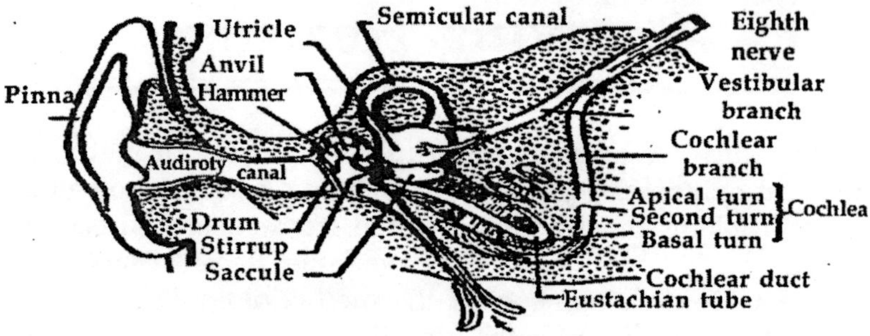

Fig. 5.1. Diagram of the ear.

The stippled regions represent bone, and the shaded portions indicate cavities filled with perilymph. R = round window, o = oval window. (After Czermak, from E. Boring, H. Langfeld, and H. Weld, *Introduction to Psychology*. Reprinted by permission of the authors and John Wiley and Sons.

concerned, and then placing an electrode in contact with the active cells for as close to them as possible, with a second electrode near by, usually in inactive tissue. There will generally be a difference of potential between the two regions under the electrodes, and this difference will change when

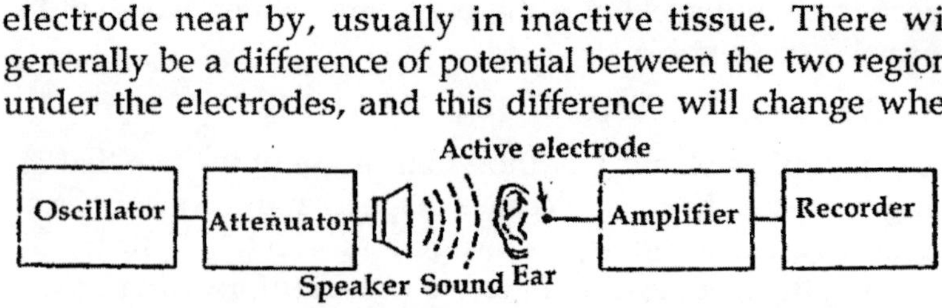

Fig. 5.2. Apparatus for study of audioelectric responses.

one region becomes active. The changes are amplified to whatever degree necessary—usually something of the order of 60 to 120 decibels—in order to operate a chosen recording device. The specific arrangements vary with the problem at hand, especially in the recording of the electrocochelear responses and the various forms of nerve action potentials. See fig. 5.2.

The electrocochlear responses are produced by the hair cells of the organ of Corti. We observe them most readily with an electrode on the membrane of the round window, from which there is a good conducting path formed by the cochlear fluids. The electrode is usually a piece of silver foil or some other conductor that is flexible enough to maintain a good contact despite accidental movements and yet imposes no serious restraint on the membrane.

The recording method varies; three instruments are especially useful, and at times all are employed in a single investigation. The amplified signals can be led into a telephone receiver or loudspeaker and then studied by listening. In this method we simply make use of the animal's ear as a microphone. We stimulate his ear with sound and ascertain the character of the responses. It is astonishing on first experience to find that the stimulating sounds are reproduced with great fidelity; indeed, if we select the right kind of ear, *e.g.*, a guinea pig's, we can equal the performance of the finest commercial microphones. This method is best employed for general exploration and qualitative studies, not for precise measurements, because the observer's ear does not discriminate loudness changes very well.

A second method employs the cathode-ray oscillograph, where the electrical changes are presented as a visible wave. Precise observations of amplitude and wave form are easily carried out. A decide advantage is that the equipment will withstand a sudden overload without damage.

A third method employs a wave analyzer, which is a vacuum tube voltmeter that can be adjusted so as to be sensitive to a single narrow hand of frequencies. For a given signal, measurements at a number of frequencies will reveal the composition of the potential wave. A sample analysis is shown in Fig. 5.3.

The cochlear responses, when studied for various kinds of acoustic stimuli, give information on the nature of the ear's activities up to the hair cells. The method is useful for a vast number of problems. It has been applied in the investigation

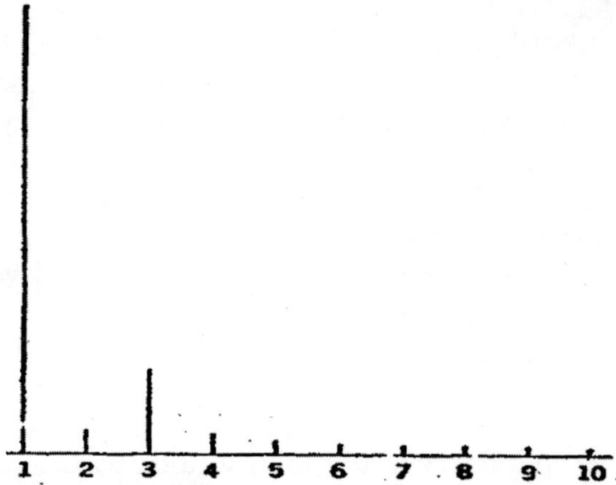

Fig. 5.3. Analysis of the cochlear response in a guinea-pig ear when stimulated strongly with a 1000-cycle tone.

The heights of the lines represent the magnitudes of the components. The line to the left, marked 1, represents the 1000-cycle component, the next line the 2000-cycle component, and so on.

of the functions of the various parts of the conduction mechanism, the nature and locus of distortion, the roles of the tympanic muscles, the action of drugs on the cochlea, the destructive effects of excessively loud sounds, the comparative efficiency of the ears of different species of animals, and many other problems. In fact, the method can be used to investigate any function of the peripheral mechanism that has to do with the tranismission and utilization of sound. A word of caution is necessary, however : these indications are not synonymous with "hearing," for hearing involves processes beyond the cochlear. Thus, for example, the fact that the cat's cochlea gives potentials to tones as high as 30,000 cycles does not thereby signify that this animal hears, such tones ; the matter must be investigated further by other methods.

The study of nerve potentials at the auditory nerve or at higher levels requires further attention to special techniques. The active electrode must be placed in intimate contact with the neurons, without damage to them. Because the nerve elements are left *in situ* and remain closely surrounded by fluids and other tissues, a considerable fraction of their potentials is shorted away; consequently the amplification must be greater than that ordinarily required in recording impulses from isolated nerves. The most suitable recording instrument is the cathode-ray oscillograph. Problems which have made use of the auditory nerve responses include the representation of intensity, the maximum frequency of nerve impulses, the locus of masking, the specificity of the fibers, and others bearing particularly on the theory of hearing.

THE AUDITORY RANGE

The physical vibrations that we call sounds may vary in frequency from zero indefinitely upward, yet tests carried out on any particular ear show sensitivity only within a limited range. A determination of the upper and lower limits of this range is one of the primary problems in the study of hearing.

The Upper Limit of Hearing

If we present to the ear a simple sound whose frequency is gradually raised, we hear a tone that grows higher and higher in pitch until ultimately it can no longer be perceived. For a young person of good hearing the point at which the tone disappears will be somewhere beyond 20,000 cycles, perhaps around 23,000 cycles, provided the stimulus is sufficiently strong. A weaker stimulus will become inaudible at a lower frequency. The upper limit of hearing therefore must be stated, not as a function of frequency alone, but of intensity as well. This situation may seem to mean that, if the intensity were raised sufficiently high, the frequency range would be extended indefinitely; if we attempt to test this possibility, however, we encounter a further condition that imposes a practical and final limitation. The tone becomes painful, and it is pain that cannot be ignored. Not only does the subject object to it, but if we should persist the ear would be damaged irreparably, as animals experiments have proved. We therefore define the upper limit of hearing as the terminal frequency at which pitch is perceived, for intensities that are below the pain or injury threshold.

Actually we do not have as yet any complete information regarding the upper limit as thus strictly defined, both because investigation in the neighbourhood of a pain threshold is disagreeable and somewhat dangerous, and because the production of tones of the necessary frequency and intensity is physically difficult. Our determinations approach the true limit and show the region of frequency beyond which it lies; and for most ordinary purposes we may be content with this approximation.

Early methods of producing high tones made use of small whistles or metal bars. Galton devised a miniature whistle with a variable plunger that could be screwed in or cut to change the pitch, and he fitted it to his walking stick so that he could test the reactions of his friends and also of the animals he visited in the zoological gardens. Unfortunately, Galton's whistle—and the same is true of later improvements on it—becomes erratic in performance when screwed down to a very short length and also is subject to variations according to the blowing pressure. Equally serious is the fact that its tone is accompanied by a hiss containing various low frequencies produced by the rushing stream of air, and a subject's ability to disregard this sound in favour of the proper one is often open to question.

A steel bar lightly suspended by stings placed about a quarter-length from the ends will vibrate transversely after being given a smart blow at the midpoint. Such bars are known as Koenig bars, being named for the famous acoustician and instrument-maker. A different bar must be cut for each frequency. So far as accuracy goes, this instrument is decidedly superior to the Galton whistle. The frequency varies slightly with temperature, but this variation can be calculated if desired. The noise made in striking the bar is, however, a drawback.

There are two modern developments of the metal-bar method, each of which avoids the noise of striking by employing an electrical form of excitation. In one, an electromagnet is mounted opposite one end of the bar (which is firmly held at its midpoint), and an oscillating electric current is sent through the electromagnetic coils to produce periodic magnetic attractions. A non-magnetic metal like aluminum may be used for the bar if an iron disk is cemented to the driven end. The periodic stretching of the bar, when carried out at the resonance frequency, quickly builds up an energetic vibration, which in this case is longitudinal rather than transverse.

A second form of excitation, which also gives longitudinal vibrations, employs the principle of magnetostriction. Certain metals and metallic alloys—nickel, cobalt, and especially nickel-iron and nickel-copper alloys—undergo a change of length when exposed to a magnetic field. If a coil is placed about the middle portion of a rod of such metals, and an oscillatory current sent through it, periodic alterations will be produced, and by choice of the proper frequency a resonance can be established, just as in the electromagnetic method. The electrically actuated rod has the further important advantage over the simple Koenig bar that the intensity can be varied at will by control of the electrical input.

Given a suitable source of high-frequency sound, the procedure for determining the upper limit of hearing is simple. The subject, seated comfortably in a soundproof room, is instructed to report at each trial whether he hears a tone. The constant-stimulus mode of psychophysical procedure is the most suitable.

Because the upper limit generally declines with age and is particularly susceptible to the effects of ear disorders, the experimenter should make careful record of the age of his subjects, their history of ear diseases, and any present condition like head colds, sinus infections, or pressure sensations referred to the eardrum.

The Lower Limit of Hearing

For several reasons, as will be seen, the lower limit of hearing is more difficult to determine than the upper limit. In the first place we need to distinguish between a lower limit of *pitch* perception and a lower limit of frequency at which *stimulation* occurs. These two limits are not the same; the ear is still stimulable by frequencies that are below the lower pitch limit. The lower limit of pitch is the problem on which we have the most information at the present time, but the other, the stimulation limit, also deserves consideration.

The experiences that appear on stimulation with pure tones of very low frequency are complex in nature, and their appreciation and analysis make severe demands on the subject's attention and skill. A good deal of preliminary practice is necessary to acquaint him with his task. If the stimulation frequency is set first around a few hundred cycles per second and then is progressively lowered, several qualitative characteristics emerge. The tone first becomes rough, and as the frequency is further reduced the roughness grows greater. Somewhere in the neighbourhood of 30 cycles the roughness grades into intermittence, a quality in which the separateness of the wave pulses is evident. The roughness too becomes greater as the frequency falls, until it passes through a maximum perhaps around 15 cycles. Between 15 and 20 cycles—often around 17 cycles—a new quality arises, called a thrusting effect, which is partly auditory and partly non-auditory; there occurs within each stimulation cycle a burst of high-frequency sound, like a hiss, and at the same time there appear kinesthetic and tactual sensations which are referred to the middle ear. At the very low frequencies, below about 15 cycles, where no low pitch remains, the stimulation is heard as a pumping noise whose pattern is determined by numerous high-frequency components. Although only the lower pitch limit may be the object of investigation in a given experiment, it is obvious that a subject must be aware of these other qualitative characters and must analyze the pitch out of the total complex. These other phenomena might be the objects of investigation also.

Low tones of pure (sinusoidal) form are difficult to produce and to handle. Sinusoidal currents can be generated by electrical means, but not very conveniently, and unless unusual precautions are taken their forms will be distorted by the circuits through which they are passed and especially by the instrument used to convert them into sounds. The most satisfactory apparatus for low-tone production is the pistonphone, a miniature pump driven by a crank mechanism which converts uniform rotary motion into simple harmonic motion.

The frequency is varied by controlling the motor speeds, and here a stroboscope or a tachometer is needed to indicate the speeds. Because the motor used to drive the piston is noisy, good soundproofing is needed to isolate this part of the equipment from the terminal part, where the ear is placed. Also, since some of the motor noise penetrates to the volume of air on which the piston is working, acoustic filters are required to prevent its passage along the line to the ear; these filters are of the "low-pass" type and allow the desired tones to continue unabated. The acoustic pressure set up at the end of the acoustic line is a simple function of the volume displacement of the piston and the total volume of air enclosed in the system, so that a reasonably convenient method of controlling the intensity is to vary this volume. Volume chambers of various sizes may be inserted in the system to give the desired intensity. The changing of volume chambers takes time, however, so that quick modifications of intensity are not easily provided. The system must be airtight, and the terminal end of the line fixed in the external meatus of the ear; with animals a cannula is tied into the ear, but with human subjects a satisfactory junction can be made with a tube having a bulbous ending, like the end of a physician's stethoscope, and a bit of vaseline smeared on the outside to form a seal.

PITCH DISCRIMINATION

The difference lime for pitch is defined as the frequency change in a tone that a subject is able to perceive 50 per cent of the time, under certain specified conditions. If we designate the frequency of the tone by f, then the symbol Δf may be used to represent the statistical value of the difference limen. The ratio of these quantities $\Delta f/f$ is called the *relative* difference limen and is especially useful as an indication of pitch sensitivity, because throughout the middle portion of the range of frequencies it remains reasonably constant.

Any of the standard psychophysical methods may be used to determine the difference limen for pitch. The method of constant stimuli is generally preferred as the most precise. According to this method, the subject is given two tones in immediate succession and is called upon to judge the pitch of one with respect to that of the others, several variables in the situating must receive attention. They include the duration of the tones, the time interval between the members of a pair, the intensity level, the number of ears—whether one or two—with which the subject listens, and especially the region of the frequency scale in which the measurements are made. The

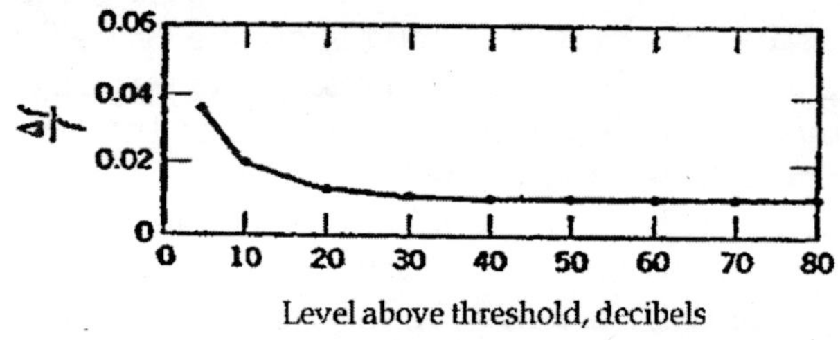

Fig. 5.4. Variation of relative difference limen with intensity.

duration of the tones should be 0.5 second or over, for if it is too brief the discrimination will be impaired. The interval between the tones is a significant condition, and in general should be as short as manipulations of the equipment will allow; the longer this interval, the poorer the discrimination. The intensity level or, more strictly, the level above the subject's threshold, is particularly important for the low-frequency tones, and for these its variations can produce changes as great as two-or threefold in the size of the limen, as Fig. 5.4 illustrates. As the intensity is raised from bare audibility, the value of the limen diminishes—the discrimination improves—

until a level of about 40 decibels above threshold is reached, after which intensity changes have little further effect. Ordinarily a level of about 60 decibels is suitable, but for the very low and very high tones, for which the ear is relatively insensitive, a lower level may be advisable to avoid pain or other extra-auditory sensations. The selection of a suitable level usually requires exploratory tests on each subject. The number of ears used is determined by the interests of the experiment and the experimental arrangements. If the sounds are made by a loudspeaker in the open air, it is more convenient to allow the subject to use both ears; but more often a telephone receiver is used as the source, and but one ear is stimulated. Discrimination is a little better for two ears. As already mentioned, the relative difference limen is fairly constant in the middle of the frequency scale, but it becomes somewhat larger for the high tones, and very much larger for the low tones, as shown in Fig. 5.5.

A comparatively new method for the study of pitch discrimination is the warble method, which is distinctive not only in the mode of presentation but also in certain of its psychological aspects [2]. Instead of presented two separate tones of different frequency, this method employs a sustained tone whose pitch is made to vary periodically. The subject is required merely to report whether he hears a steady or a

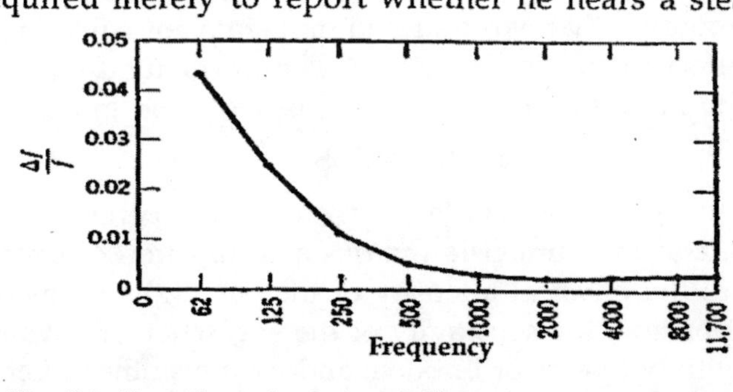

Fig. 5.5. Variation of relative difference limen with frequency. All tones were given at an intensity 40 db above threshold.

varying pitch. The warble rate, or the rate at which the frequency is changed back and forth, becomes a significant variable, and something like 2 cycles of change per second has been indicated as the optimal rate. Also important is the manner of switching : whether abrupt or gradual. An abrupt change has the disadvantage that it converts some of the acoustic energy into various high frequencies which the subject hears as a series of clicks. A sinusoidal form of transition is theoretically the most suitable, as it gives a minimum of such transient sounds, and in practice has been found satisfactory. With low tones the abrupt changes produce smaller limens, but the subject is probably using the transient patterns to some extent rather than judging merely on the low tones themselves. It is to be expected that the warble method will give smaller limens than the standard methods, because it is easier to judge continuity, as against discontinuity, than to appreciate a difference and correctly indicate its direction. As yet, however, there has been no systematic comparison of these two types of procedure.

For both procedures the electric oscillator is the most convenient source of stimulation, and for the warble method with sinusoidal variations it is indispensable. In the warble method the frequency variation is produced by rotating a small condenser in the tuned circuit of the oscillator.

As is usual, care should be taken that the tones are pure, but it is reported that harmonics in moderate amounts do not greatly affect pitch discrimination. The lower the frequency region, the more serious they would be expected to be.

LOUDNESS

The psychological magnitude of an auditory experience is its loudness, and this dimension varies as a function of several condition : the physical intensity of the sound, its frequency and composition, the sensitivity of the ear, whether listening is done with both ears or but one, and perhaps others. Let us first consider the physical intensity and the problems presented in its measurement and control.

The intensity of a sound is defined as the rate of flow of wave energy through a given region. It is expressed in power per unit area (ergs per second per square centimeter or watts per square centimeter). In no practical case, however, do we measure this power directly, but rather some other characteristic of the sound from which the power can be calculated. Measurements can be made of the amplitude of movement of the air particles, or the mean velocity of their vibratory motion, or the pressure that they exert when they strike a surface. A simple but very useful instrument for measuring sound pressures is the Rayleigh disk, pictured in Fig. 5.6. It consists of a thin disk, usually of mica, suspended by a slender thread. When exposed to a sound, the disk tends to turn its surface at right angles to the direction of flow of the sound, and from this torque the pressure can be determined.

Fig. 5.6. Rayleigh disk.

Because the ear has an extraordinarily extensive range of sensitivity it is necessary, if we use absolute units, to deal with numbers that are rather cumbersome. Thus the minimum power that will excite the ear is given by Sivian and White [3] as 0.24×10^{-16} watt, whereas the maximum that can safely be withstood is about 0.0023 watt. The variation over the intensity range is thus a thousand-million-millionfold! For convenience, therefore, we often employ a logarithmic scale, which compresses this range of numbers into a tolerably simple array. It ought to be mentioned at once that, however convenient it is to use the logarithms of numbers to compress their range, this manipulation carries one important restriction—it does away with any true zero point. The smallest logarithm that we can mention represents some quantity greater than nothing. For this reason it is not altogether proper to refer to a series of logarithmic values as representing a scale; more strictly speaking, they are ratios, and as with any ratio we must know both quantities that are being compared. In othe words, a conversion of acoustic intensities into logarithmi terms requires us first to choose a reference level; all ou quantities then are so-many logarithmic units above or belov that level.

Although any number of logarithmic conversions ar possible, the one is current use is the decibel scale. It uses th expression

$$N = 10 \log_{10} \frac{I_{10}}{I_0}$$

where N is the number of decibels, I_1 is the sound power ir question, I_0 is the reference level, and the ordinary decimal o Briggian logarithms are used. A good many reference level have been employed, so many that it is imperative that ir every use of decibels the level be explicitly given. Telephon engineers have sometimes used a "phonic level" of 1 microwatt. Others, in making pressure measurements, hav chosen a "zero level" of 1 dyne per square centimeter. Somewhat more useful for auditory work is a level tha approximates the human threshold. Unfortunately, though, this threshold is different for different tones. The threshold intensity for 1000 cycles has been used and also a rather rough average of threshold values through the middle of the range has been taken as 0.001 dyne per square centimeter. Again, many experimenters use as a reference point the threshold intensity for the particular tone in question, which of course is different for each tone and, strictly speaking, varies somewhat for every individual subject; the advantage (though a limited one) of this practice is that it avoids the necessity of any absolute measurements. Finally, in an attempt to reduce this confusion, a standardization committee of the Acoustical Society of America adopted a "reference intensity" of 10^{-16} watts per square centimeter, which is expected ultimately to supplant all the others. Table 5.1 shows these various reference levels and their relations the ASA standard.

Table 5.1

Refference Levels for Sound-Intensity Measurements

Designation	*Numerical Value*	*Decibels above ASA standard*
Phonic level	10^{-6} watts	100
Zero level	1 dyne-cm^{-2}	73.8
Mean threshold level	0.001 dyne-cm^{-2}	13.8
1000-cycle threshold level	2.4×10^{-16} watts	3.8
ASA reference intensity	10^{-16} watts	0

*Sivian and White's results for monaural listening [3].

AUDITORY ACUITY MEASUREMENTS

Measurements of auditory acuity are of two types : the precision measurements used generally in experimental investigation, and the more rough-and-ready procedures employed for clinical and other routine testing purposes. In experimental work we desire the most exact indications of the ear's characteristics and can take the pains to control the stimulus thoroughly, train the subjects well, and repeat observations systematically according to standard psychophysical procedures. In clinical and similar testing the exigencies of the situation do not allow so much attention to detail, and a less exacting programme must be carried out. Despite the limitations the results of such tests are of great value, not merely for diagnostic use but also in many instances for more fundamental understanding of auditory functions.

The Experimental Methods

In the study of auditory acuity two arrangements are used. In one, which corresponds to the natural method of listening, the source of sound is at a distance, and the ears are open. In the other the source of sound, an earphone, is fitted closely to the head, and the ear therefore is closed. These two methods give results that usually are somewhat at variance, because the ear is mechanically altered by closing it. There are other variables in the measurement situation also. With the open-ear method the observer may use only one ear the other being plugged. Whether he uses one ear or two, he can face the source or take various other angular positions with respect to it. In the closed-ear situation, if two earphones are provided, both ears may be stimulated simultaneously. For both the open-and closed-ear arrangements it is further necessary to make measurements of the sound intensity that stimulates the ear, and each arrangement presents special problems in this regard.

Once the physical problems are disposed of, the measurement of auditory acuity presents no very serious difficulties. Any of the psychophysical procedures may be followed.

Clinical Testing : Audiometry

The clinical testing methods were developed by otologists for diagnostic purposes. Until recently the procedures and techniques have been seriously limited by the instruments available for sound production. Of the cruder tests, there are the watch test and the whisper or voice test, which use means of sound production that are readily available but subject to little control. Tuning-fork tests represent a notable advance, for they use tones that are reasonably pure and, when handled expertly, give useful quantitative information. After it is struck, a tuning fork dies down rapidly and finally comes to rest, and if it is struck and then held in a standard manner, its curve of decay is fairly constant. The time that a person continues to hear it thus can be used as a measure of his acuity at that frequency.

The most modern methods of clinical testing, with which we shall be chiefly concerned, employ electrical means of generating and varying the tones. The electrical apparatus for this work, when assembled in one unit, is called an audiometer, and the technical procedures in its use constitute the special field of audiometry.

Air-conduction Tests

Audiometers are designed primarily for tests by air conduction. They consist of two main parts, an electric oscillator, which generates oscillating currents, and a resistance network or attenuator, which is used to control the power that is fed to a telephone receiver over the subject's ear. The oscillations cover a considerable frequency range, sometimes almost the whole audible scale. In some instruments there are only fixed steps of frequency, whereas in others a continuous variation is possible. The Council on Physical Therapy of the American Medical Association has specified that, if fixed frequencies are provided, they shall include at least the following seven octave tones : 128, 256, 512, 1024, 2048, 4096, and 8192 cycles per second. Some instruments provide in addition some of the semioctave or sometimes smaller intervals and it is especially desirable that they be included in the frequency region above 1024 cycles.

The output into the receiver, when in its usual position on a subject's ear, is calibrated for each individual frequency in decibels above a "normal" threshold for that frequency. Each instrument maker has done his own calibrating and has used for the purpose a rather limited number of subjects. Consequently, the calibrations do not represent the "normal" for the population at large, and of course they vary for different makes of audiometer. A good many data are available, however, for the more popular models of audiometers to permit correction of the dial readings; but, on the other hand, the alteration and discontinuance of models make many of these results obsolete.

The receiver is usually provided with a soft rubber cushion, which not only makes it more comfortable against the ear but also gives a more soundtight contacts. For ordinary testing the subject holds the receiver in his hand and adjusts it by trial to give an optimum signal. Ordinarily, intensity steps of 5 decibels are provided.

The intensity range usually varies for each frequency, partly on account of variations in the output of the receiver and partly on account of variations in sensitivity of the ear. It is desirable to provide sufficient range to reach the pain threshold at any frequency in order that persons with a grave degree of deafness may be tested, but no present instrument does so. Most fall short of this need at both ends of the frequency scale.

For a test of hearing, a soundproof room is highly desirable but must be dispensed with at times, either because it is not available, or because patients are severely ill an cannot be moved. In these events the examiner must make the best of existing circumstances, perhaps by selecting a time of day when the level of disturbing noise is low. A notation is made on the record to indicate the conditions under which the test was carried out.

In making the test, it is best to have the subject choose his better ear, if he has any preference, and to begin with a tone of medium frequency. This tone is set at an intensity that is expected to be easily audible, and the subject is required to indicate by word or signal whether he hears it. It is then reduced a step at time until it is no longer audible. Then a setting at an even lower intensity is given, and the intensity raised by steps until the subject reports that he hears the tone. Another descending series, and then an ascending series; will ordinarily complete the test for this tone, unless inattention and inconsistency call for more trials. Here the training and judgment of the examiner weigh heavily, especially with very young and with very ill subjects.

If the subject is properly attentive, the judgments will be so consistent that there is little question of the location of the threshold; the reason is that intensity steps of 5 decibels are large in relation to the difference limen for intensity, and if one step is barely heard, the next lower will commonly be inaudible. The examiner forms a "guessed average" or judgment of the threshold and records that single figure.

This same procedure is then carried out in turn on the remaining frequencies, and the whole performance repeated for the other ear. All the data, when plotted, constitute an audiogram, as illustrated in Fig. 5.7. In this figure the zero line represents the "normal," according to the instrument's calibration, and distance below the line show the amounts of hearing impairment. One curve, as indicated, is for the right ear and the other for the left.

When there is a considerable difference in the acuity of the two ears, it is necessary to use masking in the better ear to exclude if from operation. Otherwise, since there is always some leakage of sound through the air from the receiver to

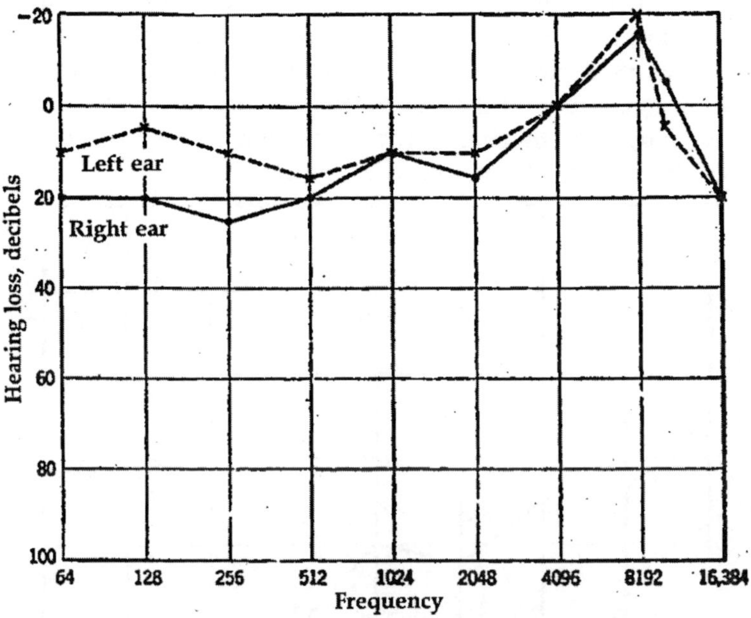

Fig. 5.7. Audiometer curves.

the other side of the head, and also some conduction through the skull itself, the sound may reach the better ear in sufficient intensity to give a false perception. This effect is strikingly shown in persons who have suffered a complete loss of hearing in one ear. An audiogram can be secured on the deaf ear, which actually is only a "shadow curve," representing the acuity of the good ear as reduced by the "shadow" of the head. Figure 5.8 shows such a curve, along with the true acuity curve of the good ear, and it will be noted that the shadow curve follows fairly closely the form of the other but lies about

60 decibels below it. This means than 60 decibels is the amount of attenuation offered by the head under the conditions. Sometimes, when the receiver does not fit well over the ear, or the rubber cushion on the receiver is omitted, the leakage is greater than this, and the curves will be closer together. The necessary amount of masking varies somewhat in every test, for it is a function of the acuity itself. It must be sufficient to prevent hearing of the cross-conducted sounds, yet must not be so great as itself to cross over to the tested ear and impair its performance. The usual course is to test both ears without masking and then to repeat the measurements on the poorer ear, with the better ear masked with a sound that is about 40 decibels above its threshold.

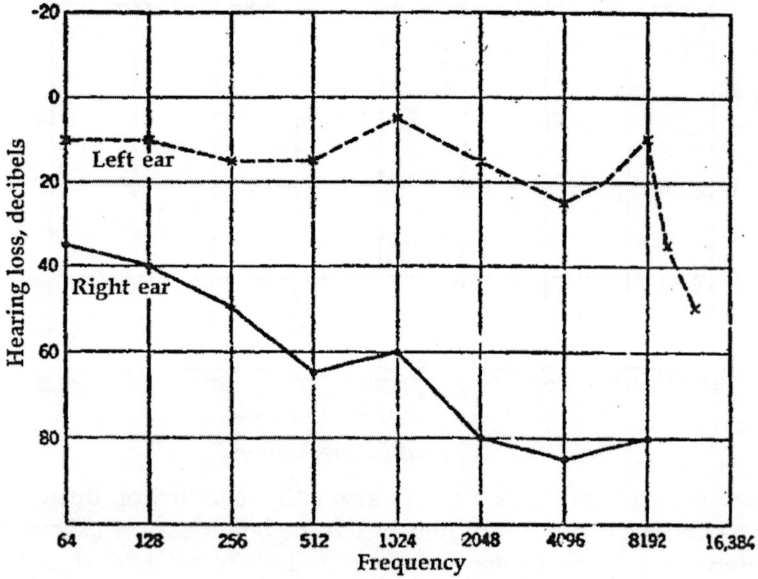

Fig. 5.8. Shadow curve.

The best type of sound to use for masking is a noise made up of a very broad band of frequencies. Such a noise is effective and at the same time (because it is qualitatively very different from the test tone) occasions the least disturbance to perception in the ear which is being tested.

Bone-conduction Tests

It frequently happens that a test of a person's hearing in the usual manner, by air conduction, reveals an impairment of acuity, yet a test by bone conduction shows that the cochlear endings and nervous elements are functioning normally. A bone-conduction test consists of the application of acoustic vibrations to the skull, through which they are conducted to the inner ear. By this route it is possible to stimulate the ear in spite of obstructions or interruptions in the usual path of transmission through the middle ear.

Most bone-conduction tests have been carried out with tuning forks. The stem of the vibrating fork is held firmly against the mastoid bone, just behind the ear. Most recent models of audiometers are provided with a bone-conduction receiver, which is mechanical vibrator actuated by the oscillating currents. This receiver has an advantage over the tuning fork in affording good control of both frequency and intensity. Its calibration curve will be quite different from that of the air-conduction receiver.

Both tuning forks and mechanical vibrators suffer from certain limitations. It is difficult with both to secure the amplitude of vibration often needed without so overburdening the instrument that it seriously distorts the sound produced. Also, both radiate a good deal of energy into the air, and the examiner must be alert to the possibility of stimulation by air conduction. This air-conducted sound may not be troublesome if air-conduction acuity is low for both ears, but it is a possible source of error if only one ear is so affected.

Momentarily stopping the meatus will often give a clue as to whether error from this source is present, but the tests ought not to be carried out with the ears closed, as this closure will affect the bone-conduction acuity.

The pressure with which the instrument is applied to the mastoid should be as constant as possible; there is more danger in too light pressure than too heavy, but care must be taken not to use one that will be painful.

A special difficulty appears when bone-conduction tests are attempted with the low frequencies. The stimulus will give tactual sensations as well as sounds, and an inexperienced observer may mistake one for the other. A few trials with the vibrator placed elsewhere on the body, say over a bone on the hand, aids in the desired discrimination.

Masking is even more important in bone-conductions tests than in air-conduction tests. Vibrations applied to one mastoid bone are readily conducted across the head, and they reach the opposite ear at a level little lower than that at the ear it is desired to test. The opposite ear, therefore, must be excluded by masking. This masking is always produced by an aerial sound, and the usual precautions are necessary to prevent its leakage to the ear under test.

In bone-conduction tests it is difficult to ascertain in preliminary trials which is the better ear. Accordingly, it is advisable to make the measurements on each ear while masking the other.

The Upper Limit of Loudness

Acoustic stimuli, when raised in intensity, eventually reach a level at which their effects are not wholly auditory. They excite a variety of other sensations, which vary somewhat with the frequency. At low frequencies excessive stimulation arouses tactual and kinesthetic sensations, which are referred to the middle ear, and also labyrinthine effects, which include dizziness, nausea, vague bodily sensations, and sometimes eye and head nystagmus. Middle frequencies give rise to tactual sensations, which are more of a pressury quality, and also sensations of pain. High tones have similar effects, with perhaps more emphasis on pain.

In the past, attempts have been made to determine one curve as an upper limit of loudness in order to guide the design of hearing aids for the deafened. The foregoing description shows that there is no one curve which forms this boundary, but a family of functions, one for every sensory quality. The determination of these functions remains to be made. The subject will need to be trained to recognize each sensory quality even when it appears in a complex of others. Then a determination, according to the usual psychophysical procedures, can be made for this quality at each frequency at which it appears.

Loudness Discrimination

Methods for the study of loudness discrimination parallel those used in the discrimination of pitch. There are two types. The more usual is one in which two discrete, steady tones are presented, one at greater intensity than the other and the subject makes a relative judgment. Here, as with pitch, the variables of frequency region, intensity level, duration of the stimuli, and especially the time interval between stimuli must receive attention. The second method is the warble method, in which the intensity is varied at a determined rate, and the subject is asked to report whether he perceives a steady or a wavering sound. The rate of warbling is of course a factor, and, according to Riesz [1], the optimum discrimination appears with a rate around 3 per second. As would be expected, this procedure gives smaller limens than the other, in which the subject must report the direction as well as the presence of a change.

Equal-loudness Curves

The task of comparing the loudness of tones which differ in frequency might be compared, in character and difficulty, to the problem of heterochromatic photometry. The equating as to loudness of sensations of different pitch is one of the most trying exercises that can be given a subject. Certainly intensive practice in this type of judgment is essential, and even then the task will never be carried out with much comfort or confidence. Therefore, to aid the subject and stabilize his judgments it is desirable to modify the usual psychophysical procedures somewhat, and to use a considerably broader range of stimuli than would ordinarily be considered necessary. The relatively easy judgments that will appear from time to time will fortify the subject's confidence and tend to prevent alterations in his criteria of judgment.

In the past, particular interest has centered on the equation of the loudness of various tones with a standard tone of 1000 cycles. The loudness of the 1000-cycle tone is used as a scale by which the loudness of any tone can be designated. The *loudness level* of a tone is then referred to as the equivalent loudness of the 1000-cycle tone; specifically it is the number of decibels above the reference intensity that a 1000-cycle tone must be raised in order to be judged equal to the tone in question. The reference intensity is 10^{-16} watts per square centimeter, or sometimes the 1000-cycle threshold.

INTERACTION PHENOMENA

A number of phenomena result when two or more simple tones act upon the ear simultaneously. Some of these are beats, combination tones, and masking.

Beats

In the observation of beats two oscillators are used, tuned to somewhere near the same frequency. Both may be operated into the same telephone receiver, but it is better to use two receivers in order to avoid any electrical interaction between the oscillators. Both the tones are conducted to one or to both of the subject's ears (not to separate ears, as this arrangement will not produce beats). The intensity of the stimuli will have to be adjusted to somewhat the same level for greatest perceptibility of the beating.

The quality of the experience varies with the beat frequency. It also varies with the frequency region from which these stimuli are taken, and to a lesser extent with the loudness relation. At low rates of beating there is perceived a slow waxing and waning of loudness, at higher rates a pulsing or pounding in which the sound seems to come in sudden thrusts, and at still more rapid rates only a sort of rough whirring in which the individual cycles of variation can no longer be distinguished.

The upper limit of perception of beats naturally depends upon the qualitative criterion selected : if it is the pulsating or intermittent quality described as the intermediate stage, the limit will be lower than if the whirring or roughness characteristic is chosen. In determining the limit, according to any criterion, the general intensity and also the intensity ratio are adjusted so as to provide the most favourable conditions for observation. A fairly high level of intensity is desirable, and a ratio that keeps the loudness of the two components somewhat near equal. The frequency region is an important variable; the higher this region, the higher is the limit of perceptible beats.

At high levels of stimulation two or more beat rates may be present at the same time, and the subject will need to differentiate them. He does so both by the perceived rates and by loudness cues : the more rapid beats are fainter.

It is generally claimed that in the slower beats there is a periodic variation of pitch as well as of loudness, and the observer must be prompted to report this qualitative change along with the others.

Combination Tones

Much the same stimulating conditions as described for beats will give combination tones, when the difference in frequency of the two tones is sufficiently large—perhaps 30 cycles or more. These tones appear in addition to the two primary tones, as products of their interaction in the inner ear. There are a great many of these interaction products, with frequencies indicated by the following expression :

$$\overline{Mh \pm nl}$$

where h is the frequency of the higher stimulus tone, t is the frequency of the lower stimulus tone, and m and n are simple whole numbers : the bar above the expression indicates that the absolute value of the quantity is to be used. We distinguish two classes of combination tones, called *difference tones or summation tones*; the difference tones are those that arise when we use only the minus sign in the formula, and the summation tones when we use the plus sign. The multipliers m and n take all integral values from 1 on; but as they grow greater, the magnitude of the resulting combination tone falls off rapidly, so that practically only the lower values or *orders* of combination tones need be considered. The *order* [6] of a combination tone is determined by the size of both m and n; it is defined numerically as $m+n-1$. For example, if $m = 2$ and $n = 3$, the combination tone is either $2h + 3l$ or $2h - 3l$, and since $m + n - 1 = 4$, we have a summation or difference tone of the fourth order.

Three methods have been found useful for the study of combination tones. The first is *simple listening*, in which the subject seeks to perceive and identify some one of the interaction products. This is a difficult matter, comparable to an identification of the several notes comprising a musical chord, and requires special talent and training. The risk is aided by a judicious selection of the frequency region for the primaries, in order to throw the combination tone into a part of the auditory range in which the subject's sensitivity is high, and also to get its frequency as far away from the primary frequencies as possible. It is aided also by variation in the intensities of the primaries, the manner of which can be determined only by trial, as it depends in part upon the particular sensitivity function of the subject's ear. For rough guidance it may be said that each primary must be raised in intensity as m or n increases in the expression for the combination tone sought for. Further, it is practically essential that the subject be presented from time to time with a tone corresponding to the frequency of the combination tone he is to listen for.

The second is the *exploring tone method*. It employs a third tone, in addition to the primaries, which is adjusted to a frequency a little different from that of the expected combination tone and therefore gives beats with that tone. It is varied in intensity to make the beats as marked as possible, which, it is assumed, happens for equal loudness of the combination tone and exploring tone. The intensity of the exploring tone them can be used as an indication of the effective magnitude of the combination tone.

A third method employs the electrical response of the

cochlea and so far has been practicable only in animals below man. When the stimulus is two pure tones, a vast array of combination tones is found in the potential waves generated in the cochlea. The study is made with a wave analyzer, an instrument by which a component of any desired frequency can be measured in isolation. At high levels of stimulation the greater part of the stimulus energy is transformed into overtone and combination tone frequencies, and scores of components, including some as high as the twentieth order, have been observed. Only by this method has anything approaching the full pattern of combination tones been revealed, and their functional relations to the stimuli worked out.

Masking

When two tones similar in frequency but considerable different in intensity are applied simultaneously to the same ear, only the stronger will be heard; the weaker is said to be *masked.* The study of masking in its simplest form is essentially the determination of thresholds for a given tone in the presence of another that in successive determinations is varied systematically in frequency and intensity. We can study masking also for complexes of tones and for noises.

THE LOCALIZATION OF SOUND

When we perceive a sound under natural conditions, we nearly always localize it in space. This aspect of perception logically may be considered as involving two features, direction and distance. Experimental methods have been developed for the determination of the accuracy of our judgments of these features and also of the cues employed.

Investigation soon shows that most of our cues are secondary, involving the perception of likely sources of the sounds we hear and inferences made from the character of the sounds. When we exclude the secondary or inferential cues and rely upon hearing alone, we find our perceptions considerably reduced. They are even more reduced when the head and the perceived object are kept stationary. We then have left only the ability to judge direction along the right-left dimension, based upon differences in the stimulation of the two ears [8]. Let us consider first this static function.

Two general procedures have been employed for the study of localization as a function of binaural differences. One, the more natural method, consists in listening, with both ears, to some source of sound that is a little distance from the observer and can be moved to various positions. The observer is prevented from using visual or other non-auditory cues and must depend on the binaural stimulation alone to judge the location of the sound.

An instrument called the sound cage is often used in this procedure. The observer, blindfolded, is seated in the center of a metal frame-work that represents several circles or parts of circles on the surface of an imaginary sphere, and a sound source, usually a telephone receiver, is moved to various positions along these circles. After a sound is produced at any desired point, the observer must indicate the angle from which it seems to come. He may make his judgment known by pointing or by verbal reference to some schema.

This natural method suffers from certain disadvantages. Control of the stimulus is a difficult matter. A sound produced in the manner indicated, in an experimental room, will reach the observer's ear not only by the direct path, but also circuitously after reflection from the walls or near-by objects. These reflected sounds have various, and usually unpredictable, angular positions. The pattern of stimulation is extremely complex, and even if its character were known it would present too difficult a problem for the observer to deal with. Reflections can be reduced by treating all surfaces with sound-absorbing materials, but ordinarily it is not practicable to carry this treatment far enough to eliminate them altogether. What is needed is to suspend the observer in free space and to make the stimulating equipment so unobtrusive as not to disturb the sound field. An approach to this condition is obtained by working on a high, flat roof, preferably with the observer elevated on a pedestal of some kind, and locating the sound source on a slender arm that can be given various positions.

A more serious disadvantage of the natural method is that it presents various binaural cues all at once and does not reveal which ones are operating at any given time or how they may be interacting. With pure tones as stimuli, three kinds of cue are possible : differences of intensity, time of incidence, and phase at the two ears. With complex tones there are also differences of timbre ; they arise because the head casts more of a sound shadow for high frequencies, and hence the ear away from the sound will hear it with the high components relatively unfeebled. The method can tell us what our capacity for localization is under usual circumstances but will not provide an analysis or explanation of the process.

In the second method the physical conditions are under better control, and the binaural cues can be studied one at a time. The two ears are stimulated separately by means of telephone receivers or tubes through which the waves are conducted. The experimenter can determine as accurately as he will the character of the binaural pattern. It has been customary to vary one kind of cue at a time and to keep the others constant (or try to), but there is no great difficulty in presenting any sort of combination of cues by this method.

In the early development of this method, sound-conducting tubes were used for separate stimulation of the ears, and by various manipulations a change was made in the stimuli reaching the ears. Partially obstructing one tube, for example, by pinching it, will reduce the intensity on that side. Changing the length of one tube is usually designed to alter the phase relation, but unfortunately this manipulation does other things too. By altering the resonance characteristics of the tube it changes the intensity; and of course, if time is considered apart from phase, it alters the time relation also.

The use of telephone receivers on the ears is much to be preferred. The electrical circuit which actuates the receivers can be adjusted so as to give any desired change of intensity, time, or phase, independently of one another. Intensity is controlled with attenuators, one in a branch of the circuit leading to one ear, another in a second branch to the other ear. Time can be controlled with mechanically operated switches. Phase control involves a special circuit in which resistance, capacitance, and inductance are altered. An electrical method can also be devised for control of the character of a complex sound : a filter network of the low-pass type may be inserted in the circuit to one receiver to reproduce the differential screening action of the head.

One further measure is advisable in the use of this method. Since two telephone receivers may not have identical electrical and mechanical characteristics, it is desirable to pick up the sounds as they actually appear at the two ears and record them on an oscillograph. By this means we may check our manipulations and be certain that the desired differences are present.

Whichever of the foregoing procedures is used, the observer's task is simply defined. Although his ears are stimulated differently, he ordinarily hears but one sound. Subjects often report what is called a "sound image" or "phantom" which may be purely auditory but more often has a visual character also, and they perceive this image at a more or less definite point in space.

In indicating the angular position with respect to the observer, for both the true location of the sound source and the observer's judgment of it, we employ such terms as azimuth, altitude, or angle of elevation. Azimuth refers to position in the horizontal plane. Altitude and angle of elevation refer to position with respect to the vertical axis; they are defined as the vertical angle between any position and the horizon.

When either the object or the head is permitted to move, we add a dynamic factor to localization. We are able to integrate cues over a period of time and thereby increase their significance and reliability. We are able also, by tipping the ears out of their usual horizontal plane, to enlarge the scope of operation of the binaural differences [4].

When the sound is of constant character and familiar to the subject, we can demonstrate certain limited capacities for the judgment of distance. As we know from common experience, sounds grow faint as they become farther away. Under natural conditions, however, this function is interfered with by reflections, which upset the relation of intensity and distance. To study the phenomena exactly requires fee-space conditions or as near an approximation to these as possible. If a complex sound is used as the stimulus, attention should be given to the possibility of timbre cues in this situation, for even in free space the different frequencies are not transmitted quite equally, and the presence of obstructing objects may cause significant modifications of the wave composition.

EPILOGUE

The foregoing pages have introduced the techniques and procedures for dealing with the more fundamental problems in the field of hearing. It has been shown that with the refinements of apparatus that recent electronic developments have provided we can produce and handle all kinds of acoustic stimuli and do so with a precision heretofore unknown.

In our enthusiasm over our material equipment, however, we must not lose sight of our other problems—of the more strictly psychological matters of the control of the subject's attitude, his criteria of judgment, and the psychophysical procedures required for systematic measurements. In this area too, by a slow growth over the years, we have at our disposal a wealth of technical knowledge. Finally, through recent physical developments, we have the electrophysiological methods, which have opened up new fields of investigation and already illuminated many problems formerly obscure. We can look to the future for a continuing expansion of our understanding of hearing in all its aspects.

REFERENCES

1. Riesz, R.R., Differential intensity sensitivity of the ear for pure tones. *Phys. Rev.*, 1928, *31*, 867-875.
2. Shower, E.G., and R. Biddulph, Differential pitch sensitivity

of the ear. *J. Acoust. Soc. Amer.*, 1931, *3*, 275-287.

3. Sivian, D.J., and S.D. White, On minimum audible sound fields. *J. Acoust. Soc. Amer.*, 1933, *4*, 288-324.
4. Wallach, H., The role of head movements and vestibular and visual cues in sound localization. *J. Exper. Psychol.*, 1940, *27*, 339-368.
5. Wever, E. G., The electrical responses of the ear. *Psychol. Bull.*, 1939, *36*, 143-187.
6. Wever, E.G., The designation of combination tones. *Psychol. Rev.*, 1941, *48*, 93-104.
7. Wever, E.G., C.W. Bray, and C.F. Willey, The response of the cochlea to tones of low frequency. *J. Exper. Psychol.*, 1937, *20*, 336-349.
8. Young, P.T., The role of head movements in auditory localization. *J. Exper. Psychol.*, 1931, *14*, 95-124.

6

Study of Skin Senses

Biologically the skin senses are more important to the human being than is either sight or hearing. The blind man and the deaf man are merely handicapped, but a man totally without skin sensitivity would have a poor chance to survive at all. Pain guards the body from external injury. The temperature senses at as external thermostats in the vital task of regulating the temperature of the blood. Even touch, although less essential, provides a critical aid in darkness. Yet, compared with sight or hearing, the skin senses have attracted relatively little attention, and they remain a rich field for further investigation. There are three persistent problems of major interest, and most research techniques have been directed toward their solution. These problems concern the number of skin senses, the nature of the receptors and receptor processes, and the measurement of the actual manner of their stimulation.

In connection with the number of skin senses, touch, pain, warm, and cold are commonly assumed to be the four basic ones, but this view has not been universally accepted. Many years ago Head [41] proposed two separate cutaneous systems, the epicritic and the protopathic, each having a separate set of four senses. Katz [30] suggested a separate vibration sense, independent of touch. At the other extreme, Nafe [35] would like to reduce warmth, cold, and some kinds of pain to sensations from dilating and constricting blood vessels, thus eliminating these as separate skin senses. The problem is further complicated by the presence of deep pain and deep pressure sensitivities; which are difficult to distinguish from the strictly cutaneous reactions.

In regard to the nature of the receptors and the way in which they work mapping the skin with small stimulators shows that there are points of high sensitivity—the warm, cold, pain, and touch spots—with relatively insensitive regions in between. It has often been assumed that each of these spots corresponds to a single receptor. However, direct microscopic study fails to confirm this simple theory, and indirect evidence suggests that the situation must be much more complex.

As to the actual nature of receptor stimulation, it is evident that mere description of external physical stimuli is insufficient. The critical questions are : What happens in the skin itself when it is stimulated? How is the skin distorted to produce an experience of touch or vibration? What are the significant temperature changes in the tissues which accompany sensations of warmth and cold? We are concerned with such questions as these when we deal with the problem of the actual nature of stimulation.

There are, of course, many additional phases of skin sensitivity which invite study. Some are peculiarly cutaneous problems, *e.g.*, the accuracy with which a stimulated point can be localized, the minimum distance at which two points can be sensed as separate, and the limits in discriminating the size of objects pressed against the skin. Some of these problems involve routine measurements similar to those made for the other senses, such as reaction times, adaptation times, stimulus limens, and difference limens. Still others deal with the perception of form, pattern, and movement by the skin senses, including illusions which are strikingly like those in vision.

In this chapter, methods related to the three basic problems are covered first, and then other problems and methods are briefly discussed. Finally, the various ways in which the skin can be stimulated are summarized.

METHODS OF SEPARATING THE SKIN SENSES

The problem here is essentially to determine the number of skin senses by experimentally *dissociating* them. This can be accomplished in a number of ways: by anesthesia, by cutting or blocking a nerve, by mapping after removing successive slices of skin, and by establishing differential chronaxies.

Disappearance and Recovery under Anesthesia

Under local anesthesia, warm, cold, touch, and pain do not disappear and reappear all at the same time, but straggle out and straggle in again. To anesthetize a section of skin, the most widely used method is electroendosmosis [9]. A pad saturated with novacain or some similar anesthetic is placed on the skin. On top of the pad is fastened the active metal electrode. A large metal plate or a vessel of salt solution is applied to some other part of the body as an inactive electrode. Direct current of low amperage is employed to drive the anesthetic into the skin. Sensitivity to warm, cold, touch, and pain stimulation is tested at intervals during the process of anesthetizing and again during the recovery period.

Although investigators do not wholly agree on the exact order of disappearance and reappearance, some dissociation has been found in every case. In general, warm and cold go out first and come back last.

Regeneration after Nerve Section or Nerve Block

Complete loss of sensitivity followed by long-delayed recovery may be produced by cutting or crushing a nerve or by injecting it with alcohol. Alcohol injection [31] has the double advantage of requiring no surgery and leaving no permanent injury. Figure 6.1 shows a sample of the dissociation of touch and warmth during recovery after alcohol injection. Effects of shorter duration may be obtained by injecting novacain around a nerve, by blocking a nerve with pressure, or by cutting off the blood supply with an inflated rubber cuff. When novocain is injected around a nerve [6], recovery occurs over a matter of hours. All these methods brings about some measure of dissociation, although, the exact order of reappearance varies with the method employed.

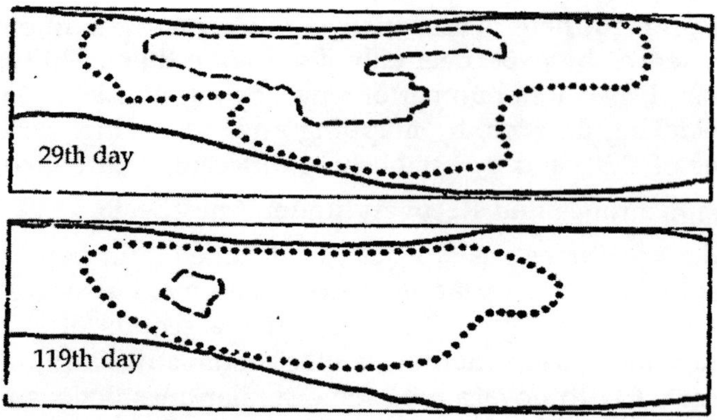

Fig. 6.1. Dissociation of warmth and touch during recovery from nerve block by alcohol injection. (Adapted from Lanier [31].)

Removing Successive Slices of Skin

An interesting if somewhat heroic method was developed by Woollard [51]. He first mapped an area on the thigh, exploring the region systematically with small stimulators to locate the points of maximum sensitivity to cold, touch, and pain. These cold spots, touch spots, and pain spots he marked on a map of the area. He then removed five successive thin slices of skin. After the removal of each slice and after healing had occurred, he retested the area and made comparisons with the original map. Again, some dissociation was evident.

Measurement of Chronaxies

Chronaxy is the minimum time for a current of double the threshold strength to produce a clear sensation of warm, cold, touch, or pain. It is measured with a device which delivers a very brief but accurately timed pulse of electrical stimulation, for example, by the discharge of a condenser. Different chronaxies are found for warm, cold, touch, and pain [28, 29], thus supporting the idea of four separate skin senses.

The general preponderance of evidence seems to favour the existence of four cutaneous senses : warm, cold, pain, and touch, and there appears to be no reason for adding to the number, as proposed by Head [41] or by Katz [30]. On the other hand, the reduction suggested by Nafe [35] leaves too many facts unexplained.

METHODS FOR STUDYING RECEPTORS AND RECEPTOR PROCESSES

Numerous attempts have been made to obtain evidence of the identity of the skin receptors by examining portions of skin under the microscope. In addition, there have been efforts to answer the more limited question of the relative depths of the receptors below the skin surface. There are also a number of studies which are of interest because their results have some hearing on the nature of the receptor processes.

Microscopic Examination

In the direct approach to this problem, portions of the skin are carefully mapped, and the points of maximum sensitivity marked. Then the pieces of flesh are removed surgically, sliced into thin sections, stained, and examined under a microscope [9]. Results that accrue technique have been rather consistently negative; *i. e,* no receptors are seen under the microscope which correspond consistently to warm sports, cold spots, etc. The negative results may be due to inadequate staining methods or simply to the fact that there are no gross receptors which can be identified in this way.

In the indirect, approach the warm, cold touch, and pain spots are separately counted. Then the same area of skin is sectioned, stained, and examined microscopically to determine the number of each type of ending. The counts of spots and endings are compared [4]. For example, if there are fifteen cold spots and the microscope shows fifteen Krause endings, it is assumed that Krause endings are the receptors for cold. Such a correlation of numbers, however, may be quite accidental, even for the special region investigated. Furthermore, in the skin on most parts of the body no Krause endings can be found [17]. Thus the evidence from indirect studies remains inconclusive.

Estimating Receptor Depth

An interesting attempt at a direct approach to the problem of receptor depth is the method of punctiform [12]. In this scheme warm and cold spots are first mapped and marked. The skin at each spot is then punctured to a measured depth, and a drop of Novocain solution placed on the puncture. Warm spots, it is found, must be punctured to a greater depth than cold spots for the Novocain to produce loss of sensitivity, suggesting that warm receptors lie deeper below the surface of the skin. Several methods of indirect estimation of depth have been employed, but these are invalid because they depend upon speculative assumptions concerning the nature of the receptors, the process of stimulation, or the rate of heat conduction through the skin—no one of which is adequately established.

Nature of the Receptor Processes

No direct approach has been made to the study of cutaneous receptor processes in human beings. The effects of chemicals upon adaptation in the skin of the frog [23] or of nerve currents from stimulation of the cornea of the cat [45] are suggestive only by analogy. There are, however, a number of methods which are significant because they bear indirectly upon the problem.

The *critical flicker frequency*, or the minimum time interval at which successive stimulations can be sensed as separate, is important in indicating the speed of receptor action. For warmth and cold, this can be determined by using radiant heat or dry ice and a rotating shutter to interrupt the stimulation [15]. Accurate measurement requires the use of not more than two successive stimulations at a time, because repeated exposure changes the skin temperature and thus its differential sensitivity. Warm and cold stimuli separated by approximately 0.2 second can be sensed as separate, indicating a quite rapid recovery in the receptor process. In the case of touch, an extremely rapid receptor process is indicated. At low rates of stimulation the successive touches are sensed as separate. As the rate is increased, the separate touches blend into a smooth vibration, which can be sensed clearly up to several thousand vibrations per second.

Adaptation to warm and cold has been studied with an apparatus in which the stimulator is surrounded by a neutral-temperature field to minimize the effect of spread to surrounding areas [24]. Under these conditions, complete adaptation to warm or cold takes place in a few seconds when a 1-millimeeter stimulator is used. With larger sizes, the time for complete adaptation is found to be greater for a narrow rectangular stimulator than for a circular stimulator of the same area, and still greater when the same area is presented in the form of a ring.

Also significant are the effects of *stimulator size and temperature*. Interesting relationships are discovered when the same skin area is mapped repeatedly with different stimulator sizes [26] or with the same size at different temperatures [27]. For such studies a checkerboard pattern of 2- or 3 -millimeter squares is stamped on the skin. The squares are stimulated in random order alternately with different sizes or different temperatures. The subject reports 0, 1, 2, or 3 to indicate the experienced intensity from each stimulation. After the mapping has been repeated six or more times, reports from the most consistent subjects are used to determine the relations.

Some unexpected results are encountered. To take a single example assume that the checkerboard is mapped with temperatures of 38, 41, 44, and 47 degrees. Intensity of warmth experienced from the higher temperatures does not rise uniformly all over the map. Some squares yield consistent reports of 1 at 38 degrees and continue to give 1 at 41, 44 and 47 degrees. Other squares give 0 at 38 degrees, 0 at 41 degrees, and then suddenly become 2 or 3 at 44 degrees. Many other varieties of response are found, indicating that receptor action is not a simple matter of uniformly graded response. Similarly curious relations are found when the same skin area is mapped with different sizes. For example, a larger stimulator covering two squares of differing sensitivity typically yields a report consistently *lower* than the maximum of the two individual squares.

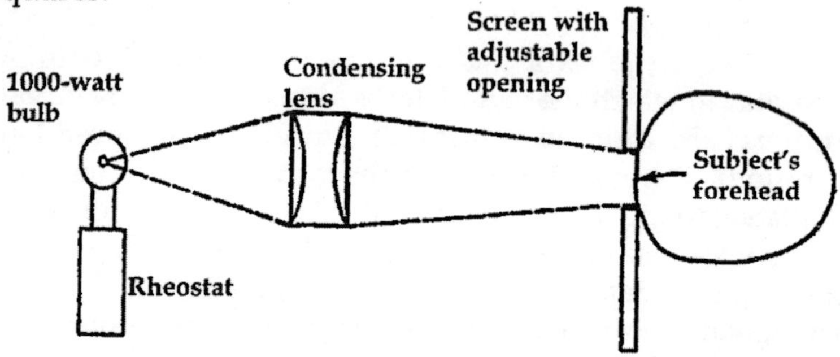

Fig. 6.2. Radiant heat stimulator. (Adapted from Hardy [37].)

Radiant stimulation produces different results from those obtained with metal stimulators brought in contact with the skin. As the radiated area is enlarged or the radiant intensity increased, the experienced warmth rises quite regularly [22]. In contrast are the irregular changes just described with contact stimulation. Why radiant stimulation and contact stimulation have such different effects has not yet been satisfactorily explained.

An excellent method of using radiant stimulation has been developed by Hardy and his coworkers [21]. Heat from a 1000-watt lamp is condensed by a lens and focused on an aperture of the desired size, as shown in Fig. 6.2. The length of exposure is controlled by a shutter. The exact strength of radiant stimulation is measured by substituting a radiometer for the subject's skin after each set of stimulations. The same apparatus can be employed to study pain from radiant heat by using much higher intensities.

Warm and cold can be aroused by various forms of *inadequate stimulation*, as well as by the usual increase and decrease of temperature. Perhaps the simplest demonstration is the chemical effect of menthol, which gives a sensation of coolness, and of chloroform (applied under a watch glass to prevent evaporation), which produces mild warmth. Warm and cold can sometimes be obtained by electrical stimulation, as in chronaxy determinations, or by mechanical stimulation of spots of high sensitivity with a blunted wooden matchstick. Some cold spots will respond with a cold sensation when touched with a small stimulator at 45 degrees centigrade—paradoxical cold. Similarly, some warm spots will respond with a warm sensation to 20 degrees centigrade—paradoxical warmth. Considerable patience is required to find such responsive spots on most subjects.

Changing the skin temperature affects sensitivity to touch, vibration, and pain. The temperature in a limited area may be raised by exposing it to a radiant heater or lowered by holding a block of dry ice near the surface. Sensitivity to touch, vibration, and pain can then be tested while the skin surface is at various temperatures. Lowering the skin temperature merely reduces sensitivity. Raising the skin temperature at first makes the skin more sensitive to touch, vibration, and painful stimulation, but with still further increase the sensitivity rapidly falls off [49].

Although these various phenomena do not give a clear and consistent picture of the nature of the skin receptor processes, they do warn against the ready acceptance of any oversimplified theory of their operation.

METHODS OF STUDYING THE ACTUAL NATURE OF STIMULATION

Attempts have been made to measure what actually happens in the skin when mechanical and thermal stimuli are applied, and some illuminating if only partial answers have been obtained.

Mechanical Distortion

To produce an experience of touch, the critical factor is the bending or distortion of the skin and not pressure as such. In small areas, careful pulling on a stimulator glued to the skin produces sensations which are indistinguishable from those obtained by pressing down gently on the same stimulator [8].

No way has been found to estimate the total amount of

skin distortion in any meaningful fashion, but the depth of its depression can be measured. Perhaps the most precise determinations were made by von Bagh [47], who used two different types of apparatus. In one, weights were applied to a balanced arm bearing a stimulator which rested on the skin, as shown in Fig. 6.3. in the other, the stimulator was forced into the skin to a measured depth. With both methods, measurements were made of the minimum depression necessary to arouse a sensation of touch, and the minimum difference in depression which could be detected. Effects of different stimulator areas were also compared. Apparently no similar measurements have been made of stimulation by pulling up instead of pressing down on the skin. The *rate* at which the stimulus is applied is found to be an important factor [20], since the experienced intensity is greater with a faster rate.

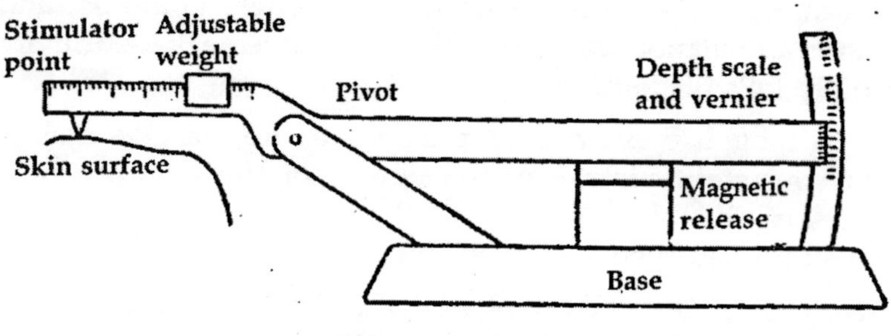

Fig. 6.3. Tactile stimulator. (Adapted from von Bagh [47].]

Skin Vibration and Spread

In vibratory stimulation, measurement is more difficult because the skin is in constant motion. A neat solution involves the use of a neon light interrupted at the same frequency as the vibrating stimulator. Proper adjustment of the light frequency causes the skin to appear to stand still or to move very slowly up and down. The extent of the swing can then be measured on a microscope scale by focusing first at the upper and then at the lower limit of the movement [16]. The amount of spread of vibration to surrounding areas can be determined by using a lightweight phonograph pick-up suspended so as just to make contact with the skin, and then amplifying the result so that it can be measured in a cathode-ray oscilloscope. Vibration applied to the skin at a single point is typically found to spread over a considerable area.

Thermal Changes

Accurate measurements of the heat absorbed by the skin from radiant stimulation can be made by substituting a Hardy radiometer for the subject's skin and repeating the stimulation [37]. Estimates of the actual skin temperature at the instant of stimulation have been attempted by making radiometric measurements 15, 30, and 60 seconds after radiant stimulation [38], but extending this curve of cooling backward to the time of stimulation gives results that are too unreliable to have much meaning. The technique might work better if measurements could be begun immediately after stimulation.

Measurement of temperature changes below the surface of the skin has been attempted with fine wires drawn through the skin to form thermocouple loops [3]. When an ordinary metal stimulator is brought against the skin above the thermocouple junction, the temperature at even a slight depth never fully reaches that of the stimulator. This discrepancy is probably due to the stabilizing action of blood circulation. However, the relatively slow-moving string galvanometer used in this method probably does not reveal the true rate at which the temperature changes occur.

OTHER PROBLEMS AND METHODS

What is actually the greatest bulk of experimental investigations of the skin senses may be grouped under this more miscellaneous heading. Though numerous, these experiments have relatively little to contribute in the way of interesting methods. Problems of localization, two-point threshold, and tactile extent and linearity are peculiar to the skin senses but involve rather simple techniques. Measurements of stimulus thresholds, differential thresholds, reaction times, and adaptation times mainly parallel those in other sensory fields. Perception of the form and motion of objects pressed against the skin follows much the same rules as in visual perception.

Measurements Peculiar to the Skin Senses

Localization two-point threshold, and other problems of spatial discrimination have been studied mainly in relation to touch, although similar questions arise in connection with warm, cold, and pain, where the use of "pure" stimuli uncomplicated by touch is an essential difficulty to be overcome.

If the skin is touched while the subject has his eyes closed, how accurately can he locate the stimulated point ? Results very according to the method of designating the locus, whether by exploring the skin with another stimulator, by pointing to the spot, or by describing its location in relation to coordinates stamped on the skin [34]. Among the factors which have been studied are the influence of age and of training, the effect of moving the stimulated part, comparison of blind and sighted subjects, and the ability to localize two simultaneous stimulations [42]. Localization of painful and thermal stimuli has been less extensively studied.

If the skin is stimulated at two points simultaneously, how far apart must the points be in order to be clearly sensed as separate? This is not a simple matter to determine. Introspectively the change from one to two points is not clean cut but involves a series of transition figures, such as ovals and dumbbells [7]. Consequently, the subject's self-instruction is important. If he reports "two points' as soon as the stimulation is no longer clearly sensed as a single point, the obtained limen is much smaller than if he waits until he clearly perceives two separate points. Partial control of suggestion in this instance might be achieved by actually using oval- and dumbbellshaped stimulators, as well as two separate points. Among the variables studied in the tactile two-point limen are the relative accuracy across the midline of the body, as compared with two stimulations on the same side, the influence of the strength of the stimuli, and the effect of moving the stimuli. Measurement of the successive two-point limen, in which the subject judges whether two successive stimulations are at the same or different places, seems to be simply a special phase of the problem of localization.

How well can a subject discriminate the difference in length of two cardboard edges pressed against the skin [13]? If three points in a line are pressed against the skin, how far must one be displaced to become noticeably out of line? In such experiments it should be noted that pure tactile sensitivity is involved only when the stimulators are pressed against the skin. When the fingers are run along a stimulator, kinesthetic as well as tactile sensitivity comes into play.

Routine Psychophysical Measurements

Determinations of cutaneous stimulus limens, difference limens, reaction times, and adaptation times are basically similar to the analogous measurements in other sensory fields.

The *stimulus limens* for pain, warm, cold, and touch have been measured on various parts of the body, with different sizes of stimulators and under different conditions of adaptation. The more important types of apparatus, such as the Hardy radiant stimulator for warm, cold, and pain, and the von Bagh apparatus for tactile determinations, have already been described. Of special interest in connection with pain is the influence of various drugs, such as aspirin, upon the pain threshold. With vibratory stimulation, thresholds are found to vary at different frequencies, much as is found in hearing. A number of studies have dealt with "threshold lability" [46]. *i.e.*, the tendency for threshold values to rise rapidly under the influence of intermittent stimulation, a condition found most strikingly in certain nervous disorders.

Difference limens, or the smallest detectable difference in pain, warm, cold, and touch, can be measured by applying successive stimulations of different intensity or by changing the intensity of an applied stimulus. The *rate* of stimulus change is an important factor which has frequently been neglected. For example, the difference limen for detecting a change of pressure on the skin is much smaller if the change is made suddenly than if it is introduced gradually.

Reaction times to cutaneous stimulation are measured by the usual chronoscope and reaction-key methods. Reactions to touch involve no complications, but contact stimulation of pain, warm, and cold are complicated by the presence of simultaneous touch, which has a shorter reaction time. Instructing the subject to neglect the touch is scarcely a satisfactory solution. Efforts must be made to eliminate the touch element completely. In radiant stimulation this difficulty does not appear [14].

The measurement of *adaptation time*, or the time for a cutaneous sensation to disappear under continued stimulation, is greatly affected by the standard used by the subject in deciding that a sensation is completely gone. A subject can be trained to give consistent results, but there is no way of telling whether his standard of complete results, but there is no way of telling whether his standard of complete disappearance is the same as that of another subject. Consequently, comparisons from subject to subject are apt to be meaningless. With thermal stimulation the spread of the stimulus can be minimized by surrounding the stimulated area with a metal ring maintained at skin neutral by circulating water. With mechanical stimulation the skin must be fixed in position to prevent movements which would accidentally arouse adjacent regions.

An interesting effect in connection with adaptation is the tendency for a sensation to wax and wane, sometimes disappearing completely and then spontaneously reappearing [43]. Another topic which has not been thoroughly investigated is long-term adaptation in the sense of "getting used" to painful or thermal stimulation as the result of repeated exposure.

Cutaneous Perception

There is a striking similarity between visual perception and cutaneous perception of forms, movement, and apparent movement. Tactile perception of forms and illusions of form have been studied by pressing wooden squares, triangles, etc., against the skin [40]. Tactile perception of actual movement has been studied by moving an air jet across the skin [11]. Tactile appearent movement can be obtained by touching a series of points in rapid succession, giving the illusion of an object being drawn across the skin surface [36]. Thermal perception of form and pattern is rather poor. It has been investigated with warm and cold metal stimulators of various shapes and also by radiant stimulation without contact [44].

Analyses have been made of the experiences of tickle, itch, and burn, but mainly at the level of introspective description. Also attempts have been made to synthesize the experiences of roughness and smoothness [1], moisture [32], and heat [25] by combining various cutaneous stimuli. For example, an illusion of "wetness" can usually be produced by a stimulator that is both cold and slippery, although entirely dry. Some subjects report "heat" when stimulated with a grid of alternate warm and cold tubes, although the effect is difficult to obtain in most naïve individuals. An interesting finding is the dependence of the *Anziehungseffekt* (tendency of a weak touch to seem displaced toward a stronger touch) upon the *perceived* separation of the two points, rather than upon their actual physical separation [33]. This suggests that conditions as perceived might be more important than conditions as they are in our other psychophysical measurements.

SUMMARY OF METHODS OF CUTANEOUS STIMULATION

Although a variety of methods of stimulating the skin have been mentioned in connection with specific problems, it seems well to summarize the chief methods, with some comments on their limitations.

For Touch

The traditional stimulators for mapping touch spots are hairs of differing stiffness, which bend at known pressures. An esthesiometer or a stiff wire operating against a spring acts in a similar fashion. These hand-operating stimulators give control of the maximum pressure applied, but not of the rate of application. For any precise measurements, some sort of mechanically or electrically controlled stimulator is desirable, so that the *rate* of application can be controlled and the depth of the skin distortion measured. The von Bagh apparatus (fig. 3.) represents a type of device that is useful in a number of different kinds of experimental work. Little has been done toward developing methods stimulating the skin by traction (pulling up instead of pressing down), although the same sort of apparatus could be readily adapted for this purpose. Another neglected field is the controlled stimulation of individual hairs on the skin, which, like the cat's whiskers, are extremely sensitive indicators.

For Vibration

Practically all experimenters now use an oscillator to generate the desired frequencies and the analog of a dynamic speaker to transform the electrical oscillations into mechanical vibrations. The use of an interrupted neon light and a microscope to measure the amplitude of skin movement has already been mentioned. Alternating currents applied directly to the skin produce effects similar to those obtained with mechanical vibration [18], although the actual nature of the stimulation is different. An interrupted air jet has also been used for vibratory stimulation, but is a poor method because of the inertia of the individual air puffs.

Vibratory stimulation readily spreads to other parts of the skin, even when the stimulator is a fine needle point. Anesthetizing the skin under the stimulator does not prevent such spreading and may in fact aggravate it, since the anesthetized area tends to vibrate as a whole [48]. The actual extent of spread can be checked by using a lightweight pick-up suspended so a just to make contact with the skin. In addition to spread, another source of confusion is the presence of deep sensitivity, which continues to respond to vibratory stimulation after the skin itself has been completely anesthetized.

For Pain

The chief ways of arousing pain experimentally are by pricking and burning. Any of the devices used for tactile stimulation may be employed to prick the skin by substituting a fine needlepoint for the tactile stimulator. A very fine needle will sometimes penetrate the skin so smoothly as to give pure pain without any accompanying sensation of touch. Heavy pressure with larger stimulators may arouse deep pain, causing some confusion.

Radiant heat has no touch element, and the burning pain can be subjectively discriminated from painless warmth and heat. The Hardy apparatus (Fig. 6.2) is excellent for this purpose. There is some evidence, however, that deep pain can be aroused by strong radiant heat, even when the skin has been anesthetized [39]. Electrical stimulation with high-voltage, low-amperage current give a painless prick which becomes painful with stronger stimulation [5].

For Warm and Cold

Warm and cold sports are usually mapped with a water-circulated stimulator having a circular tip approximately 1 millimeter in diameter [10]. For repeated mapping of a checkerboard pattern, square and oblong stimulators which exactly fit the checkerboard squares may be used [26]. The subjects must be trained to neglect the simultaneous touch sensation and report only experiences of warm and cold.

In the measurement of adaptation times, difference limens, and stimulus limens, the stimulator at neutral temperature can be allowed to rest on the skin until tactile sensation has disappeared. Then the desired temperature can be applied by suddenly changing the temperature of the circulating water. With a very small stimulator, touch can be virtually eliminated by applying the stimulator through a small opening in a neutral field to such a level that the skin is not distorted.

For radiant stimulation the Hardy type of apparatus is

admirably adapted. A block of dry ice can be substituted for the heating clement to obtain "radiant cold." The heat absorbed or lost by the skin during stimulation can be accurately measured by radiometer. Since results obtained from radiant stimulation appear to differ markedly from those secured with contact stimulation, parallel investigations using the two forms are desirable. Diathermy has also been used for thermal stimulation [50], and thermal sensations are aroused when blood circulation is cut off and then suddenly released [2].

Especially in studies of adaptation, false results may arise from the spread of the stimulus beyond the desired area. Spread can be minimized by surrounding the stimulator with a metal ring maintained at skin temperature on by anesthetizing the surrounding region by electroendosmosis [9]. Constriction or dilating of the blood vessels usually accompanies thermal stimulation, but these vascular changes must be considered part of the normal stimulus situation.

REFERENCES

1. Basler, A., and H. Schuster., Uber das Erkennon von "rauh" und "glatt." Z. *Sinnesphysiol.*, 1935, *66*, 33-44.
2. Bazett, H.C., and B. McGlone, Studies in sensation. III. Chemical factor in the stimulation of end-organ giving temperature sensation. *Arch, Neur. Psychial.*, 1932, *28*, 71-91.
3. Bazett, H.C., B. McGlone, and R.J. Brocklehurst, The temperatures in the tissues which accompany temperature sensations. *J. Physiol.*, 1930, *69*, 88-112.
4. Bazett, H.C., B. McGlone, R.G. Williams, and H. M. Lufkin, Sensation. I. Depth, distribution, and probable identification in the prepuce of sensory end-organs concerned in sensations of temperature and touch; thermometric conductivity. *Arch. Neur. Psychict.*, 1932, *27*, 289-517.
5. Bishop, G.H., Responses to electrical stimulation of single sensory units of skin. *J. Neuroplysiol.*, 1943, *6*, 361-328.
6. Bishop, G.H., The peripheral unit for pain. *J. Neurophysiol.*, 1944, *7*, 71-80.
7. Boring, E.G., The stimulus error. *Amer. J. Psychol.*, 1921, *32*,

449-471.

8. Clark, G.P., On certain characteristics of the pressure sensations of the human skin. *Amer. J. Physiol.*, 1898, *1*, 346-358.
9. Cummings, S.B., The effect of local anesthesia on tactile and vibratory thresholds. *J. Exper. Psychol.*, 1938, *23*, 321-338.
10. Dalienbach, K.M., The temperature spots and end-organs. *Amer. J. Psychol.*, 1927, *39*, 402-427.
11. DeCillis, O.E., Absolute thresholds for the perception of tactual movement. *Arch. Psychol.*, No. 294. New York : 1944.
12. Endres, G., Punktions-narkose von Rezeptoren. *Z. Biol.*, 1930, *89*, 436-540.
13. Gatti, A., The perception of space by means of pure sensations of touch. *Amer. J. Psychol.*, 1937, *50*, 289-296.
14. Geblewicz, E., La relation entre l'intensite du stimulus et le temps de reaction pour les excitations thermiques en duree indefinie et en duree breve. *Compte rend. soc. biol.*, 1933, *119*, 1362-1364.
15. Geblewicz, E., L'influence de l'intensite sur la persistence apparente des excitations thermiques pour deux stimulations sucessives. *Compte rend. soc. boil.*, 1933, *127*, 173-175.
16. Geldard, F.A., The perception of mechanical vibration. II. The response of pressure receptors. *J. Gen. Psychol.*, 1940, *22*, 271-280.
17. Gilbert, R.W., Dermal sensitivity and the differentiated nerve terminations of the human skin. *J. Gen. Psychol.*, 1929, *2*, 445-461.
18. Gilmer, B. von H., The sensitivity of the finger to alternating electrical currents. *Amer. J. Psychol.*, 1937, *49*, 444-449.
19. Gilmer, B. von H., The glomus body as a receptor of cutaneous pressure and vibration. *Psychol., Bull.*, 1942, *39*, 73-93.
20. Grindley, G.C., The variation of sensory thresholds with the rate of application of the stimulus. II. Touch and pain. *Brit. J. Psychol.*, 1936, *27*, 189-195.

21. Hardy, J.D., and T.W. Oppel., Studies in temperature sensation. III. The sensitivity of the body to heat and the spatial summation of the endorgan responses. *J. Clin. Investig.*, 1937, *16*, 533-540.

22. Herget, C.M., L. P. Granath, and J.D. Hardy., Warmth sense in relation to skin area stimulated. *Amer. J. Physiol.*, 1941, *135*, 20-26.

23. Hoagland, H., Adaptation of cutaneous tactile receptors. VI. Inhibitory effects and potassium and calcium. *J. Gen. Physiol.*, 1936, *19*, 943, 951.

24. Jenkins, W.L., Studies in thermal sensitivity. 3. Adaptation with a series of small annular stimulators. *J. Exper. Psychol.*, 1938, *22*, 164-177.

25. Jenkins, W.L., Studies in thermal sensitivity. 5. The reactions of untrained subjects to simultaneous warm + cold stimulation. *J. Exper. Psychol.*, 1938, 22, 451-461.

26. Jenkins, W.L., Studies in thermal sensitivity. 12. Part-whole relations in seriatim cold-mapping. *J. Exper. Psychol.*, 1939, *25*, 373-388.

27. Jenkins, W.L., Studies in thermal sensitivity. 16. Further evidence on the effects of stimulus temperature. *J. Exper. Psychol.*, 1941, *29*, 413-419.

28. Jones, F.N., The chronaxy of cold and warmth. *Amer. J. Psychol.*, 1940, *53*, 216-228.

29. Nones, F.N., and M.H. Jones., The chronaxy of pain. *Amer. J. Psychol.*, 1941, *54*, 240-242.

30. Katz, D. ,The vibratory sense and other lectures. *Univ. Maine Bull.*, 1930, 32, 90-104.

31. Lanier, L.H., An experimental study of cutaneous innervation. *Proc Assoc. Res. Neru. Ment. Disease*, 1935, *15*, 437-456.

32. Lauterbach, C.E., and R. E. Crouser., Sensation cues to moisture. *J. Exper. Psychol.*, 1933, *126*, 328-338.

33. Madlung, K., Uber anschauliche and funktionelle Nachbarschaft von Tasteindruckern. *Psychol. Forsch.*, 1935, *19*, 193-236.

34. Munn, N.L., Tactual localization without over localizing

movements and its relation to the concept of local signs as orientation tendencies. *J. Exper. Psychol.*, 1937, *20*, 581-588.

35. Nafe, J.P., Toward the quantification of psychology. *Psychol. Rev.*, 1942, *49*, 1-18.

36. Neuhaus, W., Taktile Scheinbewegung. *Arch. Ges. Psychol.*, 1932, *83*, 519-562.

37. Oppel, T.W., and J.D. Hardy., Studies in temperature sensation. I. A comparison of the sensation produced by infra-red and visible radiation. *J. Clin. Investig.*, 1937, *16*, 517-524.

38. Oppel, T.W., and J.D. Hardy, Studies in temperature sensation. II. The temperature changes responsible for the stimulation of heat and organs. *J. Clin Investig.*, 1937, *16*, 525-531.

39. Rein, H., Beitrage zur Lehre von der Temperaturempfindung der menschlichen Haut. *Z. Biol.*, 1924, *82*, 189-212.

40. Revesz, G., Suystem der optischen and haptischen Raumtauschungen. *Z. Psychol.*, 1934, *131*, 296-375.

41. Rivers, W.H.R., and H. Head, A human experiment in nerve division. *Brain*, 1908, *31*, 323.

42. Schobel, R., Uber die absolute Erkennung zweier Druckreizorte. *Z. Sinnesphysiol.*, 1934, *64*, 310-324.

43. Sjostrand, T., Uder die Enstehung von wiederholten Stichempfindungen, Hyperalgesie, Rotung and Oedem bei kontinuerlicher mechanischer Reizung der Haut mit dem Algesimeter. *Skand. Arch. Physiol.*, 1938, *78*, 17-39.

44. Stone, L.J., An experimental study of form perception in the thermal senses. *Psychol. Rec.*, 1937, *1*, 234-338.

45. Tower, S.S., Unit for sensory reception in cornea. *J. Neurophysiol.*, 1940, *8*, 486-500.

46. Tschlenoff, L., Sensibilitatstudien an Nervenkranken. II., Uber die Schwellenlabilitat der Hautsinne. *Deut. Z. Nervenheilk.*, 1931, *122*, 89-113.

47. Von Bagh, K., Weitere Versuche uber die Summation von gleichzeitigen Beruhrungs. Hzw. Druckreizen. *Deut. Z. Nervenheilk.*, 1936, *140*, 95-101.

48. Weitz, J., Vibratory sensitivity as affected by local anesthesia.

J. Exper, Psychol., 1939, 25, 48-64.

49. Weitz, J., A further study of the relation between skin temperature and cutaneous sensitivity. *J. Exper,Psychol.*, 1942, *30*, 426-431.

50. Windisch, E., Untersuchungen uber den adequaten Reize fur Warmerezeptoren. *Z. Biol.*, 1931, *91*, 126-136.

51. Woollard, H.H., Observations on the terminations of cutaneous nerves. *Brain*, 1935, *58*, 352-367.

7

Studying the Senses of Taste and Smell

The flavour of food, which we often uncritically call taste, is usually a complex experience or perception depending not only on the sense of taste but also on the sense of smell and the

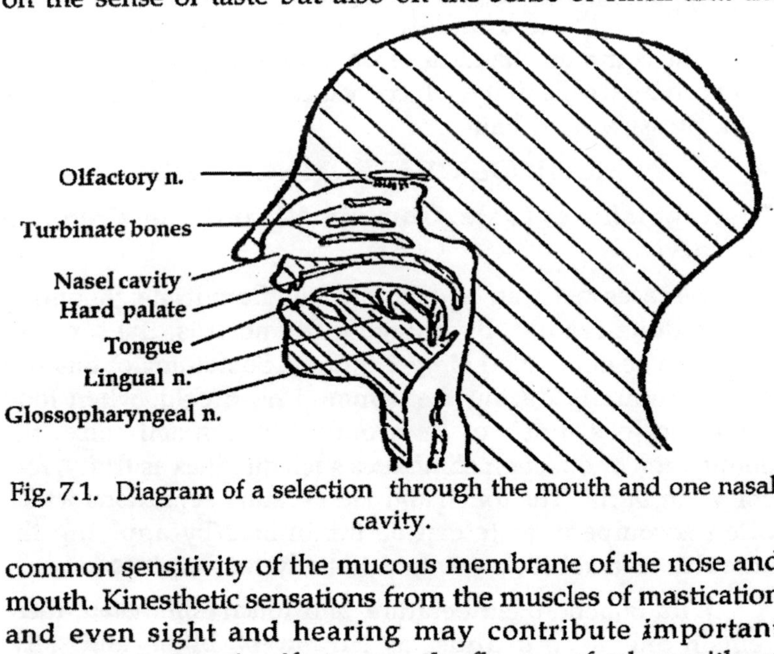

Fig. 7.1. Diagram of a selection through the mouth and one nasal cavity.

common sensitivity of the mucous membrane of the nose and mouth. Kinesthetic sensations from the muscles of mastication and even sight and hearing may contribute important components. Imagine if you can, the flavour of celery without the cool, crisp feel and crunchy sound as you chew the fresh, stalk. Coolness, feel, and sound are not true taste qualities. It is with true taste that you appreciate the flavour of salt, citric acid, sugar, or quinine ; it is largely by odor that you know the flavour of fruit, coffee, or butter.

Anatomical studies have shown that olfactory sense organ consists of small patch of nervous tissue located in the upper recesses of the nasal passages. The sense organs of taste consist of small goblet- shaped sense cells primarily in the fungiform and circumvallate papillae of the tongue, although some taste buds may be found on adjacent structures, such as the epiglottis and soft palate. The sense organs of the common sensitivity are nerve endings throughout the mucosa of the nose and mouth. The relative position of these sensory areas is shown in Fig. 7.1.

This chapter will discuss methods of investigating taste and smell. For the present purposes the sensitivity of the mucous membrane to mildly irritating chemicals, called by some the common chemical sense, will be included under the term common sensitivity, which includes sensitivity to warmth, cold, pressure, and pain.

METHODS OF STUDYING TASTE

Distinguishing Taste from Smell and the Common Sensitivity

In some cases taste can be distinguished from its neighbouring senses quite readily. By plugging the nostrils, the sense of smell can be eliminated almost entirely. Something of this sort occurs naturally during the common head cold, when food seems to lose much of its aroma. More specifically, the elimination of olfaction eliminates such qualities as fruity, foul spicy , or burnt. The touch and temperature sensations which often accompany taste can be minimized by applying the stimulus as a solution warmed to body temperature.

With olfaction, temperature, and touch eliminated, there remain only such qualities as our, sweet, bitter, and salty. These are the true taste qualities, for they can be elicited only from areas knows to possess taste buds. Very weak acid solutions, for example, will arouse no sensation from the gums, cheeks, or undersurface of the the tongue, but will call out a definite our taste on the tip and sides of the tongue, where taste buds are found in great abundance. Stronger acids may call out the additional quality of pain or sharpness. This however, occurs everywhere in the mouth and must therefore be an added component form the common sensitivity of the mucosa.

Methods of Studying Taste Qualities and Their Sensory Basis

The relation of taste quality to stimulus composition is most commonly investigated in man by one of the integrative stimulation methods, in which the solution spreads over a large part of the tongue surface to stimulate as many receptors as possible. In general such methods are standardized versions of normal sipping or tasting. In other cases small amounts of fluid are dropped on the partially extended tongue by means of a pipette or medicine dropper (drop method). Appropriate intervals (1/2 to 5 minutes) between stimuli avoid adaptation or contrast effects, and a delay of 2 or more hours after eating minimizes taste aftereffects from the food .

In certain experiments the subject is asked merely to describe the taste experience as accurately as possible. In other instances he may compare the test sample with standard solutions possessing pure salty, sweet, sour, or bitter tastes. Both methods show that many different substances have pure sweet, sour, or bitter tastes, whereas the pure salty taste is elicited only by sodium chloride. All other salts give rise to complex tastes which can be matched by mixtures of solutions, as specified by the following mixture equation [40, p. 455] :

$$N = xA + yB + zC + vD$$

where N is the concentration of substance giving the compund taste, matched by a mixture of x. y, z, and v concentrations of the bitter, salty, sour, and sweet standard solutions, respectively. It is important to specify the concentration at which such qualitative comparisons are made, for taste quality often changes as the concentration increases. Saccharine in dilute solutions tastes sweet ; in stronger solutions the taste is bitter.

In general it may be said that acids have a sour taste, a large number of alkaloids a bitter taste, many carbohydrates a sweet taste, and many salts a complex salty taste. It should be pointed out, however, that there are many exceptions to this simple rule. Certain substances radically different from the sugars in chemical composition, such as saccharine, lead acetate, and various alcohols, have sweet tastes that are indistinguishable from each other.

In the method of punctate stimulation the stimulus is restricted to a single point or small area on the tongue. It was by a gross form of this method, as mentioned above, that the end organs for taste were identified. The qualities of salty, sour, bitter and sweet could be elicited only from areas known to contain taste buds.

"Inadequate" stimulation by electric currents is well suited to the punctate method. Since stimulation takes place through metal wire or wick type of electrodes, these can be placed on a particular tongue region with great accuracy. There is no danger of the stimulus diffusing away from the point of application, as might occur with solutions.Monopolar stimulation occurs when one terminal of a battery is connected to a single electrode on the tongue, and the other terminal to a large indifferent electrode on some other part of the body. If the tongue electrode is attached to the positive pole of the battery, a sour taste will result ; if the tongue electrode is negative, the taste is alkaline [29]. With bipolar electrodes, *i.e.*, both leads on the tongue, or faradic or alternating currents, the taste may be complex. The essential point for our purpose is that no "electric taste" is elicited from these regions devoid of taste buds.

To use the punctate method with liquid stimuli, small brushes saturated with taste solutions are most commonly

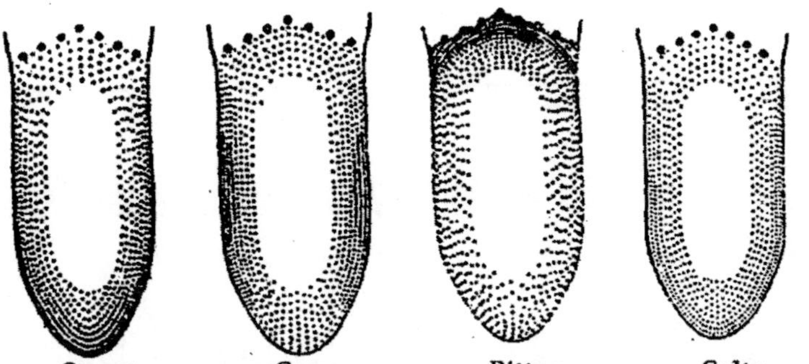

Fig. 7.2. Diagram showing the relative sensitivity of the tongue for the different tastes.

The regions of greatest sensitivity, *i.e.*, with the lowest threshold by the greatest density of dots. (After Hanig [19].)

employed. By this means the sensitivity of the tongue to each of the four basic tastes has been mapped. The tip of the tongue is most sensitive to sweet, the sides to sour, the back to bitter, and the tip and sides to salty, as shown in Fig. 7.2 [19]. This distribution suggests that the four qualities of taste are mediated by four types of receptor organ. If all tastes depended on the same receptor organ, every region of the tongue should be equally sensitive.

If very small brushes are used, so that individual papillae can be stimulated, the majority of papillae will be sensitive to all taste stimuli. A small number, however will respond exclusively to salt, sweet, or sour stimuli [26]. This suggests that certain papillae may contain only one type of taste receptor.

The four taste qualities can be further dissociated by the suppressor action of certain durgs. In weak concentrations cocaine primarily reduces bitter sensitivity ; another substance, gymnenic acid, depresses sweet sensitivity [39].

It will be noted that the methods so far described are indirect, in that they depend on correlations between the stimulus and response of the intact organism. Changes in threshold or in the quality of the sensation are believed to reflect changes in the sense organ, providing, of course, that

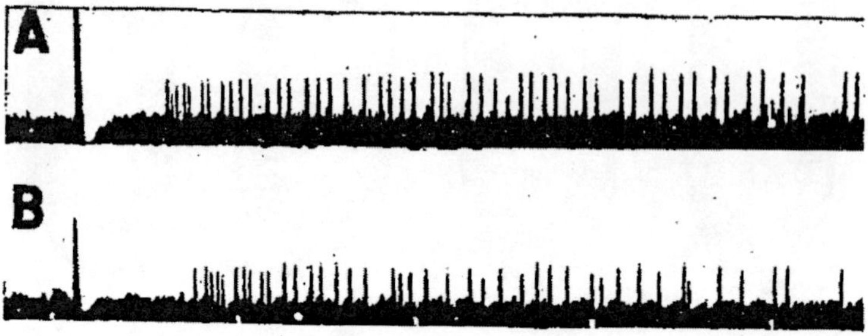

Fig. 7.3. Record of a single nerve fiber preparation responding to acid on the tongue.

The large initial upward deflection signals the time of applying the stimulus. This is followed by the train of nerve impulse spikes. (A) stimulus 0.5 N acetic acid. (B) stimulus 0.01 *N* hydrochloric acid. Each white time mark at base of record (B) indicates 1/10 second.

such factors as fatigue, inattention, and practice have been adequately controlled. The development of electrophysiological methods in recent years permits a more direct attack on the analysis of sensory function. It is now possible to record with an electronic amplifier and oscillograph the nerve impulses in a sensory nerve fibre following stimulation of its associated sense organ. In one study single afferent nerve fibers in the nerves from the tongue of the cat were dissected under a binocular microscope and placed upon the recording electrodes. The discharge in a typical single nerve-fiber preparation from the chorda tympani nerve is illustrated in Fig. 7.3. Instead of four type of single nerve fiber, each responding only to acid, salt, sugar, or quinine, as might have been expected from the evidence presented so far, only three types of single nerve fibre were found. One was activated only by acids, a second by both acids and sodium chloride, and a third by acids and quinine. No single fibre preparations responsive to sugar were found. These results confirm the view that there are different types of taste receptor but suggest further that these receptor types do not necessarily correspond to the four fundamental taste qualities [34].

Methods of Studying Taste Sensitivity

Most techniques in this category are primarily concerned with taste sensitivity as a whole. Differences in sensitivity from one part of the tongue to another are averaged by applying the stimulus to a large area of the tongue. In man the stimuli may be applied by any of the integrative methods already

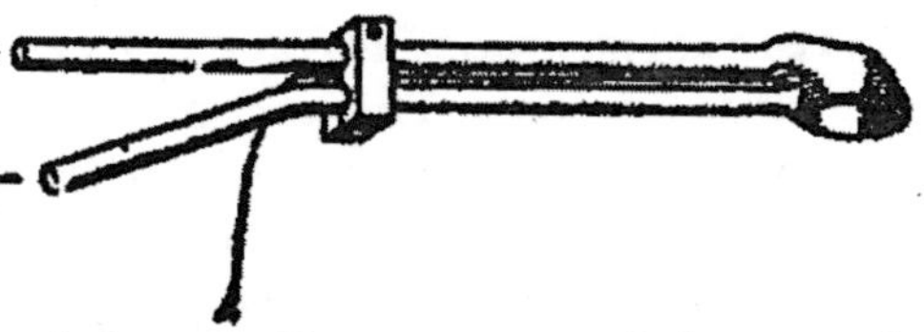

Fig. 7.4. One type of glass applicator to control the area of taste stimulation.

The applicator operture is placed on the subject's tongue. The inlet is connected to a system of tubes so that various solutions can be directed through apparatus.

described, such as the drop method or sipping method. Of these, the sipping method will give lower and less variable values of the absolute threshold [38]. In certain cases where precise control of such factors as the area, pressure, temperature, and duration of stimulation is required, some form of applicator may be employed [17, 23, 32]. One such device is shown in Fig. 7.4. The most frequently employed psychophysical procedures are the methods of constant stimull, single stimuli, and limits. In the method of limits the descending series is often omitted, because the aftertastes of the suprathreshold stimuli in the early part of the descending series tend to mask the weaker stimuli in the later part of the series.

Studies indicate that marked differences in taste sensitivity may exist even in a relatively small group of individuals. In a group of forty-seven subjects the thresholds for different taste stimuli distribute over the ranges shown in Fig. 7.5. Note that one substance, phenyl thiocarbamide (PTC), has an unusually wide range of thresholds [7]. This substance has been employed in tests of "taste blindness." Persons unable to taste PTC crystals are known as "non-tasters." Actually such individuals are not taste blind. They are only relatively insensitive, for with sufficiently strong stimuli their thresholds can be reached. In Fig. 7.5. their values would lie in the upper part of the distribution curve for PTC. The notion of taste blindness as an all-or-none attribute gained credence largely as a result of early tests with the commercial crystals. In this form the stimulus cannot be graded in intensity so that the subject either tastes or does not taste. This dichotomy is quite arbitrary [7]. If the commercial crystals are purified, a more effective stimulus can be obtained, and some of the "non-tasters" will become "tasters." This is an important point of methodology, for it shows how experimental results may be influenced by the method of measurement.

It is of particular interest that taste sensitivity in the same person may change from day to day and even during the same day. Such variations probably reflect changes in the physiological state of the individual. The direct action of chemical agents in the blood has been demonstrated in a number of cases. For example, decholin (a bittertasting substance) gives rise to a bitter taste shortly after injection directly into the blood stream [20]. Stimulation sufficient to elicit a sensation in this way probably occurs only if the change in the blood takes place suddenly. Normally, the taste receptors are in a state of equilibrium with the chemicals in the blood. As these blood factors change slowly, there may be corresponding changes in the sensitivity of the receptor. With high concentrations of sodium chloride in the blood, for example, it would be expected that the threshold for the same substance applied to the tongue would be high. With a lower concentration the threshold might be lower.

Methods which depend upon unlearned feeding preferences or aversions have been employed primarily in animal studies. To determine sodium chloride preference thresholds, for example, the animals, placed in individual living cages, are provided with two graduated drinking bottles. After they have become adjusted to situation and are drinking about

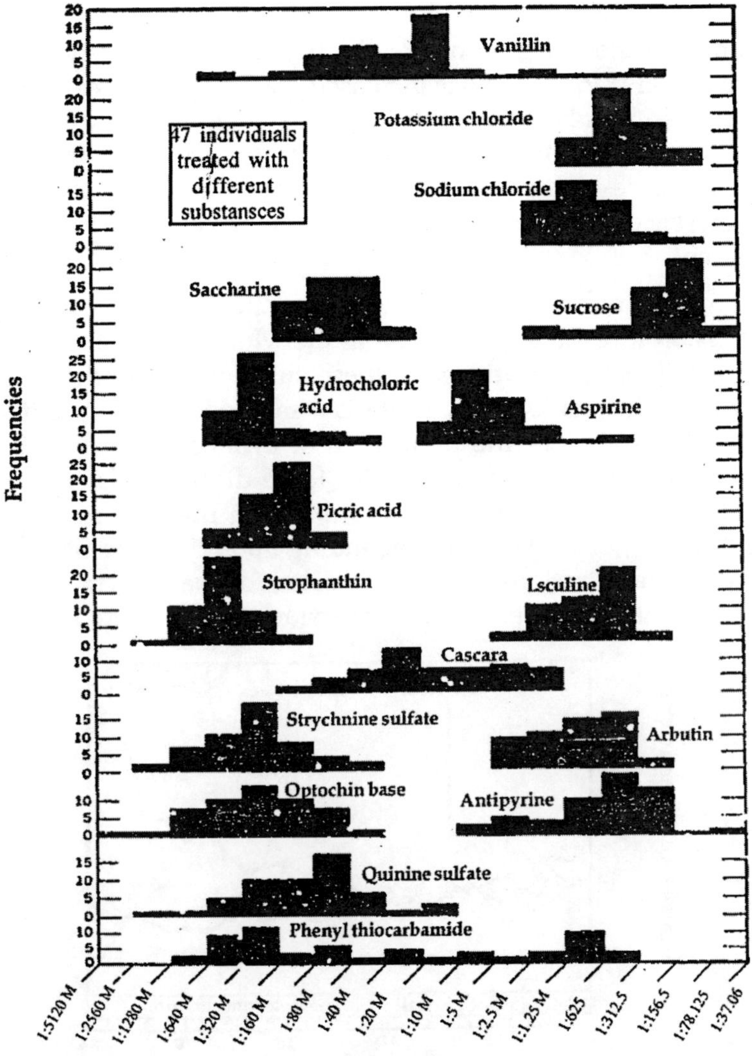

Fig. 7.5. Graphs showing the distributions of thresholds in 47 individuals for different substances.

Values indicated at the base line range from a dilution of 1 part in 5,120,000 (1.5120m where m = 1000) to 1 part in 39.06 parts of water (1.39.06). (From Blakeslee and Salmon [7].)

equal amounts of water from each bottle, sodium chloride is added to the water in one of the bottles. On successive days the concentration of salt is increased gradually until the animal consistently takes more salt than water. The concentration at which the animal first shows a preference for salt is the preference threshold concentration. See Fig. 7.6. This preference is abolished when the taste nerves to the tongue are cut.

The preference threshold for sodium chloride and the aversion threshold for quinine in the white rat agree with the threshold concentrations for these substances found in man by other means [37, 42]. There is a methodological question, however, whether the preference or aversion threshold is a true index of sensitivity. Studies to be discussed later show that in man, the same taste substance may be pleasant, indifferent, or unpleasant, depending upon the concentration. Weak concentrations of quinine sulfate, for example, may have a pleasant taste. Preference or aversion may be related to that

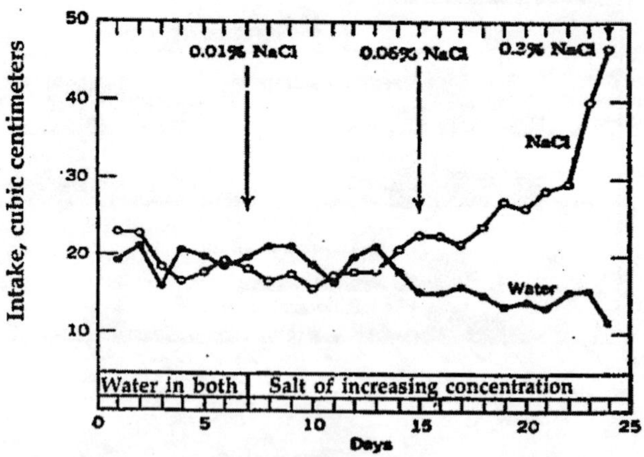

Fig. 7. 6. Graph showing the sodium chloride preference threshold for 12 rats.

At 0.06% the animals begin to show a definite preference for salt solution, which becomes greater as the concentration increases. (from unpublished results of J.K. Bare.)

factor in man known as the pleasantness or unpleasantness of taste.

Closely related to the above procedure is the method of observing reflexes or the modifications of reflex activities after taste stimulation. The sucking response is particularly suited to suited to studies of taste in infants and young mammals. Although the early workers simply observed the sucking movements when taste stimuli were introduced into the mouth,

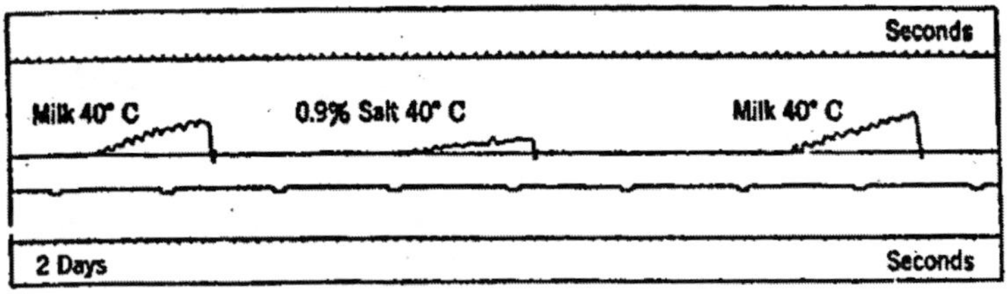

Fig. 7.7. Polygraph record showing a differential response to 0.9% sodium cholride compared to the normal sucking response to milk. (After Jensen [24].)

later investigators graphically recorded the sucking reflex by utilizing pressure and volume changes in the nursing bottle as the fluid was sucked out [24, 33]. A modified nursing bottle was connected by a system of tubes to the recording bellows of a polygraph or kymograph. Figure 7.7 shows the response to 0.9 per cent sodium chloride, a concentration above threshold for the particular child studied. Thresholds defined as the concentration that caused a just noticeable distortion of the sucking response were found to range between 0.2 and 0.9 per cent for one group of infants.

Methods for Studying Suprathreshold Stimuli

The disignation or specification of taste intensity for concentrations above the threshold is of practical as well as theoretical interest [8]. One common method for designating the strength of a sweetening agent is in terms of a standard substance, such as cane sugar. The sweetness grade is given by the number of grams of cane sugar required to match 1 gram of test substance in sweetness when both are dissolved in equal volumes of water. By this measure, fructose was found

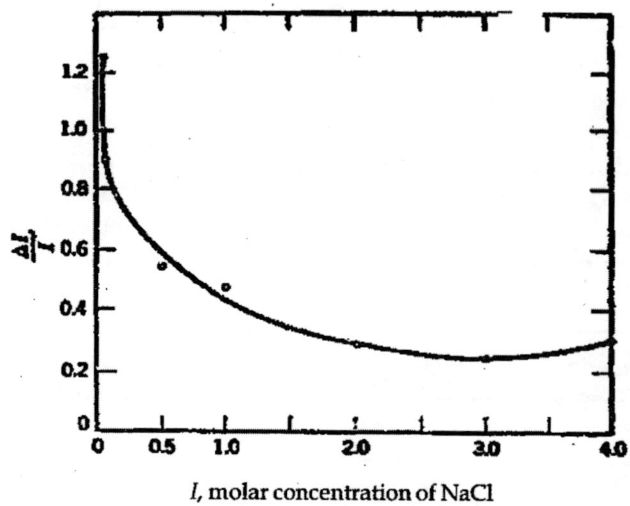

Fig. 7.8. The change in the value of the Weber fraction ΔI/I as a function of intensity I. (From A. H. Holway and L. M. Hurvich [22].)

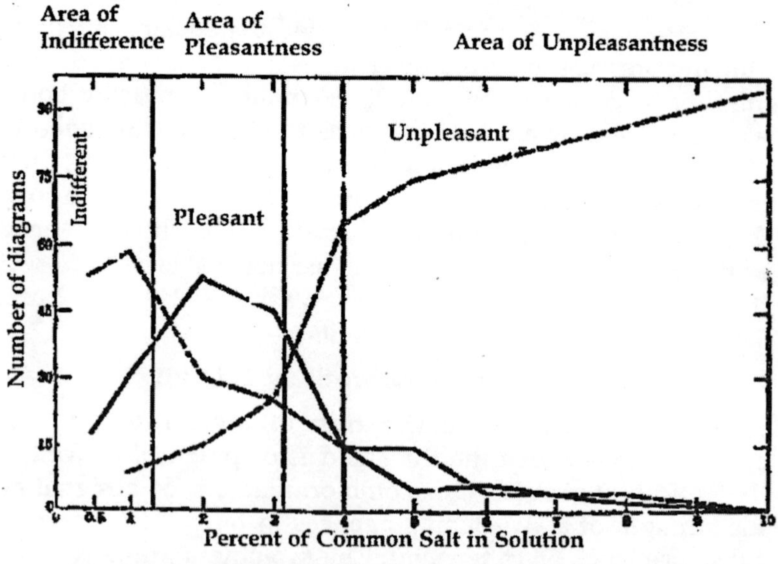

Fig. 7.9. Graph showing the number of indifferent, pleasant, and unpleasant judgments made by 7 observers for different concentrations of sodium chloride.
(After Engel [14].)

to have a value of 1.05. Since 1.05 grams of sucrose were required to match 1 gram of fructose, fructose is the sweeter of the two substances. Glucose and lactose have values of 0.53 and 0.27 respectively and are therefore less sweet. This method holds only for the particular concentration at which the comparisons are made. As concentration increases, some substances become relatively less sweet [40].

That latter effect presumably depends on the fundamental relation between subjective intensity and objective stimulus intensity. The study of intensity discrimination in taste shows a relation similar to that for other senses [22]. As the concentration increases, the value of $\Delta I/I$ for the taste of sodium chloride decreases as shown in Fig. 7.8. At higher intensities, a relatively smaller increase in the stimulus is required in order to produce a just noticeable increment in taste.

In addition to these effects, changes in the intensity of taste stimulation are usually associated with changes in the pleasantness or unpleasantness of taste. When we use salt, pepper, vinegar, or other condiments to improve palatability of food, our recipe usually calls for just enough to give a good taste, but not so much as to be too strong and unpleasant. The relation of hedonic tone, *i.e.,* pleasantness or unpleasantness, to the intensity of stimulation can perhaps be demonstrated better in taste than in any other sense field. In Fig. 7.9. the degree of pleasantness or unpleasantness of salt solutions of different concentration is shown [14]. The method of single stimuli was employed. The subject reported whether the taste was pleasant, unpleasant, or indifferent. For weak concentrations around 0.5 percent the judgments of indifferent predominate. At 2 per cent the pleasant judgments predominate ; for concentrations for 4 per cent and up the taste is mostly unpleasant. Acid solutions show the same progressive changes as intensity is increased. Certain other substances, like sugar, are pleasant for nearly all concentrations, whereas others, like quinine, are unpleasant in nearly all but the weakest concentrations.

Such findings are representative of most individuals. Nevertheless, there are certain persons whose judgments of pleasantness and unpleasantness may diverge. Whereas most people dislike strong salt, a few may like it. Although most people find sugar pleasant in all concentrations, some may dislike it. In one experiment two subjects were found who had such a dislike for sugar. Their judgments for concentrations above 9 per cent, which most people like, were predominantly unpleasant. Both subjects reported excessive indulgence of sweets in their youth. Just how such past experiences or current daily variations in physiological state in response to nutritional needs may influence the hedonic tone of taste stimuli is not yet understood and is a fertile field for further investigation.

METHODS OF STUDYING OLFACTION

As we have seen, independent stimulation of smell or taste is possible only under certain conditions. In olfaction, it is particularly difficult to eliminate those extraneous effects due to the common sensitivity of the nasal mucosa. Such double action occurs with ammonia, which has, in addition to its characteristic odor, a strong, irritating effect leading to such obvious reflex acts as crying and sneezing. The methods by which these effects have been shown to depend on the nerve endings of the nasal mucous membrane as well as on the sense of smell will be discussed in the following section.

In all investigations of olfactory sensitivity, several general precautions must be observed. Wherever possible, pure chemicals are employed to avoid contamination by small amounts of impurity, which are capable of severely altering the odor. The experimental rooms for olfactory investigation are well ventilated, and precautions against the clinging of odorous substances to rubber tubing, stoppers, glassware, etc., are taken. Stimulation in most cases is achieved by introducing the odorous vapor into the nostrils, either through a system of tubes inserted into the nostrils or by active sniffing on the part of the subject when a flask is brought close to the nostrils. The odor may be applied to both nostrils (dirhinic) or to one nostril (monorhinic), or a different odor may be presented to each nostril separately (dichorhinic).

Methods of Distinguishing Olfaction from the Common Sensitivity and Taste

The difference between true smell and the common sensitivity can be demonstrated rather simply by means of a menthol nasal inhalator sold commercially for the relief of head colds. When the inhalator is inserted in the nostrils in the usual way, the cool sharp menthol odor is perceived. If the subject now places the inhalator to the lips while holding the nostrils closed, the sharpness and coolness will be felt in the mouth. The aromatic true smell of menthol will not be experienced, however, until the nostrils are opened and the air currents of normal respiration can carry the odor into the nasal passage by way of the posterior nares. The contribution of taste to other odors can be investigated similarly with inhalators containing other substances.

Surgical dissociation of olfaction and the common sensitivity has been employed in animal experiments [3]. It is possible to remove the nerve supply to the mucous membrane of the nose by cutting certain branches of the Vth cranial nerve (trigeminal), so that only the sense of smell remains. This preparation is known as an olfactory animal. In other animals the sense of smell can be removed by cutting the Ist cranial nerve (olfactory), leaving only the common sensitivity in a so-called trigeminal animal. The insufflation of ammonia or other irritants leads to marked changes in respiration and blood pressure in both types, as well as in the normal animal. Both olfaction and the common sensitivity therefore are stimulataed by such irritants. Animals so prepared have been employed in other experiments on olfaction.

The method of localization, an indirect method for use in man, assumes that only those stimuli which activate the common sensitivity can be localized in the right or left nostril when monorhinal stimulation is employed. Pure olfactory stimulants cannot be so localized [40]. Another indirect method, that of stream injection [13], defines pure olfactory stimulants as those which do not lead to pain or crying when a stream of the odorous vapor is continuously injected into the nostrils at a known rate of flow. During such tests the subject breathes through the mouth. Very few odors have been found that do not lead to pain. Even many of the stimuli classed as pure olfactory stimulants by the method of localization have been found to produce pain under these conditions. Clinical experience with this test suggests that certain brain tumors may impair true olfaction with little effect on the common sensitivity.

Methods of studying Olfactory Qualities and Their Discrimination

Early classifications of odors were based in part on the literature of the perfume industry and to some extent on apparent resemblances and relations among groups of odors as experienced by casual observers. The work of Henning [21] is noteworthy as an attempt to derive a classification based on the description of odors by both trained and untrained observers and on the serial arrangements of odors when a number of scents were presented to the subject for such arrangement. Over 400 scents were employed in these experiments. They were contained in wide-mouthed, stoppered bottles which could be held under the subject's nostrils for dirhinic stimulation.

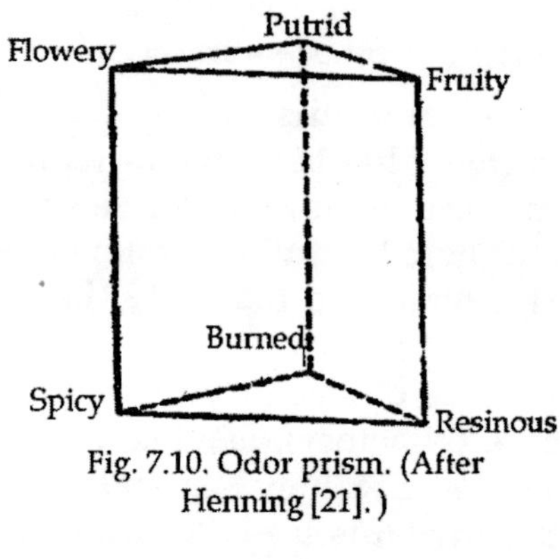

Fig. 7.10. Odor prism. (After Henning [21].)

The schema shown in Fig. 7.10 was devised to show the interrelations among the various odor qualities as indicated by these experiments. This is the odor prism, of which only the surfaces represent the psychological dimensions. No odor qualities are represented in the interior. Odors along an edge resemble the corners bounding that edge; the odors on the surface resemble all corners in proportion to the distance from the point to each of the corners. Other workers attempting to validate this schema have obtained variable results [11, 16, 30]. All agree that the precision of representation on this figure does not compare with that for the colour double pyramid. On the other hand, the odor prism more or less represents the relations existing in the manifold of odor sensations. More recently, other workers [9] have reduced these six salient qualities to four—fragrant, acid, burnt, and caprylic or goaty—in developing a nomenclature for practical work.

The method of differential exhaustion should be mentioned for completeness, although it has not yet been successfully applied to the analysis of the fundamental olfactory qualities [29]. This method depends on the fact that olfactory fatigue is often selective. Fatiguing the sense of smell by ammonium sulfide reduces the sensitivity to hydrogen sulfide, hydrochloric acid, and bromine, whereas the sensitivity to etherial oils is unaffected. The conclusion seems warranted that all of the first group of substances act on the same sense organs, whereas the etherial oils stimulate a different group of receptors. Such groupings might serve as the basis for a classification of odors.

The correlation between the stimulus for smell and the quality of the odor is difficult to establish, largely because the exact nature of the adequate stimulus is unknown. In many cases the aromatic fraction of naturally occurring odorous objects has been isolated and identified. The odor of roses, for example, is due in great measure to geroniol, yet the odor of the natural plant extract can be matched only if a small amount of the genuine extract is added to synthetic geroniol, [35]. Of the chemical elements, only the halogens—bromine iodine, fluorine, and chlorine—appear to be odorous. The great majority of odorous substances are organic compounds, *i.e.*, compounds containing carbon.

The electrophysiological technique has proved less effective for investigations of olfaction than for taste. So far, the electrical activity in the olfactory bulb, olfactory tract, and other parts of the brain has been recorded [2,5]. All these structures are one or more synapses removed from the primary sense cells. The latter are virtually inaccessible, since the fine nerve filaments leading from the olfactory epithelium pass through perforations in the floor of the cranium to enter the olfactory bulb of the brain directly.

The earliest studies on the olfactory sensitivity of animals were based simply on observations of their general behaviour when confronted with olfactory stimuli. Numerous incidental observations on olfaction have been made in connection with studies of maze learning, food selection, and mating behaviour. For the white rat the standard discrimination box of the Waston-Yerkes type, modified to permit olfactory stimulation, has not proved very successful [27]. More success has been obtained with a technique in which the animal can reach a food box by digging through one of two tunnels filled with scented wood shavings. One of the scents is the cue for the open tunnel. On successive trials the odor stimuli are alternated from one side to the other in chance order. Discrimination between butyric acid and a disinfectant, trail scent and gasoline, anise and a disinfectant, and male and female odors was established [41]. Another method was employed recently, in which the stimulus containers were fashioned from three small blocks of wood, each containing a smaller well provided with glass container at the bottom and covered with a perforated sliding metal cover, which the rats could pull open [28]. The blocks were impregnated with paraffin so that they could be washed and recoated to remove odors. One block was placed in each of the three corners of a square cage, and the rat was admitted at the fourth corner. Milksoaked bread was placed in one well, and cotton with a few drops of oil of wintergreen was placed in the others. The position of the blocks was varied in random order during the trials. Any attempt by the rat to open the cover of a well not containing food was counted as an error. The discrimination between milk-soaked bread and oil of wintergreen established in this situation was lost when the olfactory bulbs were removed.

Conditioned reflex methods were early applied to the determination of the olfactory sensitivity of the dog [36]. In a recent study leg withdrawal to electric shock was conditioned to the presentation of an odorous vapor 7 seconds before the shock [4]. Stimuli were presented in wide-mouthed bottles held before the animal's nostrils. Bottles containing no odor were presented periodically as a control. In some cases the stimuli were delivered by means of a system of tubes opening close to the animal's snout. This proved less convenient because of the time between trials required to free the room of the odor. Normal, olfactory, and trigeminal dogs could be conditioned in 15 to 25 trials. Certain substances, such as cloves, lavender, anise, and asafetida, give rise to conditioned reflexes only in the olfactory animal. Camphor, butyric acid, ether, and chloroform could be conditioned in both olfactory and trigeminal animals.

Methods of Studying Sensitivity

Absolute threshold values in man are frequently stated in terms of the minimal concentration, *i.e.*, milligrams per liter of air, that can be detected. Starting with a given weight of odorous material evaporated in a container of known volume, the subject sniffs at the mouth of a series of flasks of increasing dilution until he is no longer able to detect the odor. For ethyl alcohol the threshold figure is 200 milligrams per liter; for musk vanillan or skatol the figure may be as low as 0.001 milligram per liter. The actual quantity as the stimulus will be some fraction of this figure, since only a portion of the inspired air reaches the olfactory receptor [10].

Other more elaborate ways of controlling the strength of odor have been employed. In one apparatus [6] a series of flow meters indicated the rate at which pure air bubbled through a chamber containing the odorous material. From the weight lost by the material after known volumes of air had passed over it, the concentration could be calculated. This concentration could be diluted by mixture with air in varying proportions, as indicated by another system of low meters. The stimuls mixture was led to a funnel placed over the subject's nostrils. Artificial musk could be detected with this apparatus in concentrations as low as 0.00004 milligram per liter of air.

Threshold values stated in relative terms have proved useful for measures of the lower threshold in different individuals, for measures of differential sensitivity, for measures of changes in sensitivity in the same individuals as a result of adaptation or other factors, for studies of the interaction or neutralization of odors, and for studies of the relative stimulating efficiency of different substances. One simple procedure is to determine the greatest distance from the blindfolded subject at which the odor of an opened odor bottle can be detected. The more sensitive subject will detect the odor at a greater distance A more quantitative procedure makes use of the olfactometer devised by Zwaardemaker [43]. The essential feature of this instrument is an odor tube of glass which can be slipped inside a larger rubber tube or hollow kaolin cylinder impregnated with odorbearing material, as in Fig. 7.11. The outer kaolin cylinder is encased with glass or otherwise sealed from the atmosphere of the room. When the glass tube is pushed all the way through the odor tube, no odorous material is imparted to the air stream being drawn though the tube. As the glass tube is pulled out to expose more and more odor-bearing surface, the concentration of the odorous material in the air stream is said to increase proportionately to the extent of the surface exposed. One end of the glass tube is curved upward, so that it can be inserted into the nostrils. The flow of air through the olfactometer is

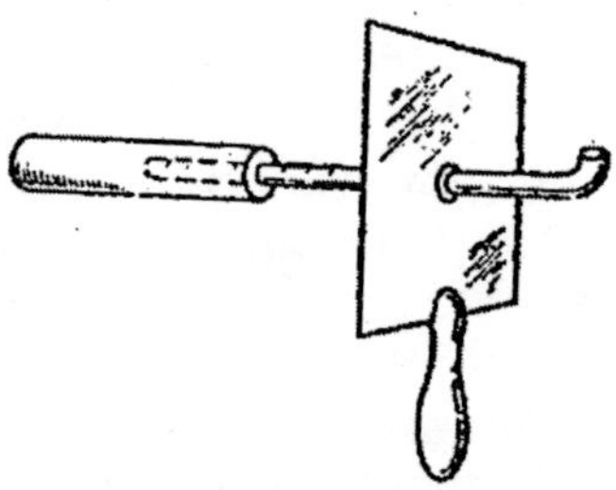

Fig. 7.11. Olfactometer. (After Zwaardemaker [43].)

controlled by the subject's inspiration. All parts of the apparatus except the nasal tip are concealed by a screen. Sensitivity is measured in terms of the *olfactie,* the length of the odor-bearing surface exposed to the current of air as measured in centimeters. Stimulation may be monorhinic, dirhinic, or with the double olfactometer, consisting of two odorous cylinders leading separately to each nostril, dichorhinic. It is by the use of the double olfactometer that the interaction and neutralization of odors have been most extensively studied Various modifications of this or similar principles have been developed for practical purposes [15].

In most of the procedures so far discussed, the subject draws the odorous vapor into the nostrils by inspiration. Variations in the force and rate of inspiration might influence the values obtained. These factors have been controlled in recently developed procedure, the blast injection method, in which the odor is forcefully injected into the subject's nostrils [12]. The odorous material is contained in a 500-cubic-centimeter bottle closed by a stopper except for an inlet and outlet tube. The inlet is connected to a hypodermic syringe ; the outlet, to a double or single nasal tip by means of a rubber tube that is normally closed by a strong pinch clip. The pressure in the bottle is raised by injecting a few cubic centimeters of air into the bottle with the syringe. If the nosepiece is then inserted into the nostrils and the pinch clip suddenly released, a volume of odorous gas equal to that introduced into the bottle is injected into the nostrils. Thresholds are stated in terms of the number of cubic centimeters that must be injected before the olfactory sensation occurs or the substance is correctly identified. From an analysis

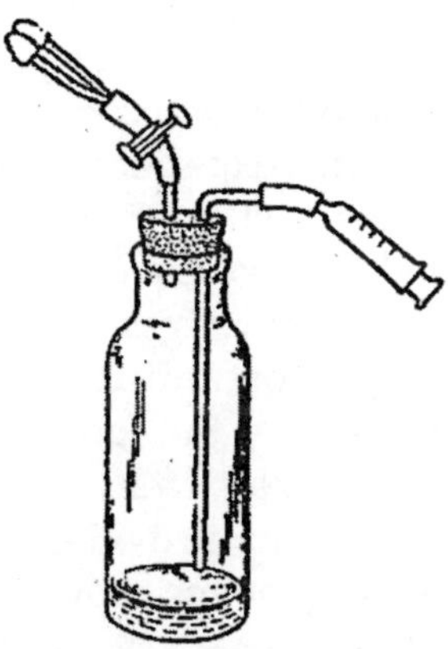

Fig. 7.12. Blast injection method. (After Elsberg [12].)

of pressure-volume relations it appears that the pressure of the injection, and not the amount of vapor injected, is directly related to stimulation [25]. Approximately the same injection pressure is required over a wide range of volumes when bottles of different volumes are employed as the odor container. The exact significance of this fact in terms of the process of stimulation is not clear. Further investigation of this point is needed.

CONCLUSION

The student will have noted that the analytical and quantitative approach to the study of taste and smell has been emphasized. To be sure, our daily experiences with these senses is rarely analytical in character. Our selection and enjoyment of food is based on flavour, the composite of taste, smell, and the common sensitivity. Yet the contribution of each to the composites must be known if we are to understand how the complex experience comes about. The professional tea or wine taster distinguishes between the nose and the tongue in making his tests. He first smells and then tastes the sample under investigation according to a schedule that will avoid adaptation and fatigue effects. A recent volume on flavour written for the food industry says, "Sensation analysis. . . . , considered first from a theoretical and then a practical standpoint, provides a unifying basis for a mass of otherwise heterogeneous matter" [9].

We have seen that there are at least two major difficulties in the study of taste and smell. The first is largely instrumental, resulting from the difficulty of presenting the chemical stimulus in a convenient and highly controlled way. Although various applicators and injectors have been developed, these do not approach the accuracy of control which is attainable with visual and auditory stimulation.

Even more fundamental is our lack of knowledge of the true stimulus for taste and for smell. The stimulus property that makes sugar and all other sweet-tasting substances sweet has not yet been determined. There is no logical unification of the many relations between chemical constitution and taste and smell. It is for this reason, perhaps, as much as any other, that the experimental study of taste and smell has been retarded.

REFERENCES

1. Abrahams, H., D. Krakauuer, and K.M. Dallenbach, Gustatory adaptation to salt. *Amer. J. Psycholl.*, 1937, *49*, 462-469.
2. Adrian, E.D., Olfactory reactions in the brain of the nedgehog. *J. Physiol.*, 1942, *100*, 459-473.
3. Allen, W.F., Effect on respiration, blood pressure, and carotid pulse of various inhaled and insufflated vapors when stimulating one cranial nerve and various combinations of cranial nerves. *Amer. J. Physiol.*, 1929, *88*, 117-29.
4. Allen, W. F., Olfactory and trigeminal conditioned reflexes in dogs. *Amer. J. Physiol.*, 1937, *118*, 553-539.
5. Allen, W. F., Distribution of cortical potentials from insufflation of vapors into the nostrils and from stimulation of olfactory bulbs and pyriform lobe. *Amer. J. Physiol.*, 1943, *139*, 553-555.
6. Allison, V.C., and S.H. Katz., An investigation of stenches and odors for industrial purposes. *J. Indus. Eng. Chem.*, 1919, *11*, 336-338.
7. Blakeslee, A.F., and T.H. Salmon, Genetics of sensory thresholds : individual taste reactions for different substances. *Proc. Nat. Acad. Sci.*, 1935, *21*, 84-90.
8. Cameron, A.T., The relative sweetness of sucrose, glucose, and fructose. *Trans. Roy. Soc. Can.*, 1943, 37, 11-27.
9. Crocker, E.C. Flavour, New York : McGraw-Hill, 1945.
10. Crozier, W.J. Chemoreception, In *Handbood of General Experimental Psychology*. C. Murchison, Ed., Worcester, Mass : Clark University Press, 1934, pp. 987-1036.
11. Dimmick, F.L., The investigation of the olfactory qualities. *Psychol. Rev.*, 1927, *34*, 321-335.

12. Elsberg, C.A., and I. Levy, The sense of smell. I. A new and simple method of quantitative olfactometry. *Bull. Neurol. Inst.*, 1935, *4*, 5-19.

13. Elsberg, C.A., I. Levy, and E.D. Brewer, The trigeminal effects of odorous substances. *Bull. Neurol. Inst.*, 1935, *4*, 270-285.

14. Engel, R., Experimentelle Untersuchungen uber die Abhangigkeit der Lust and Unlust von der Reizstarke beim Geschmackssinn. *Arch. ges. Psychol.*, 1828, *64*, 1.

15. Fair, G.M., and W.F. Wells, The air-dilution method of odor determination in water analysis. *J. Amer. Water Works Assoc.*, 1934, *26*, 1670-1677.

16. Findley, A.E., Furether studies of Henning's system of olfactory qualities. *Amer. J. Psychol.*, 1924, *35*, 436-445.

17. Hahn, H., and H. Gunther, Uber die Reize and die Reizbedingungen des Geschmackssinnes. *Pflug. Arch.*, 1932, *321*, 48-67.

18. Hahn, H., Die adaptation des Geschmackssinnes. *Z. Sinnesphysiol.*, 1934, *65*, 8-145.

19. Hanig, D.P., Zur Psychophysik des Geschmackssinnes. *Phil. Studien*, 1901, *17*. 576-623.

20. Hartridge, H., Importance of taste and smell in nutrition. *J Physiol*, 1945, *103*, 34P-35P.

21. Henning, H., *Der Geruch.* Leipzing : Barth, 1924.

22. Holway, A.H., and L. Hurvich, Differential gustatory sensitivity to salt. *Amer. J. Psychol.*, 1937, 49, 37-48.

23. Holway, A.H., and L. Hurvich, On the psychophysics of taste. I. Pressure and area as variants. *J. Exper. Psychol.*, 1938, *23*, 191-198.

24. Jensen, K., Differential reactions to taste and temperature stimuli in newborn infants. *Genet.Psychol. Monog.*, 1932, *21*, 361-479.

25. Jerome, E.A., Olfactory thresholds measured in terms of stimulus pressure and volume. *Arch. Psychol.*, 1942. No. 274.

26. Kiesow, F., Schmeckversuche an einzelnen papillen. *Phil. Studien*, 1898, *14*, 591-615.

27. Liggett, J.R., An experimental study of the olfactory sensitivity of the white rat. *Genet. Psychol. Mong.*, 1928, 3, 1-64.

28. Lashley, K.S., and R.W. Sperry, Olfactory discrimination after destruction of the anterior thalamic nuclei. *Amer. J. Physiol.*, 1943, *139*, 446-450

29. Luciani, L., *Human Physiology*. Vol. 4, *Sense Organs*. New York : Macmillan, 1917.

30. Macdonald, M.K., An experimental study of Henning's system of olfactory qualities. *Amer. J. Psychol.*, 1922, *33*, 535-553.

31. Moncrieff, R.W., *The Chemical Senses*. New York : John Wiley, 1946.

32. Pfaffmann, C., Apparatus and technique for gustatory experimentation. *J. Gen. Psychol.*, 1935, *12*, 446-447.

33. Pfaffmann, C., Differential responses of the new-born cat to gustatory stimuli. *J. Genet. Psychol.*, 1936, *49*, 61-67.

34. Pfaffmann, C., Gustatory afferent impulses. *J. Cell. Comp. Physion*, 1941, *17*, 243-252.

35. Poucher, W.A., *Perfumes and Cosmetics*. New York : Van Nostrand, 1923.

36. Razran, H.S., and C.J. Warden. The sensory capacity of the dog as studied by the conditioned reflex method (Russian schools). *Psychol. Bull.*, 1929, *26*, 202-222.

37. Richter, C.P., Self-regulatory functions. *The Harvey Lectures*, 1942, Series 38, 63-103.

38. Richter, C.P., and A. Maclean. Salt-taste thresholds of humans. *Amer. J. Physiol.*, 1939, *126*, 1-6.

39. Shore, L.E., A contribution to our knowledge of taste sensations. *J. Physiol.*, 1892, *13*, 191-217.

40. Skramlik, E.V., Die Physiologie des Geruchs and Geschmackssinnes. *Handbuch der Physiologic der niederen Sinne*, Bd. 1. Leipzig : Thieme, 1926.

41. Swann, H.G., the function of the brain in olfaction. I.

Olfactory discrimination and an apparatus for its test. *J. Comp. Psychol.*, 1934, *15*, 229-241.

42. Wedell, C.H., Taste sensitivity of the white rat. *J. Comp. Psychol.*, 1936, *21*, 233-244.

43. Zwaardemaker, H., Prufung des Geruchssinnes und der Geruche. *In Handbuch der biologisches Arbeitsmethoden.* R. Aboderhalden, Ed. Abt. V, Teil 7, Heft 3, 1920

8

Studying Proprioception

We maintain an upright posture, we alter this posture and move about in a coordinated manner, and we are aware of our postural attitudes and of our movements. Our ability to make these postural and locomotors adjustments and our awareness of what we do are dependent upon the activity of several of our sensory systems, principally, vision, touch, and *proprioception*. Of these three, proprioception is of primary importance.

The proprioceptive system is made up of two major parts : (*a*) the *kinesthetic division*, which includes end organs or *proprioceptors* in the muscles and tendons, the peripheral nerves which connect the proprioceptors with the central nervous system, and the related nerve tracts and centers in the central nervous system; and (*b*) the *vestibuler division*, which includes the proprioceptors in the non-auditory part of the inner ear and the associated neural structures.

In reviewing methods of studying proprioception it is important to bear in mind that activity of the proprioceptive system, unlike that of the other sensory systems, is characterized by a lack of conscious experience. Postural and locomotor adjustments are carried out to a large extent on a reflex level. We shall find, therefore that methods involving discriminatory responses, *e.g.*. psychophysical methods, will not be of such fundamental importance as they are in studying vision, hearing, or any of the other senses. Instead, we shall see that most of our present knowledge about proprioception has come from experiments in which the activity of end organs or connecting nervous structures was examined directly or from experiments in which the reflex responses of individual muscles or muscle groups were carefully recorded and analyzed.

METHODS USED IN STUDYING KINESTHESIS

Anatomical Methods

The proprioceptors, which are stimulated by the activity of the muscles of the body, were discovered by the anatomists of the eighteenth and nineteenth centuries through histological techniques. Three main kinds of receptors were isolated and described : (1) encapsulated nerve endings (Pacinian corpuscles), located in the sheaths of muscles and tendons; (2) muscle spindles, which lie within voluntary muscles and end upon individual muscle fibers; and (3) Golgi tendon organs, which are found at the juncture of muscle fibers and tendons. see Fig. 8.1. Free nerve endings may also be stimulated by muscular movement and thus serve a kinesthetic function. It is usually suggested, however, the these endings mediate pain.

Discovery of histological structures which, because of their location in or near muscles or tendons and their connection with nerve endings, appeared to be the sensory and organs stimulated by movement of the muscles was suggestive, but additional evidence was needed to establish the true nature of these receptor-like structures.

Sherrington [29] showed that the muscle spindles were supplied by sensory nerve fibers. By cutting the motor roots of peripheral spinal nerves of experimental animals, he caused all motor fibers to a given muscle of the lower limb to degenerate. He then examined the muscle spindles and their nervous connections under the microscope and found that every spindle still was supplied by sound, undegenerated nerve fibers. These fibers could have come only from the dorsal spinal roots, which are the paths for sensory fibers entering the cord. Similar techniques were used to show that the Golgi tendon organs and Pacinian corpuscles are innervated by sensory nerve fibers.

The anatomical studies which have been described provided no direct evidence of the *function* of the proprioceptive system; however, they did provide evidence upon which shrewd inferences could be based, and they paved the way for studies using methods by which the function of the kinesthetic system could be directly examined.

Selective Ablation

In any dynamic system where many parts act together, information concerning the function of a part or of the whole minus that part can be obtained by destroying the part and studying the activity of the remainder. Classic examples of the use of selective ablation may be found in experiments of Sherrington, Magnus, Fulton, and their coworkers. Their investigations, although concerned chiefly with analysis of the postural and locomotors reflexes, produced a major portion of the knowledge which we now possess of the kinesthetic system.

To illustrate how the selective-ablation technique is used, we may describe briefly an experiment by Pi-Suner and Fulton[25]. These investigators were interested in the reflex coordination of the movements of the front and hind limbs in quadipedal locomotion. In order to study one aspect of the problem, *i.e.*, how impulses set up in the proprioceptors of hind-limb muscles affect the posture of the fore limbs, they limited the functional parts of the system under examination as follows :

1. Voluntary control of limb movement was eliminated by decelerating the experimental animals (cats).

2. Reflexes initiated by cutaneous stimulation were ruled out by cutting the appropriated sensory nerves.

3. The exact manner of stimulation of individual muscles or muscle groups in the hind limbs was brought under control by destroying the nerve supply to the other muscles and by

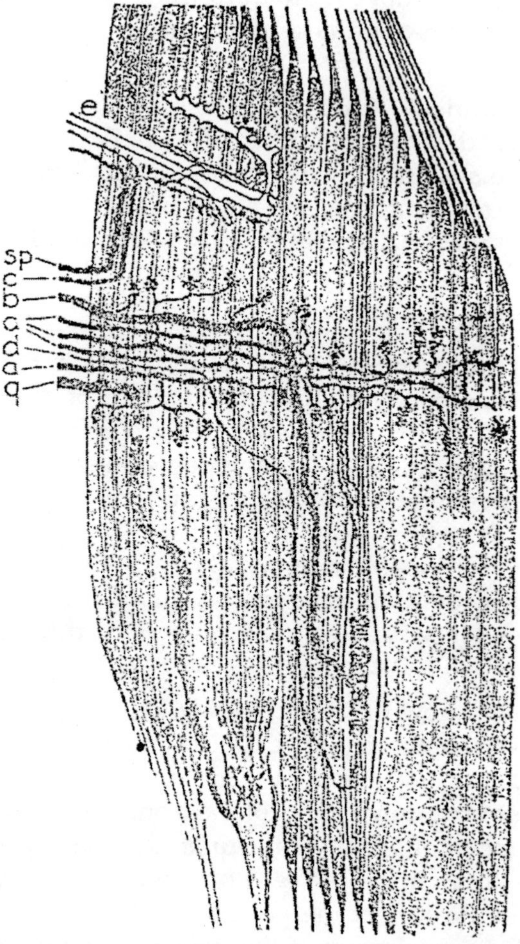

Fig 8.1. Denny-brown's diagram illustrating the sensory and motor innervation of group of 23 mammalian muscle fibers.

The motor innervations comes from 4 fibers : *a, a, a, a.* the muscle spindle is made up of 3 intrafusal fibers, each one innervated by branches of moter nerve fibers *a, a, a, a.* The spindle has one large annulospiral ending, *b*, and *a* single flower spray ending connected with the nervous system by a fiber of relatively small diameter, *d*. There is *a* single Golgi tendon organ, *g*, and *a* sympathetic plexus, sp, accompanied by a small myelinated pain fiber, *c*, from the blood vessel, *e*. (From Fultion [14], by courtesy of the Oxford University press.)

dissecting out those to be stimulated. Some muscles were detached from their tendons, and stimulation was applied artificially.

It was found that, when certain proprioceptors in the quadriceps muscles of one hind limb were stimulated in a manner similar to that which occurs during flexion of the knee joint, reflex responses occur in the other three limbs, so that the fore limb of the opposite side is flexed and the fore limb of the same side and the opposite hind limb are extended. This reflex pattern is at once suggestive of movements which occur during locomotion in the quadruped. By a number of experiments such as this one it has been shown that the series of progressive movements which constitute locomotion are in large part dependent upon reflex responses set off by stimulation of muscle proprioceptors.

Electrical Stimulation and Recording

Kinesthetic receptors and their nervous connections were discovered by anatomical methods; individual reflex arcs and integrated patterns of reflexes were found and carefully examined by means of selective ablation. Exact analysis of the function of individual parts of the system, *e.g.*, isolated receptor units, had to await the invention of suitable methods of stimulating and recording action. Development of such methods has closely paralleled the development of electronic instruments.

An outstanding example of the application of the electrical recording method in the study of proprioception is the experiment in which Matthews [22] distinguished four kinds of receptors corresponding to the four kinds of endings which had formerly been described by the anatomists. Matthews isolated a muscle and its sensory nerve in the limb of a cat and then, under the dissecting microscope, used sharpened needles to divide the nerve into separate bundles of fibers had to destroy these bundles one by one. After each bundle and been cut, electrodes were placed on the nerve central to the lesion, so that the point at which the fibers were cut was between the electrodes and the muscle ; the muscle was then stretched, and the electrical response of the intact nerve fibers recorded. This procedure, namely, redividing the nerve and sectioning successive bundles, was repeated until stretching of the muscle gave rise to a single rhythmic discharge in the fibers remaining uncut. The response thus finally obtained was from a single kinesthetic receptor in the muscle. By varying the nature of the stimulating conditions and carefully analyzing the electrically recorded responses, Matthews was able to show that different kinds of proprioceptors in the muscles and tendons may be distinguished, not only on anatomical but also on functional grounds.

Clinical Methods

Results of histological, ablation, and electrical studies on experimental animals have been corroborated by clinical studies of man. The disturbances of movement in locomotor ataxia were described as early as 1851 [26] and were later shown to be due to degeneration of dorsal spinal roots and nerve tracts in the dorsal part of the spinal cord. Later clinicians, on the basis of postmortem examination of the central nervous system and peripheral nerve endings in the muscles of tabes dorsalis patients, reported atrophy of the kinesthetic and organs and the sensory fibers innervating them.

Innumerable studies of the symptoms resulting from lesions of the spinal cord in man have been made. The classical syndrome resulting from lateral hemisection of the spinal cord at the cervical level was first described by Brown-Sequared on the basis of his observations of patients which spinal lesions. The Brown-Squared syndrome consists of homolateral loss of voluntary movement and *kinesthesis* and contralateral loss of thermal, pressure, and pain sensibility caudal to the lesion. The clinical studies have been of value both in tracing the central kinesthetic pathways and in clarifying the role of kinesthesis in reflex activity.

Psychophysical Methods

Since the time of Fechner there have been countless experiments of the discrimination of lifted weights. Although the judgments required are based principally upon kinesthetic cues, these weight discrimination studies have contributed far more to the development of psychophysical methodology then to an understanding of the kinesthetic system. The exception to this generalization is a series of investigations conducted recently in which the effect of cortical lesions on discrimination of lifted weights was studied [27,28]. To summarize the results of these studies briefly, it was found that partial destruction of the parietal lobes produces only transient defect in ability to discriminate lifted weights; total destruction, a permanent defect. Comparison of monkey, chimpanzee, and man indicates an increase in corticalization of the function in question as the phylogenetic scale is ascended.

METHODS USED IN STUDYING VESTIBULAR FUNCTIONS

For many thousands of years man must have known that experiences such as loss of equilibrium, dizziness, and nausea are aroused when the body is subjected to certain kinds of motion, such as the pendulum-like movements of a swing, the undulations of a boat, or the gyrations of the dance. Nevertheless, he did not discover until 1824 that the inner car contains specialized receptors which are stimulated by the position or movement of the head. At that time Fluorens showed, in a series of experiments of birds and rabbits, that destruction of the semicircular canals produces severe defects in the ability of the experimental animal to maintain equilibrium and to make coordinated movements. Later experimenters corroborated Fluorina results, and during the next 100 years more than 1500 reports of studies on the vestibule system were published [16] .

It is obviously impossible to give even a brief description of all the methods employed in these studies. We shall, therefore, group the methods under three main *headings—methods of stimulation, methods of recording and analyzing responses, and ablation methods*—and we shall give representative examples of each class. First, however, the structure of the

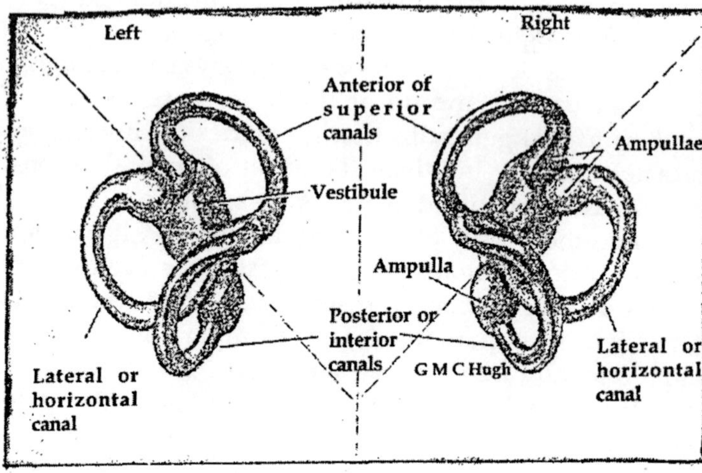

Fig. 8.2 The semicircular canals as seen from behind and above.

The distance between the two sets of canals is not scale. Note that the three canals on one side lie in planes of approximately right angles to one another and that the following pairs of canals lie in approximately the same planes : (*a*) the lateral canals, (*b*) the right anterior and the left posterior, and (*c*) the left anterior and the right posterior.

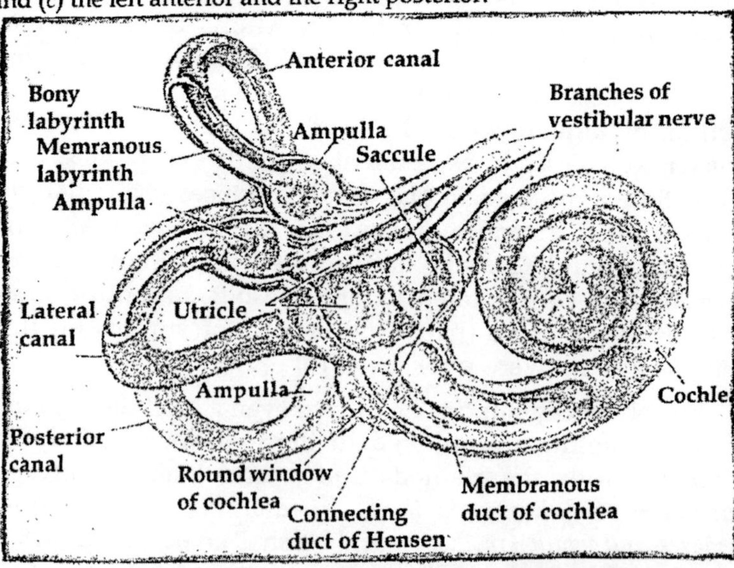

Fig. 8.3. A lateral view of the right labyrinth.

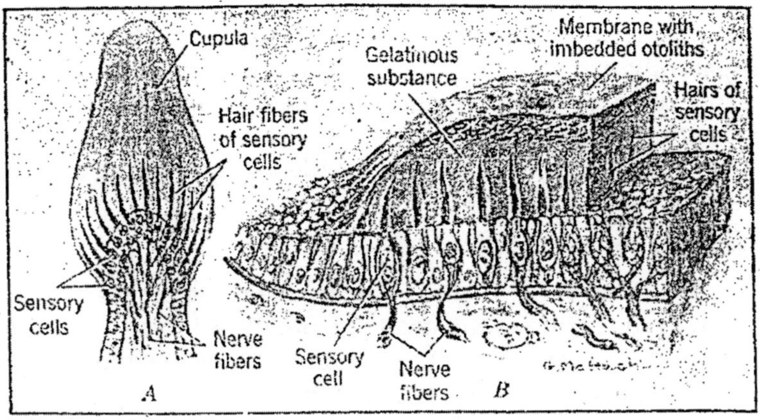

Fig. 8.4. (*A*) Cross-section of ampullar crista. (After Kumar.) (*B*) Macula in three-dimensional cross-section. (After Colmer.)

vestibular receptors and the probable functions of the individual part should be briefly mentioned.

Structure and Function of the Vestibule Receptors

The vestibular portion of the inner ear labyrinth includes the semicircular canals, the utricle, and the saccade; the remaining part, the cochlea, contains the receptors for hearing. The vestibular receptor cells are found in the ampulla cristae of the canals and in the maculae or otolith organs of the article and saccule. See Figs. 8.2, 8.3, and 8.4.

The most generally accepted view at the present time is that the acristae of the semicircular canals are the chief receptors for rotary movement, the effective stimulus being angular acceleration or deceleration. Continued rotation at constant velocity ceases to be effective. The utricular maculae are the primary receptors for position of the head and may also be the most important receptors for rectilinear acceleration and deceleration, although the relative roles of the semicircular canals and the utricle in rectilinear motion have yet to be definitely established. Futhermore, there is evidence that the semicircular canals may play a secondary role in static stimulation and that the utricle may be stimulated by marked angular acceleration. The function of the saccular maculae is uncertain. If they serve as proprioceptons, their part is apparently a minor one, since no obvious defect occurs as a result of their destruction. They have been suggested as receptors for vibration and for sounds (especially low frequencies), but experimental evidence in support of these suggestions is lacking.

Methods of Stimulation

Position. The problem of stimulating the receptors for position of the head is simple; the head is merely held fixed in various positions. Avoidance of stimulation of other receptors is not so simple. Time must elapse after any change in position in order that stimulation due to motion will have ceased. Care must also be taken to eliminate stimulation of muscle proprioceptors, because the reflex responses aroused by labyrinth position are also affected by the other proprioceptors, especially those in the neck, which give rise to reflex responses of limb and trunk muscles. Visual and cutaneous stimulation must likewise be avoided. Several techniques have been devised to eliminate stimulation of these other receptors. Plaster casts enclosing the shoulders, neck, and head are sometimes used to keep the relative position of head, neck, and body constant. Tilt boards and other mechanical devices make possible accurate control of the subject's position and minimize the stimulation of receptors other than those being investigated. Visual stimulation can be eliminated by blindfolding or, in experimental animals, by destroying the eyes. In some experiments nerve impulses arising in proprioceptors other than those of the labyrinth have been excluded by appropriate lesions in the nervous system.

Rotation. The methods of rotation which have been devised vary in complexity from simply instructing the human subject to whirl around rapidly a number of times to elaborate apparatus designed to regulate accurately rate of angular acceleration, velocity, and plane of rotation. For most experimental purposes the rotator must possess several additional features. Smoothness in starting stopping is often a requisite. In experiments where the subject is required to make discriminatory responses to vestibular cues, all other cues—visual, auditory, tactual, and kinesthetic—must be eliminated. The noise of the motor or other driving mechanism is usually kept constant under all conditions of operation through the use of suitable clutch and brake devices. Control of other extraneous cues is obtained both by design of the rotator and arrangement of the experimental situation.

The Barany chair, which has been widely used for clinical testing, is simply a straight-back chair mounted on a rotating platform in somewhat the same manner as a barber's chair. A headrest is provided to keep the head position fixed. The typical procedure is to rotate the subject 10 times in 20 seconds. Because the chair is usually rotated by hand, control of acceleration and rate of rotation is only approximate.

For more accurate experimental work many elaborate devices have been constructed for rotating both experimental animals and human subjects. Dunlap [9] designed a rotator with which smooth, constant acceleration and deceleration and a constant maximum speed may be obtained. See Fig. 8.5. The rate of acceleration and deceleration and the speed of rotation are measured on a kymograph record.

Dodge carried on a series of careful experiments on thresholds of rotation, habituation to rotation, and the effect of rotation on eye movements [4, 5, 6]. In the course of these experiments he developed a rotator with which he was able to control and measure angular displacement (*i.e.*, number of degrees of rotation), angular acceleration, and angular velocity. See Fig. 8.5

For the purpose of testing the susceptibility of military personnel to motion sickness, several investigators have recently designed modified versions of the Barany chair. Modification has been in the direction of simulating the forms of motion encountered in flying or on ships. A chair designed by Travis [38] is operated from a multiple harmonic cam, which is driven at a constant rate by an electric motor. The cam pattern is such that during one revolution of the chair seven different rates of acceleration and one period of rest are produced. A somewhat different apparatus used in experiments by Spiegel [33] is constructed so that during each rotation the head is tilted either forward or to the side, thus producing continuous stimulation of the vestibular receptors even when rate of rotation is constant.

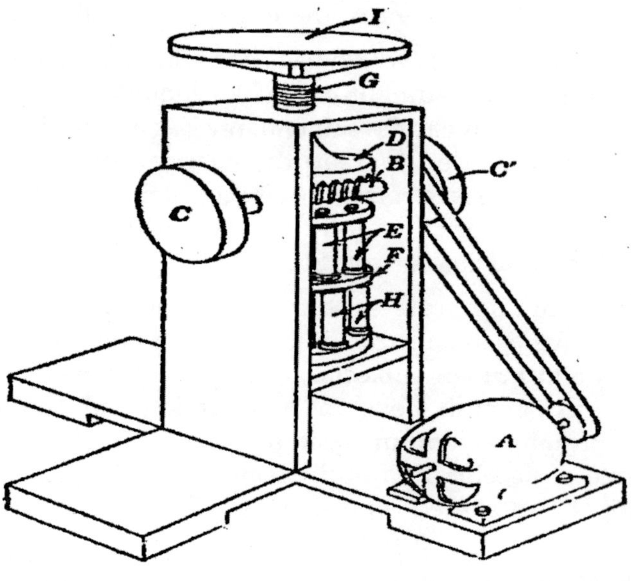

Fig. 8.6. The Dunlap rotator.

The motor (*A*) drives the horizontal shaft (*B*), which carries the flywheels (C) and (C'). Rotation of the shaft (*B*) drives the worm-wheel (*D*), which is attached to the gang of magnets (*E*). When electric current is applied to the magnets (*E*), they act as a clutch and "pick up" the iron disk armature (*F*), which is attached to the vertical shaft (*G*). The vertical shaft is thereby set into motion. The amount of "slip" of the clutch is determined by the load and by the amperage of current applied to the magnets. Acceleration may thus be controlled. To stop the rotation of the vertical shaft, the current to the clutch magnets (*E*) is interrupted, and current is applied to the set of magnets (*H*)which are firmly fastened to the framework of the apparatus. Magnets (*H*), therefore, act as a brake, the rate of deceleration depending upon the current applied. A chair a platform may be bolted to the platform (I), (After Dunlap[9.)]

Linear motion, like angular, may be readily obtained through the subject's own movements, *e.g.*, walking, running, failing, or rising. For experimental purposes, however, apparatus is required which makes possible control of velocity, acceleration., and the direction of movement with relation to the axes of the head. Elimination of nonvestioular cues is, of course, a factor in many experiments.

One of the simplest methods of obtaining approximately linear acceleration which can be accurately measured is by use of a swing, because a swing behaves according to the principles of motion governing a simple pendulum. The swing technique was widely used during World War II in experiments on motion sickness. A typical arrangement consists of a carriage suspended so that distance from the overhead bar to the swing seat is about 14 feet. To insure stimulation of the same receptors in all subjects, an exact position of the head is obtained through the use of a headrest. In experiments using this apparatus subjects were swung through an are of 150 degrees for a period of 20 minutes or until Vomiting occurred [17].

A "wave-machine," so named because it was designed to simulate the wave-like linear motion of boats and planes, has also been used in experiments on motion sickness [1]. This machine consists of a closed cab sort in a vertical shaft so that it may be raised and lowered by hydraulic pressure. Linear motion in the vertical direction is produced by this elevator-like apparatus. Acceleration, velocity, and amplitude of movement can be exactly controlled and measured.

In still other war researches experimenters have produced vestibular stimulation by movements of a Link trainer, by maneuvers of a real plane in fight, and by rotation on a human centrifuge [20, 3, 15]. The motion to which subjects were subjected in these experiments often possessed both angular and linear acceleratory components.

Caloric Stimulation. The vestibular receptors may be stimulated by the injection of hot or cold water into the external auditory canal. Apparently temperature changes set up

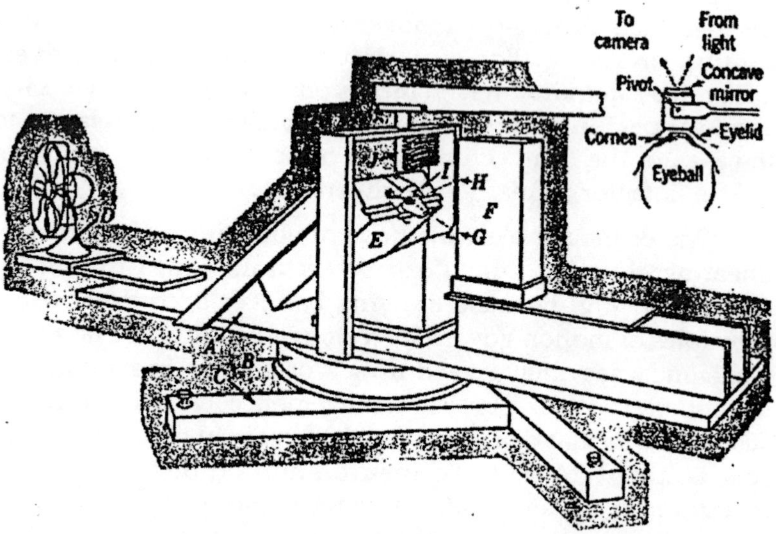

Fig. 8.6. Dodge-Wendt rotator and eye-movement recording apparatus.

The platform (A) and the equipment which it carries are mounted on an automobile wheel (B) and rotate on the bearing of the wheel. The platform may be levelled by means of the adjustable base (C). The rotator is driven by the electric fan (D). A brake applied to the rim of the wheel (B)controls starting and stopping. When the apparatus is used for animal experiments, the animal is restrained in the box (E) and its head held fixed by a head-holder. A photokymograph (F) may be mounted on the platform and the animal's eye movements recorded by directing a beam of light from (G) onto the concave mirror which rests on the closed eyelid, as shown in the insert at the upper right. The light reflects back to a vertical slit at (H) and produces a line upon the moving film of the photo kymograph. Head movements may also be recorded by means of a light beam directed upon a concave mirror attached to the head at (I). Electrical circuits are led to the platform through the slip-ring contacts at (J). (See reference [39.)]

convection currents in the endolymph, the fluid which fills the membranous labyrinth, and these currents stimulate the receptor cells. By means of the caloricstimulation technique the labyrinth of each ear can be separately stimulated. With the head in the normal upright position, the vertical canals are affected by caloric stimulation. The horizontal canals may be stimulated by tilting the head backward through 60 degrees. Injection of cold water (about 68 degrees Fahrenheit) produces eye nystagmus with the quick phase toward the side opposite that stimulated. Injection of hot water (about 112 degrees Fahrenheit) produces nystagmus with the quick phase toward the stimulated side.

Several methods of producing caloric stimulation have been used. Early investigators syringed the ear or allowed water to flow into it through a tube connected with a container suspended above the subject's head. Large doses of water (100 to 1000 cubic centimeters) at either very high or very low temperatures were used. It has since been found that a few cubic centimeters of water at temperatures only slightly above or below body temperature provide effective stimulation. When these very small quantities are used, more care must be taken to insure proper injection. A syringe with a blunt needle is usually used, and the stream of water is directed against the posterior superior wall of the external auditory canal.

The caloric method of stimulation has been used mainly for diagnostic purposes by clinicians. Most experimental studies utilizing this method have been concerned with the mechanism whereby the injection of hot or cold water into the external auditory meatus excites the vestibular receptors.

Mechanical Stimulation. One aim of the many methods that have been invented to stimulate the proprioceptors of the inner ear has been to control conditions so that different receptors can be stimulated individually ; *e.g.*, it is desirable to be able to stimulate the crista of one horizontal canal or the otolith organ of one utricle. Ewald [2] accomplished this by devising a technique to produce pressure changes in the endolymph of the labyrinths of experimental animals. He drilled a small hole in the wall of one of the semicircular canals and over this sealed a metal cylinder 1.4 millimeters in diameter and 9 millimeters in length. The cylinder contained a tapered piston by means of which pressure could be applied to the membranous labyrinth and the intralabyrinthine fluid. Using this "pneumatic-hammer," Ewald was able to stimulate each of the canals individually and to study the response made by the animal to both compression and decompression. It was assumed that compression produced movement of the endolymph toward the ampulla (ampullopetal flow), and decompression, movement away from the ampulla (ampullofugal flow). When the right horizontal canal was stimulated, it was found that compression caused turning of the head and eyes to the left, *i.e.*, away from the side stimulated ; decompression caused turning to the right or toward the stimulated side. The intensity of stimulation produced by Ewald's technique was probably greater than any resulting from natural stimulation, such as rotation under ordinary conditions.

In human patients suffering from otosclerosis, an otological disorder accompanied by alkalosis of the stapes in the oval window and a consequent reduction of hearing, an artificial window (fenestrum) is sometimes made surgically in the wall of the horizontal semicircular canal. The success of the fenestration operation depends upon the artificial window remaining open, *i.e.*, covered only by a membranous flap. In many cases it is closed by regret of bone. One test to discover whether the window has remained open is to apply pressure to it by pressing with the index finger at the appropriate point in the external auditory canal. If the fenestrum is still open, nystagmic eye movements can be produced.

Electrical Stimulation. Both direct and alternating currents have been used to stimulate the vestibular receptors of human subjects and expeiimental animals. When direct current is employed, a typical arrangement in the intact subject is to place the stimulating electrode on the mastoid bone and the neutral electrode on some other part of the body, such as the muscles of the neck. If only one car is stimulated in this manner, nystalgic eye movements are produced, with the fast phase toward the side of stimulation when the cathode is applied to the mastoid and away from the side of stimulation when the anode is applied. Alternating-current stimulation does not produce nystagmus but does give rise to rotation of the head away from the side stimulated.

What part of the vestibule system is stimulated by electric current has been a point of controversy. Some experimenters have suggested that the electric current induces movement of the endolymph ; others, that it acts upon the sensory cells in the cristae or maculae; and still others, that it acts directly upon the fibers of the vestibular nerve. This uncertainty concerning the locus of stimulation has limited the usefulness of the method; nevertheless some experimenters have attempted to analyze the effects of stimulation of individual ampullae's or maculae by applying electrodes to them and noting the resulting reflex responses. Most of the experimental evidence to date supports the view that electrical current applied to the walls of the labyrinth acts directly upon nerve fibers in the vestibule nerve.

Methods of Recording and Analyzing Responses

There are a number of different levels at which we may examine the response to stimulation of a sensory system. We may study :

1. The activity of the end organ or receptor.
2. The activity of the afferent nerve fibers, tracts, or centers.
3. The reflex responses of effectors.
4. The discriminatory responses, which in the human subject will usually be verbal reports and in lower animals will be overt learned responses, *e.g.*, conditioned responses.

In experiments on vision, hearing, small, taste, and the cutaneous senses, we depend heavily upon response of the fourth type : the verbal reports of human subjects and the discriminatory responses of lower animals. In studying proprioception we usually make use of responses which fall in one of the first three classes. This, as we have already seen, was true in experiments on the kinesthetic system, and it is equally true in the case of the vestibular proprioceptive processes. The human subject can report an awareness of position or of movement of the head, but to what extent this awareness is the direct result of sensory impulses initiated in the vestibular receptors and to what extent it is the result of sensory impulses aroused in receptors of the muscles, viscera, and skin by the reflex responses brought about by vestibular stimulation is not clearly understood. Although the bulk of the experimental data points toward the importance of the sensory impulses reflex aroused, there is some evidence for direct sensory connections from the vestibular receptors to higher nervous centers. The existence of such connections suggests, of course, the likelihood that part of our awareness of head position or movement results from the passage of impulses directly from the vestibular receptors to the brain.

Activity of the end Organ. Fluorens discovery that the inner ear contains a sense organ which is stimulated by the position or movement of the head immediately led to speculation as to what parts of the inner ear are concerned and as to the manner in which the movement or position is translated into sensory nerve impulses. The anatomy of the inner ear was already known, and it is not surprising, in view of their triplane structure, that the semicircular canals were immediately seized upon as the principal receptors. The utricle and saccule were also suggested by some as additional end organs,the cochlea being excepted as a rule because of its known auditory function. Experiments in which ablation techniques were used or in which stimuli were applied directly to different parts of the labyrinth soon showed that the inferences based upon knowledge of structure were approximately correct—the proprioceptors of the inner ear were to be found in the ampullae of the canals and in the auricular maculae. As already noted, the function of the secular maculae has not been established.

It was not so easy, however, to determine by experiment the nature of the intralabyrinthine events whereby head movement or position causes impulses to be set up in the eighth cranial nerve. Because of the microscopic size of the structures involved and the fact that in most animals they are completely encased in bone, direct observation or recording of activity within the labyrinth is almost impossible. For that reason, methods which have been developed to overcome these obstacles are of special interest.

Ewald, who is noted for the precise surgical techniques he employed in his studies of the vestibular labyrinth, introduced the "bridge method" in which he exposed a limited portion of the membranous canal of the pigeon by removing a short length of the surrounding bony canal [2,p. 43]. By introducmg a minute amount of lampblack or other coloring matter into the endolymph of the canals, Ewald and other investigators using similar surgical procedures were able to observe, under the microscope, movements of the endolymph in the exposed part of the membranous labyrinth.

More recently Steinhausen [34, 35, 36] has developed a technique whereby not only endolymph movement but also, more important, movement of the cupula of the ampullar crista can be observed. Using the pike, which has rather large

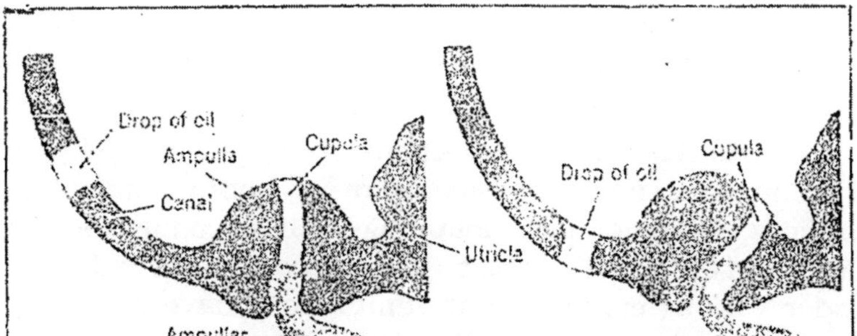

Fig. 8.7. Movement of copula and endolymph during angular acceleration.

A. Position of copula with the canal at rest. A drop of oil has been injected into the canal in order to obtain a record of fluid movement. *B*. Position of copula during angular occeleration.The fluid in the canal has moved toward the ampulla's, as indicated by the change in position of the drop of oil, and the copula has been displaced toward the utricle by the fluid movement. (After Dolman[8].)

semicircular canals the outer walls of which are of cartilage rather than bone, he exposed an ampulla and part of the adjoining canal and injected a minute amount of Chinese ink into the endolymph. He was then able to observe and photograph movements of the cupula during rotary, caloric, and mechanical stimulation. Steinhausen's studies show that, when the canals are stimulated, the endolymph exerts pressure upon the copula and displaces it to one side or the other of the ampulla. See Fig. 8.7. It is apparently through this movement of the copula and the resulting distortion of the sensory hair cells that the hydrodynamic changes produced in the end lymph are transformed into nerve impulses. The mechanism by which deformation of sensory hair cells stimulates the nerve endings is not known. In his experiments Steinhausen was also able to show that the movement of the copula is that of a heavily damped elastic system having a natural period of about 20 seconds. This finding fits well with observations by many experimenters that nystagmus ceases after approximately 20 seconds of rotation at constant speed and that the period of postrotary nystagmus is of similar duration.

Neural Activity. Connections of the vestibule labyrinth with the central nervous system were firs: aced by anatomical methods. More complete mapping of these connections and analysis of the activity going on in the nervous paths and centers under various conditions of stimulations have been made possible by electrical recording techniques.

One of the earliest studies of the electrical response of the vestibular nervous system was made by Mowrer [23]. With electrodes placed on the eight nerve of the *painted terrapin*, he recorded action potentials during and after rotation of the animal on a turntable. He reported that the action potentials lasted only a fraction of a second after rotation had ceased.

In later experiments Lowenstein and Sand used more refined techniques to record the impulses in a single nerve fiber from the ampulla's of the horizontal canal of the *ray* [21]. They found a steady flow of impulses even when the labyrinth was at rest. The frequency of impulses increased during angular acceleration when the direction of rotation was toward the side being examined and decreased when the direction of rotation was toward the opposite side. Cessation of rotation was also reflected in the rate of discharge; and during rotation at a constant speed a steady state was reached within 20 to 30 seconds, after which the frequency remained at the same rate as that during rest. See Fig. 8.8.

Although anatomical methods have so far failed to reveal

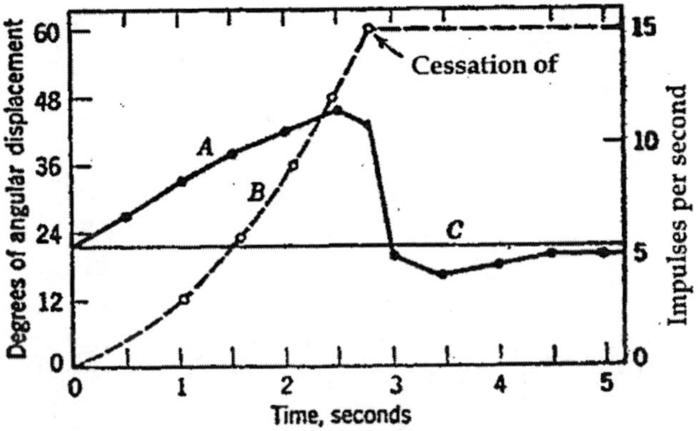

Fig. 8.8. Frequency of nerve impulses in a single nerve fiber from the ampulla of the left horizontal canal during stimulation by rotation.

The rate of angular acceleration was approximately 15 degrees per second per second. Curve *A* shows the frequency of frequency of discharge in impulses per second (read from scale at right). Curve *B* gives the degree of angular displacement from the resting position (read from scale at left). The horizontal line *C* indicates the frequency of discharge with the labyrinth at rest. Direction of rotation was toward the side from which the recording was made. (From Lowenstein and Sand[21].)

completely the paths followed by vestibular fibers between the end organs and the cortex, functional evidence indicates that direct connections do exist. Spiegel [30] found that convulsions can be produced in cats and dogs by stimulation of vestibular receptors if strychnine is applied to certain areas of the temporal loves. No convulsions occur when strychnine is applied to other parts of the cortex. In other experiments

Spiegel [31] recorded changes in the electrical activity of the cortex of the cat and monkey during stimulation of the labyrinth by rotation. See Fig. 8.9. That these changes are due to the flow of impulses directly from the labyrinth to the cortex by way of centers lower in the central nervous system, *e.g.*, cerebellum and medulla, and not from stimulation of the eyes or of receptors in the muscles or viscera was demonstrated by a series of control experiments. Visually aroused activity

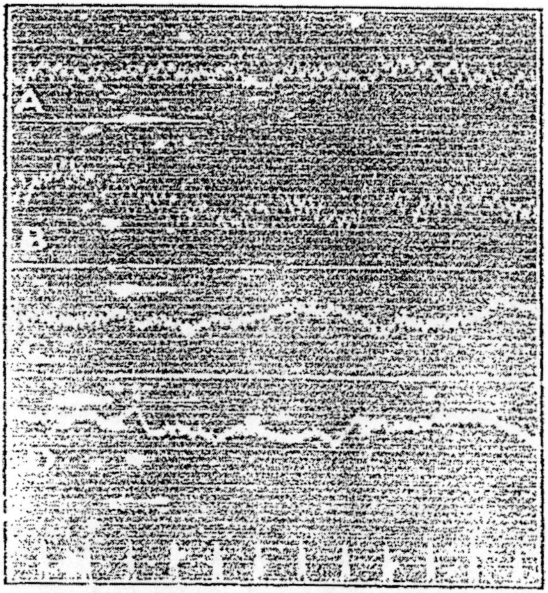

Fig. 8.9. The effect of vestibule stimulation on the electroencephalogram of the cat.

All records were taken during bulbocapnine catalepsy. The recording electrode was placed on the suprasylvian sulcus of the temporal lobe. Record *A* was taken with the head at rest, both labyrinths intact. The animal was then rotated 15 times; the change in the electroencephalogram after rotating is clearly shown in record *B*. Record *C* was taken with the animal at rest after destruction of both labyrinths. That no change in the electroencephalogram now occurs is shown by record *D*, taken after 20 ratations. (From original records of E.A. Spiegel.)

was eliminated by covering the eyes and placing the animal in the dark. Reflex and voluntary activity of the muscles was excluded by the injection of curare and bulbocapnine. Sensory impulses from the skeletal muscles and viscera were blocked by transecting the spinal cord in the upper cervical region and by cutting the vague nerves. None of these control measures eliminated the changes in electrical response of the "vestibular area" of the cortex during rotation. On the other hand, no changes in electrical activity occurred during deep ether anesthesia, after bilateral labyrinthectomy, or after undercutting of the responsive cortical area.

Evidence such as that brought forth by Spiegel's experiments lends weight to the supposition that our awareness of head position and movement is in part, at least, due to nerve impulses flowing directly from the vestibule receptors to the brain.

Reflex Responses. Since there are a great many reflex responses resulting from stimulation of vestibular receptors, it is convenient to classify them in some systematic fashion. The following scheme represents a modification of one proposed by Dusser de Barenne [10] :

I. Positional reflexes : refluxed for which the adequate stimulus is the position of the head, not the movement occurring during attainment of the position.

A. Tonic reflexes : reflexes which maintain certain patterns of tonus in the musculature :

1. Of eye muscles.
2. Of neck muscles.
3. Of limb and trunk muscles.

B. Righting reflexes : reflexes of neck muscles which restore normal position of head when it has been displaced.

II. Acceleratory reflexes : reflexes for which the adequate stimulus is angular or linear acceleration.

A. Reflexes resulting from angular acceleration(rotation) :

1. Of eye muscles.

B. Reflexes resulting from linear acceleration :

1. Of neck muscles.

2. Of neck muscles.
3. Of limb and trunk muscles.
4. Of visceral muscles.

2. Of limb and trunk muscles.
3. Of visceral muscles.

III. Artificially induced reflexes :

A. Reflexes resulting from caloric stimulation.

B. Reflexes resulting from mechanical stimulation.

C. Reflexes resulting from electrical stimulation.

Any of the three artificial stimuli may produce reflex responses of eye, neck, limb, trunk, and visceral muscles.

In many investigations experimenters have been satisfied to observe carefully the reflex responses produced by vestibular stimulation and have not tried to make quantitative measurements. This was particularly true in the first exploratory experiments and even in most of the later studies of reflex responses of the neck, limb, and trunk muscles. In some instances, as in the experiments of Tait and McNally [37], measures of the extent and duration of movement have been desired, and techniques have therefore been developed to make these measurements. These two investigators used-decelerate frogs in which one or both hind legs were divided from the remainder of the body and head except for a connecting link, the sciatic nerve. The hind leg was then mounted so that the contractions of individual muscles could be recorded by means of a muscle lever. The head body part of the preparation was placed on a tiltboard whose movement subjected the labyrinth to the stimulation of angular acceleration.

Direct observation of visceral muscle responses is impossible unless surgery is performed. The contractions of the stomach or of other parts of the gastrointestinal tract have been recorded by inserting a rubber balloon attached to a rubber tube, the other end of which is connected to a tambour recorder. The balloon is inflated after insertion so that it fills the cavity in which it rests. Contraction of the walls of the cavity will then exert pressure on the balloon, and the pressure on the enclosed air of the balloon-tube-tambour system will produce movement of the tambour diaphragm and of recording lever attached to it.

It is in the study of reflex responses of eye muscles to vestibular stimulation that the most elaborate recording and measuring techniques have been developed. To measure the tonic reflex movement of the eyes in human subjects, Benjamin's designed a special pair of spectacle frames with cylindrical eyepieces [2, p.221]. One of a pair of time cross-wires is set so that it crosses two points marked by white paste on the anesthetized cornea. After a change in head position the angle through which the eye rotates is measured by adjusting the second cross-wire to include the new positions of the two points on the cornea.

Many different techniques—mechanical, photographic, and electrical—have been employed to record the nystagmic eye movements which occur during rotation. Duster de Barenne and de Kleyn [11] recorded the movements of individual eye muscles of the rabbit. The apparatus which they used was so arranged that threads attached to each of the eye muscles operated separate levers, which recorded on the smoked paper of the kymograph. The animal was rotated about its longitudinal axis, and the reflex responses of each eye muscle were registered. By careful fixation of the head and proper design of the thread and lever system, all changes in tension on the threads as the result of rotation, except changes due to muscle contraction, were eliminated. The experimenters were able to demonstrate the reciprocal innervations of certain pairs of eye muscles.

The total movement of the intact eye during and after rotation is more often recorded than are the responses of the separate eye muscles. In some of the earliest attempts at such recording mechanical methods were used, but these were anything but satisfactory because they lacked sensitivity, annoyed the subject, and could easily have a distorting effect upon the response itself. These difficulties were overcome by the use of photographic methods. Among the first to devise a satisfactory technique of recording eye movements photographically were Dodge and Cline [7]. They took advantage of the facts that *(a)* the cornea of the eye readily reflects a light beam directed upon it and (*b*) the surface of the cornea bulges out from the spherical surface of the rest of the eyeball. Movement of the eyeball, therefore, results in changes in the angle of reflection of a beam directed upon the cornea. Although this technique was first used to study eye movements during reading, it was readily adapted to the study of the eye movements which result from stimulation of the labyrinth by rotation. For the later purpose, however, it is usually desirable to photograph eye movements with the eyes closed and during rotation as well as afterward, and it is necessary to be able to distinguish between changes in the record which are caused by head movements and those caused by eye movements. These added requirements may be met by modifying the setup. The eyelids are held shut by a clamp or by narrow strips of adhesive tape. A small, freely-pivoting wooden block on which is mounted a concave mirror is allowed to rest lightly against the eyelid directly over the cornea. See Fig. 8.6 insert. Movement of the cornea causes the block to rotate about its axis, the direction of rotation being opposite to that of cornea movement. A light beam is now directed on the mirror and reflected by it instead of the cornea. A similar concave mirror may also be mounted in fixed position on the head so as to reflect the beam form a second light onto the photographic record. With this double record detections of the recorded eye-movement line which are produced by head movements may be detected. To record eye movements during rotation it is necessary to mount the light source, camera, and associated apparatus on the same rotating platform with the experimental subject. See Fig. 8.6.

Another photographic technique which has proved useful in the study of eye movements is to take pictures of the eye with a moving picture camera. The successive frames of the film may then be examined, and, the rate at which the frames were exposed being known, a plot of movements per unit time can be made. In making such plots it is desirable to have a fixed reference point on the eyeball. This may be accomplished by fixing a small piece of reflecting material to the eyeball. Judd, who was one of the fist to use this method, placed a small particle of China white, coated with paraffin to prevent irritation, one the eyeball in the region of the iris [19]. In order to have a record of all eye movements, even during the time between successive frames of a moving picture, some experimenters have used a dual camera recording system, in which a frame in one camera is being exposed at the time the film in the other is moving in preparation for exposure of the next frame.

Changes in electrical potential during eye movements have been recorded from electrodes placed near the eye, *e.g.*, one on each temple for horizontal movements or one above and one below for vertical movements [18, 24]. These electrical records show a close correspondence to the eye-movement records obtained by photographic techniques.

Discriminatory Responses. Although we do not yet know the relative importance of sensory impulses flowing directly from the vestibular receptors to higher centers and sensory impulses from kinesthetic receptors stimulated by the positional and acceleratory reflexes, we can nevertheless in our experimental investigations make use of sensory experiences accompanying vestibular stimulation. Several early investigators, such as Wells (1792), Erasmus Darwin (1801), and Purkinje (1820), described the sensory phenomena which could be noted introspectively during and after rotation. It remained, however, for Griffith (1920) and Dodge (1923) to furnish accurate introspective reports under carefully controlled conditions.

Griffith, aroused by the mistaken notion persisting in studies on the selection of aviation candidates during World War I that lack of sensitivity to rotation was an undesirable trait in such candidates, conducted careful laboratory studies in which he was able to demonstrate that *dizziness* is subject to habituation [16]. Experienced pilots or others who had been exposed repeatedly to rotator motion were likely to show decreased responses during the typical test situation. Of less practical importance, perhaps, but of greater theoretical interest were his conclusions that the sensory experience which we call *dizziness* is the combination "of a large number of processes the most prominent of which are (1) kinesthesis from the eyes and neck and in the arms, (2) pressure room the region of the abdominal viscera, the chest, and head, and (3) certain vascular processes which supply an obscure background and which give to the whole experience a characteristic shading."

Dodge measured thresholds of rotation by having his experimental subjects report any change noticed in their position [6]. With rapid onset of rotation, he found the threshold to be about 2 degrees per second. In several studies Dodge obtained both introspective reports and records of eye movements under different conditions of stimulation by rotation. Although in some instances reports of awareness of onset or cessation of rotation coincided with appearance or disappearance of eye movements, this was not true under all stimulating conditions.

In addition to reports of awareness of movement and of *dizziness*, subjects have been asked to report feelings of discomfort and nausea and to make judgments about apparent movement of surrounding objects. Examples of experiments involving both these kinds of reports may be found in the work of aviation research groups during World War II. In a summary of experiments by several investigators Bard has listed the symptoms of motion sickness as occurring usually in the following sequence : "drowsiness, pallor, cold-sweating, nausea (usually ushered in by some degree of epigastric awareness), and vomiting (which may not occur)." He adds that "headache and dizziness are vague symptoms occurring only irregularly" and that true vertigo and nystagmus are evoked only when there is angular acceleration.

Graybiel, Clark, and associates, working at the Naval School of Aviation Medicine, Pensacola, Florida, have described two visual illusions reported by human subjects in whom vestibular stimulation was brought about by maneuvering a plane or link trainer or by rotation on a human centrifuge. One, which they call the *oculogyral illusion,* occurs during angular acceleration and is therefore thought result from stimulation of receptors in the semicircular canals. The second, named the *oculogravic illusion,* occurs when centrifugal force is acting and is thought to result from stimulation of the otolith organs. The oculogyral illusion consists of the apparent movement of a fixed object; the oculogravic illusion, of the apparent displacement of the object [3,15].

It has been stated earlier that discriminatory responses of animals have seldom been used in the study of the vestibular system. Note should be taken, however, of experiments by Spiegel and Oppenheimer, in which they report obtaining a conditioned response in dogs to changes in position and to angular acceleration [32]. The animals were carefully fastened in position on a tilt-table or rotating platform. One leg was free to flex upon application of the unconditioned stimulus, shock. Conditioned responses to slow changes in position about the horizontal axis were established not only in the intact animal but also in animals in which the following surgical ablations were carried out : (*a*) section of the posterior columns and dorsal spinocerebellar tracts at the first or second cervical level, (*b*) destruction of both labyrinths, (*c*) combination of *a* and *b*. In animals in which operation *c* was performed, the experimenter concludes that the conditioned responses must have been based upon non-vestibular sensory impulses carried by the remaining ascending tracts of the spinal cord.

The conditioned responses to angular acceleration were established readily after section of the posterior and dorsal spinocerebellar tracts and paralysis of the eye, facial, and mastication muscles by local anesthetic. After bilateral labyrinthectomy, on the other had, conditioned responses could not be obtained for a period of 1/2 to 2 months. Repeated training trials finally resulted in conditioned responses, first to rapid and eventually to slow rates of acceleration. Discriminatory reactions to direction, which were obtained in normal animals, could not be established in the labyrinthectomized dogs.

Because of their experimental findings, Spiegel and Openheimer question the adequacy of theories which account for the awareness of rotation entirely on the basis of sensory impulses from muscles whose contractions are reflex produced upon vestibular stimulation. These results, in addition to those obtained by Spiegel in other experiments suggest the need of further investigation of the direct connections of the vestibule receptors with higher nervous centers.

Ablation Methods

As in the study of kinesthesis, selective ablation has been of fundamental importance in the study of the vestibule system. It was the method employed by Fluorins in the classical experiments in which he firmly established the role of the semicircular canals in postural adjustment and coordinated movement [13]. Fluorens not only destroyed the whole of the vestibule system on one or both sides; in some experiments he sectioned individual canals and pairs of corresponding canals, *e.g.*, both lateral canals or the anterior canal on one side and the posterior on the other.

Following the work of Fluorens ablation was the method most often used to analyze further the functions of the vestibule system. Surgical procedures differed widely, and the results often reflected the exactness or crudeness of the procedure. Knowledge of the vestibule system was nevertheless rapidly advanced by the experiments in which careful, refined techniques were employed.

Not only were the experimenter's surgical skill and carefulness important in the ablation experiments but also of significance was the type of animal used. In birds and fishes the canals, utricle, and saccule can be exposed easily, and individual parts separately destroyed or damaged. In the frog, the amphibian usually studied, the small size of the labyrinth makes destruction of separate parts extremely difficult. Nevertheless, several investigators, by using a dissecting microscope, have been able to render separate parts of the labyrinth non-functional by crushing or cauterizing them or by sectioning the nerve supply.

In mammals the labyrinth lies imbedded in the very hard portion of the temporal bone. Exposure and destruction of any part of the vestibular mechanism without damage to other parts are all but impossible. Furthermore, the position of the labyrinth is such that injury may be done to cerebellum or to neck muscles, both of which are important in postural control. If unintentional damage is done to either vestibular or non-vestibular structures without the experimenter's knowledge, the results of ablation will be misinterpreted. Disagreement among many early experimenters using ablation techniques was often the result of differences in exactness of surgical procedure.

The ablation method has also been applied in studying the central nervous connections of the vestibule system. For example, in experiments on motion sickness, Bard has obtained results which throw new light upon the role of the cerebellum in controlling responses aroused by vestibular stimulation. Tests were made of the vomiting responses of dogs subjected to swing stimulation before and after ablation of parts of the cerebellum. A typical animal vomited within 8 to 25 minutes in each of 11 test periods given at weekly intervals. After destruction of all the cerebellar cortex no vomiting occurred in 14 separate test periods, in each of which swinging was continued for 60 minutes, nor in one additional period of 2 hours. Similar results were obtained in other experiments in which only limited portions of the cerebellum were ablated.

SUMMARY

The proprioceptive system consists of a kinesthetic division and a vestibular division. Kinesthetic receptors, i.e., proprioceptors in the muscles and tendons, were first discovered through anatomical methods. Selective ablation methods were then used to establish the functions of the different kinds of receptors and to investigate the role of kinesthesis in the control of posture and locomotion. With the development of electrical stimulation and recording methods it has been possible to make a more exact analysis of the functions of the receptors and nervous elements of the kinesthetic system.

Evidence from experimental studies on lower animals has been corroborated and supplemented by clinical studies of man. In a few instances psychophysical methods used in animal experiments or clinical investigations have added to our knowledge of kinesthesis. For the most part, however, methods requiring discriminatory responses have not been used.

The structures in the inner ear which make up the vestibular end organ had been described in detail by anatomists long before anyone suspected that they served as the receptors which are stimulated by position and movement of the head. Their function was first discovered by ablation methods. After this discovery progress in understanding the vestibular mechanisms depended mainly upon the development of methods of stimulation, methods of recording and analyzing responses, and improved ablation techniques.

The natural forms of stimulation of the vestibule receptors are position of the head, angular acceleration (rotation), and linear acceleration. In addition, these receptors may be stimulated artificially by caloric, mechanical, and electrical stimuli.

There are several levels at which we may record and analyze the response to vestibule stimulation. We may examine: (1) the activity of the receptor; (2) the activity of afferent nerve fibers, tracts, or centers; (3) the reflex responses of effectors; (4) the discriminatory responses of human subjects or of experimental animals. In most instances, experimenters have been interested in responses of the first three classes. A wide variety of mechanical, electrical, and photographic recording techniques has been developed. In some experiments, however, subjects have been instructed to report the least noticeable motion or to make judgments about the position and motion of objects in space or to describe such experiences as dizziness, vertigo, and nausea. In animals conditioned responses have been established to angular acceleration and to show change in position.

REFERENCES

1. Alexander, S.J., M. Cotzin, C. J. Hill Jr, E. A. Ricciuti, and G.R. Wendt. Wesleyan University studies of motion sickness. I, The effects of variation of time intervals between accelerations upon sickness rates. *J. Psychol.*, 1915, *10*, 49-62.
2. Gamis, M., *The Physiology of the Vestibular Apparatus.* (Translated form the Italian and annotated by R. S. Creed.) London : Oxford University Press, 1930.
3. Clark, B., and A. Graybiel, Visually preceived movement caused by angular acceleration and by centrifugal force during fight (abstract). *Amer. Psychol.*, 1946, *1*, 238.
4. Dodge, R., The latent time of compensatory eye-movements. *j. Expert. Psychol.*, 1921, *4*, 247-269.
5. Dodge, R., Habituation to rotation. *J. Exper. Psychol.*, 1923 6, *1* -35.
6. [illegible], R. Thresholds of rotation. *J. Exper. Psychol.*, 1923, *6*, [illegible]
7. Dodge, R., and T. S. Cline, The angle velocity of eye movements. *J. Expert. Rev.*, 1901, *8*, 145-157.
8. Dohlman, G., Some practical and theoretical points in labyrinthology. *Proc. Roy. Soc. Med.*, 1935, *28*, 1371-1380.
9. Dunlap, K., A rotator for vestibule and organic stimulation. *J. Comp. Psychol.*, 1921, *1*, 365-367.
10. Dussser de Barenne, J.G., The labyrinthine and postural mechanisms. In *A Handbook of General Experimental Psychology*. C. Murchison, Ed. Worcester, Mass.: Clark University Press, 1934.
11. Dussser de Barenne, J.G., and A. de Kleyn., On reciprocal innervations of the eye muscles in the tonic labyrinthine reflexes. *Acta Oto-Laryng.*, 1931, *16*, 97-116.
12. Ewald, J.R., *Physiologische Untersuchungen umber das Endorgan des Nervus Octavos.* Wiesbaden : Bergmann, 1892.
13. Fluorens, M.P.J., *Recherches experimentales sur les proprietes et*

les fonctions du systcmc nerveux duns les animaux vertebres. 2nd Ed. Paris : Bailliere, 1842.

14. Fulton, J.F., *Physiology of Nervous System..* New York : Oxford University Press, 1943.
15. Graybiel, A. B. Clark, K. MacCorquodale, and D. Hupp, Role of vestibular nystagmus in the visual perception of a moving target in the dark. *Amer. J. Psychol.,* 1946, 59, 259-266.
16. Griffith, C.R., *An Historical Survey of Vestibular Equilibration.* Urbana. Illnois : University of Illinois Press, 1922.
17. Hemmingway, A., Cardiovascular changes in motion sickness. *J. Aviat. Med.,* 1945, *16,* 409.
18. Jacobson, E., Electrical measurements of neuromuscular states during mental activities. *Amer. J. Physiol.,*1930, *95,* 694-702.
19. Judd, C.H., C.N. McAllister, and W.M. Steele., General introduction to a series of studies of eye movements by means of kinetoscopic photographs. *Psychol. Rev., Monog. Supp.,* 1905, *7,* 1-16.
20. Kerr. W.A., and A. Graybiel, Thresholds of stimulation of the horizontal semicircular canals in man (abstract). *Amer. Psychol.,* 1946, *1,* 237.
21. Lowenstein, O., and A. Sand, The mechanism of the semicircular canal. A study of the responses of single-fibre preparations to angular accelerations and to rotation at constant speed. *Proc. Roy. Soc. London, Series B,* 1940, *129,* 253-275.
22. Matthews, B.H.C., Nerve endings in mammalian muscle. *J. Physiol.,* 1933, *78,* 1-53.
23. Mowrer. O.H., The electrical response of the vestibular nerve during adequate stimulation. *Science,* 1935, *81,* 180-181.
24. Mowrer, O.H.T.C. Ruch, and N.E. Miller., The corneo-retinal potential difference as the basis of the galvanometric method of recording eye movements. *Amer. J. Physiol.,* 1936, *114,* 433-428.
25. Pi-suner, J., and J. F. Fulton., The influence of the proprioceptive nerves of the hind limbs upon the posture of

the fore limbs in decerebrate cats. *Amer. J. Physiol.*, 1928, *83*, 548-553.

26. Romberg, M.H., *Lehrbuch der Nerven-Krankheiten des Menschen*. 2te Aufl. Berlin : Duncker, 1851.

27. Ruch, T.C., Cortical localization of somatic sensibility. The effect of precentral, postcentral, and posterior parietal lesions upon the performance of monkeys trained to discriminate weights. *Res. Publ. Assoc. Nerv. Ment. Disease*, 1935, *15*, 289-330.

28. Ruch, T.C., J.F. Fulton, and W.J. German., Sensory discrimination in monkey, chimpanzee, and man after lesions of the parietal lobe. *Arch. Neurol. Psychiat., Chicago*, 1938, *39*, 919-937.

29. Sherrington, C. S., On the anatomical constituation of nerves of skeletal muscles ; with remarks on recurrent fibres in the ventral spinal nerve-root. *J. Physio.*, 1894, *17*, 211-258.

30. Spiegel, E.A., The cortical centers of the labyrinth. *J. Nerv. Ment. Disease*, 1932, *75*, 504-512.

31. Spiegel, E.A., Labyrinth and cortex ; the electrencephalogram of the cortex in stimulation of the labyrinth. *Arch. Neurol. Psychiat.*, 1934, *31*, 469-482.

32. Spiegel, E.A., and M. J. Oppenheimer., Conditioned reactions to position and angular acceleration. *Amer. J. Physiol.*, 1939, *125*, 265-275.

33. Spiegel., E.A.M.J. Oppenheimer, G.C. Henny, and H.T. Wycis, Experimental production of motion sickness. *War Medicine*, 1944, *6*, 283-290.

34. Steinhausen, W., Uber den Nachweis der Bewegung der Cupula in der intaken Bogengangsampulle des Labyrinths bei der naturlichen rotatorischen und calorischen Reizung. *Arch. ges. Physiol. (flugers)*, 1931, *228*, 322-328.

35. Steinhausen, W., Uber den experimentellen Nachweis der Ablenkung der Cupula terminalis in der intakten Begengangsampulle des Labyrinths bei der thermischen and adaquaten rotatorischen Reizung. *Z. Hals-Nas-u. Ohrenheilk.*, 1931, *29*, 211-216.

36. Steinhausen, W., Das Begengangssystem des inneren Ohres als Wahrnehmungsorgan fur Drehungen. Berlin : *Reichstelle*

fur den Unterrichtsfilm zu den Hochschulfilm, 1939, No. 323.

37. Tait, J., and W.J. McNally., A method of recording the responses of individual muscles to appropriate stimulation of the semicircular canals. *Amer. J. Physiol.*, 1929, *90*, 536-537.

38. Travis, R.C., Perception and bodily adjustment under changing rotary acceleration : a new technique. *Amer. J Psychol.*, 1944, *57*, 468-481.

39. Wendt, G.R., and R. Dodge, Practical directions for stimulating and for photographically recording eye-movements animals. *J. Comp. Psychol.*, 1938, *25*, 9-39.

Bibliography

Bartley, S.H. : *Vision : A Study of Its Basis.* New York : Van Nostrand, 1941.

Boring, E.G . : *Sensation and Perception in the History of Experimental Psychology.* New York : Appleton-Century, 1942, pp. 523-544.

Bunch, C.C. : *Clinical Audiometry.* St. Louis : C. V. Mosby, 1943.

Boring, E.G. : *Sensation and Perception in the History of Experimental Psychology.* New York : Appleton-Century, 1941.

Camis, M. : *The Physiology of the Vestibular Apparatus.* (Translated from the Italian and annotated by R. S. Creed.) London : Oxford University Press, 1930.

Carr, H.A. : *An Introduction to Space Perception.* New York : Longmans, Green, 1935.

Cohen, M.R., and E. Nagel : *An Introduction to Logic and Scientific Method.* New York : Harcourt, Brace, 1934.

Duke-Elder, W.S. : *Textbook of Ophthalmology,* Vol. I. St. Louis : C. V. Mosby, 1933.

Fletcher, H. : *Speech and Hearing.* New York : Van Nostrand, 1929.

Geldard, F.A. : The perception of mechanical vibration. *J. Gen. Psychol.,* 1940, 22, 243-303.

Graham, C.H. : Vision III : some neural correlations. In *Handbook of Experimental Psychology.* Worcester, Mass : Clark University Press, 1934, pp. 829-879.

Guilford, J.P. : *Psychometric Methods.* New York : McGraw-Hill, 1936. (pp. 1-70, 110-262.)

Hecht, S. Vision II : the nature of the photoreceptor process. In *Handbook of Experimental Psychology.* Worcester, Mass : Clark

University Press, 1934, pp. 704-828.

Jenkins, W.L., and L.J. Stone. : Recent research in cutaneous sensitivity. II. Touch and the neural basis of the skin senses. *Psychol. Bull.*, 1941, 88, 69-91.

Johannsen, D.E. : *The Principles of Psychophysics, with Laboratory Exercises.* Saratoga Springs, New York : the author, 1941.

Koffka, K., *Principles of Gesalt Psychology.* New York : Harcourt, Brace, 1935.

Luckiesh, M., and F. K. Moss. : *The Science of Seeing.* New York : Van Nostrand, 1937.

Parsons, J.H. : *An Introduction to the Study of Color Vision.* New York : G.P. Putnam, 1935.

Pratt, C.C. : *The Logic of Modern Psychology.* New York : Macmillan, 1939.

Ritchie, A.D. : *Scientific Method.* New York : Harcourt, Brace, 1923.

Stevens, S.S. : Psychology and the science of sciences. *Psychol. Bull.*, 1939, *36*, 221-263.

Stevens, S.S. and H. Davis,. : *Hearing, Its Psychology and Physiology.* New York : John Wiley, 1938.

Stone, L.J., and W.L. Jenkins : Recent research in cutaneous sensitivity. I. Pain and temperature. *Psychol. Bull.*, 1940, 87, 285-311.

Wood, A.B. : *A Textbook of Sound,* New York : Macmillan, 1930.

Woodworth, R.S., Experimental Psychology. New York : Henry Holt 1938.